£ 15

This book is to be returned on or before
the last date stamped below.

Breast cancer:
the decision
to screen

FOURTH

H.M. QUEEN ELIZABETH

THE QUEEN MOTHER FELLOWSHIP

1990

Breast cancer: the decision to screen

SIR PATRICK FORREST

MD, ChM, FRCS(Ed.Eng.Glasg), FRSE
DSc.(hon), LLD(hon), FACS(hon)
FRACS(hon), FRCSCan(hon), FRCR(hon)

Professor Emeritus, University of Edinburgh
Visiting Scientist, National Institutes
of Health, Bethesda, Maryland

THE NUFFIELD PROVINCIAL
HOSPITALS TRUST

Published by the
Nuffield Provincial Hospitals Trust
3 Prince Albert Road, London NW1 7SP

ISBN 09 00574 74 7

PRINTED IN GREAT BRITAIN BY
BURGESS & SON (ABINGDON) LTD
THAMES VIEW, ABINGDON
OXFORDSHIRE

HER MAJESTY QUEEN ELIZABETH THE QUEEN MOTHER FELLOWSHIP

Her Majesty Queen Elizabeth the Queen Mother, who is the Patron of the Trust and has always shown a keen interest in its work, approved the founding of the Fellowship by the Trust to commemorate her 80th birthday.

The Trustees of the Nuffield Provincial Hospitals Trust will select a Fellow who will be invited to undertake to review in a monograph a subject within the sphere of the Trust which is believed to be of particular interest to Her Majesty. The monograph will be launched by a lecture

THE AUTHOR

Professor Sir Patrick Forrest retired from the Regius Chair of Clinical Surgery in the University of Edinburgh in 1988. A student of the University of St. Andrews, he returned to Dundee following service with the Royal Navy for his surgical training, spending a year as a research fellow at the Mayo Clinic and then becoming lecturer and then senior lecturer to Sir Charles Illingworth in Glasgow. During this time he became a Fellow of all three British Royal Colleges of Surgeons and wrote theses for the degrees of M.D. and Ch.M., both of which were awarded with honours and gold medals.

In 1962 he proceeded to the Chair of Surgery in the Welsh National School of Medicine, which he occupied for nine years before accepting an invitation to go to Edinburgh. A dedicated academic surgeon he built up thriving clinical, teaching, and research departments in both schools. His personal research interest, initially in gastric but latterly and exclusively in breast disease, led to the development of a comprehensive clinical service for women with breast cancer, backed up by laboratory research: both of which have been internationally recognised. He has been Chairman of many national committees concerned with breast cancer including the Working Group which recommended the introduction of breast screening as part of the NHS, the Breast Cancer Research Subcommittee, and now the Scottish Advisory Committee on Breast Screening.

Sir Patrick has been President of the Surgical Research Society and of the Association of Surgeons of Great Britain and Ireland; a member of the Medical Subcommittee of University Grants Committee; of the Medical Research Council; of the Advisory Board for Research Councils; the Scientific Advisory Committee of the Cancer Research Campaign and the Council of the Royal College of Surgeons of Edinburgh. In 1981 he was appointed Chief Scientist (part-time) to the Scottish Home and Health Department, a position he held for 6 years.

He has received many honours, including honorary degrees from the Universities of Wales, Dundee, and the Chinese University of Hong Kong; honorary Fellowships of the American, the Royal Australasian and Royal Canadian Colleges of Surgeons and of the Royal College of Radiologists; the Gold Medal of the Netherlands Surgical Association; and in 1987 the Lister Medal of the Royal College of Surgeons of England.

CONTENTS

THE AUTHOR   vii

CONTENTS   ix

PREFACE   xi

LIST OF FIGURES   xiii

LIST OF TABLES   xvii

ACKNOWLEDGEMENTS   xxii

PROLOGUE   xxiii

1 RECOMMENDATIONS   1
SCREENING, 1; REMIT AND CONCLUSIONS, 2;
BACKGROUND, 3; IMPLEMENTATION, 5. Basic
Screen, 5. Assessment, 7. Biopsy, 8. Treatment, 9.
Numbers, 9.

2 DISSENT   11

3 BIOLOGY OF BREAST CANCER   13
Origin, 13. A Diffuse Disease, 16. Non-invasive Breast
Cancer, 19. A Threshold, 20.

4 INVASIVE BREAST CANCER   26
A HEALTH PROBLEM, 26; AN INCURABLE
DISEASE? 28. Mortality Rates, 29. Definitions of Cure, 30.
THE PROBLEM, 32. Clinical Presentation, 32.
Staging, 35. Radical Local Treatment: A False Premise, 37.
The Unorthodox, 39. Psychosexual Morbidity, 40.
ONE SOLUTION, 41. Systemic Treatment, 41. For
palliation, 41. As an adjuvant, 42. ANOTHER
SOLUTION, 45.

5 THE METHOD   46
EVOLUTION OF MAMMOGRAPHY, 46; RADIATION
RISK, 50; XEROMAMMOGRAPHY, 52; WHAT DOES
THE RADIOLOGIST SEE, 53; EVALUATION, 54.
Sensitivity, 55. Specificity, 56. The Trade-Off, 57.

Predictive Value, 58. Alternative Methods of Calculating
Sensitivity, 59. ALTERNATIVES, 60.

6 THE EVIDENCE   62
EVALUATION, 62. Lead-Time Bias, 63. Length Bias, 63.
Selection Bias, 63. Elimination of Bias, 64. Critical
Evidence. U.S. STUDY: HEALTH INSURANCE PLAN
(HIP) 65. Organisation, 68. Screening, 69. Results, 70.
Additional Analyses, 74. SWEDISH TRIALS, 76. Two-
Counties, 76. Results, 77. Malmo, 81. Results, 82.
Stockholm, 84. Göteborg Trial, 86. U.K. TRIALS, 87.
TEDBC, 87. Results, 89. Edinburgh, 90. Results, 93.
CANADIAN TRIAL, 95; CASE-CONTROL STUDIES, 96.
Nijmegen, 97. Utrecht, 98. Florence, 99. OTHER
STUDIES, 100. Gavlëborg, 101. BCDDP, 101.

7 SOME COMPARISONS   104
TRIAL WEAKNESSES, 104. Design, 104. Response, 112.
Efficiency, 116. Sensitivity, 117. Specificity, 119. Lead-
time, 120. Models, 120. Stage distribution, 121.
CONCLUSIONS, 126.

8 DOUBTS ON RECOMMENDATIONS   129
AGE, 129; SINGLE-VIEW MAMMOGRAPHY, 134;
FREQUENCY OF SCREENING, 138; BREAST SELF-
EXAMINATION (BSE), 139.

9 QUESTIONS OF MORBIDITY AND COST   147
RISKS AND BENEFITS, 147; PSYCHOLOGICAL
EFFECTS, 150; BASIC SCREENING AND RECALL, 155;
ASSESSMENT AND BIOPSY RATES, 157;
TREATMENT, 164; SELECTIVE SCREENING, 166.
Factors of Risk, 166. Sex and reproduction, 166. Race
and environment, 168. Genetic Factors, 169. Hormonal
Profiles, 169. Benign disease, 170. Application to
Screening, 172. COST, 175.

10 WHERE NOW   179
TREATMENT, 179; PREVENTION, 182. Role of
Oestrogens, 183. Plans for Prevention, 184. Anti-
Oestrogen Therapy, 184. Ovarian Ablation, 186. Diet, 188.
Risk Factors Again, 188. MAMMOGRAPHY AND
SCREENING, 189.

EPILOGUE   193

APPENDIX TABLES   194

REFERENCES   208

PREFACE

Compared to her Swedish or American counterpart, the average British woman is dismally unaware of the nature of her most common type of malignant disease. According to Mildred Blaxter, cancer has replaced tuberculosis as 'the disease to be dreaded, the disease to be mentioned without any discussion as to its cause... upon which speculation was not only fruitless... but uncomfortable' (1).

When invited by the Trustees to write a Queen Elizabeth the Queen Mother monograph for the Nuffield Provincial Hospitals Trust on some aspects of breast cancer, I set out to produce an account of its nature for the professional in all branches of health care. It is from them that education of our women must stem, replacing fear by a desire to know. But with mounting criticism against the decision to implement screening for breast cancer in Britain, Dr Ashley-Miller suggested that it would be better to attempt to address the question 'Why did Britain screen'. The monograph is still directed to the health professional in general, and not to the expert, which, as a surgeon and in these days of statistical modelling, I am ill-equipped to do.

This change in direction coincided with my acceptance of an invitation by Dr Bruce Chabner, Director of the Division of Cancer Treatment, to spend 12 months in the National Cancer Institute in Bethesda. I am most grateful to him and to his colleagues Drs Greg Curt, Charles Myers and Kenneth Cowan for allowing me the time and use of facilities to complete this task. I owe a particular debt to Dr Jack Cohen, who provided word-processing facilities in his private office, and to Ms Kathy Moore, for her superb editorial and literary skills in preparing the final script.

With the opportunity to use the unique medical library facilities in Bethesda, I re-consulted the literature I have quoted, so that the facts I have presented are only from published work. The efficient and courteous service provided by the staff of the NIH Library is remarkable, and has been greatly appreciated. In the Scottish Cancer Trials Office, Wendy Taylor, secretary to Dr Helen Stewart, continued to give willing and invaluable assistance, while, in the Medical School Anne McNeill, David Dyrom and Jim Paul provided the illustrations.

I have not attempted to mention by name the many people who have, by their knowledge and example, influenced my thinking about this disease. But they know who they are: and I hope can recognise my indebtedness. And they include the many patients with breast cancer who I have been privileged to care for, and who have taught me so much.

Finally, I wish to place on record my very deep thanks to my wife Margaret, who, during the somewhat difficult and frustrating months, has been her usual tower of strength in putting up with what she describes as my 'spastic behaviour'.

LIST OF FIGURES

1. The screening process   6

2. Proportion of women expected to attend each stage of the screening procedure   10

3. Terminal duct-lobular unit of the breast   13

4. Relationship of tumour size to node involvement in 24,740 women with breast cancer   22

5. Relationship of tumour diameter to histology of the axillary lymph nodes in screen-detected and symptomatic cancers   23

6. Relationship between tumour diameter at primary treatment and the subsequent development of metastatic disease   24

7. Model to illustrate the principle of screen detection of cancer during its 'sojourn' phase   25

8. Breast cancer mortality throughout the world (age adjusted)   27

9. Age specific incidence (1982) and mortality rate (1985) rates for breast cancer in UK   28

10. Deaths in females: UK 1985   29

11. Long-term survival of 704 patients with breast cancer treated by local surgery or radiotherapy   31

12. Breast cancer mortality: England and Wales, 1951–85   33

13. Breast cancer in England and Wales: effect of stage on prognosis is shown in Figure 13   37

14. Result of overview of randomised trials of tamoxifen adjuvant therapy in 8142 women over 49 years of age   43

xiii

15. Result of overview of randomised trials of chemotherapy as adjuvant treatment in 1692 women under 50 years of age   44

16. Radiation dose received by breast related to later risk of breast cancer   51

17. ROC curve to illustrate the principle of 'trade-off' of sensitivity and specificity   58

18. Model of estimates of efficiency. Sensitivity and specificity are applied to populations: predictive value to the test   60

19. Length bias: horizontal lines represent different durations of sojourn time, vertical line an episode of screening   64

20. Cumulative numbers of cancers detected in study and control populations in HIP trial. Catch-up is at 5–6 years after entry for 4 annual episodes of screening   71

21. Survival of women with breast cancer diagnosed within 5 years of entry to HIP trial from date of diagnosis adjusted for lead time   72

22. Cumulative mortality from breast cancer in study and control populations in HIP trial. Cases within 5 years of entry from date of diagnosis   73

23. Cumulative probability of survival from breast cancer diagnosed within 5 years from time of entry to HIP trial: calculated from date of entry to trial   75

24. Cumulative rates of stage II and more advanced cancers in Two-Counties trial   78

25. Cumulative mortality rates in Two-Counties trial. Numbers of deaths are not adjusted for randomisation ratios   80

26. Cumulative rates of stage II and more advanced cancers in Malmo trial   83

27. Cumulative mortality rates in Malmo trial   84

28. Cumulative rates of stage II and more advanced cancers in Stockholm trial. Third rate includes 'hidden' cases in control population 86

29. Cumulative mortality rates in TEDBC 91

30. Cumulative rates of stage II and more advanced cancers in Edinburgh trial 94

31. Cumulative mortality rates in Edinburgh trial 95

32. Comparison of reported results of trials and case-control studies 107

33. Comparison of cumulative rates of stage II and more advanced cancers in the Swedish and Edinburgh trials (from Table 34) 123

34. Comparison of results of trials and case-control studies in women of 35–50 years. Note contrast with Figure 32. For data consult Appendix table 24 130

35. Proportional rates of interval cancers following negative screen in women of 40–49 years of age in the Two-Counties trial 131

36. Cumulative mortality from breast cancer for cases within 5 years of entry of different ages 132

37. Survival rates from date of entry into trial for women (a) 40–49 and (b) 50–64 years of age with breast cancer diagnosed within 6 years of entry 133

38. Proportional rates of interval cancers following a negative screen in women of 59–69 years of age in the Two-Counties trial 139

39. Cancer detection rates in the Edinburgh trial comparing clinical plus mammography and clinical only screens 140

40. Cumulative mortality rates in TEDBC: for BSE and comparison districts 145

xvi

LIST OF FIGURES

41. Comparison of breast cancer mortality in the
city Utrecht (where screening was
introduced in 1974) with other urban areas
in Netherlands. Women born 1911–1925   148

42. Proportion of 94 interval and 178 control
cancers surviving in the Two-Counties trial   167

43. Annual number of operations in Kopparberg
and Uppsala counties in Sweden (a) for
benign disease (b) for cancer. Only
Kopparberg had a screening programme in
operation   178

LIST OF TABLES IN TEXT

1. Critical evidence available to Working Group   4

2. Estimated annual number of women undergoing different stages of the screening process   10

3. Incidence of atypical hyperplasia and *in situ* and invasive cancer   17

4. Frequency of diagnosis of proliferative disease and carcinoma *in situ*   17

5. Summary table of TNM clinical classification of breast cancer (from 1978 classification) as used in screening trials. In pathological TNM, size as measured on the gross specimen and node involvement by histological examination   36

6. Requirements for modern mammography   48

7. Dose of radiation to each breast for two-view mammography in the Canadian National trial   52

8. Sensitivity, specificity and predictive value   56

9. Mean and range of sensitivities and specificities available to working group   57

10A. Prospective trials from which mortality data has been reported   66

10B. Case-control studies from which mortality data have been reported   67

10C. Ongoing trials not reported   67

11. Deaths from breast cancer at 5–18 years among women with breast cancer diagnosed within five years of entry to trial   73

12. Person-years of life lost (PYLL) from breast cancer deaths at 5–18 years amongst women whose breast cancer was diagnosed within five years of entry. PYLL takes account of both number and timing of deaths   74

13. Probability of death from breast cancer amongst women diagnosed within five years of entry to trial   76

14. Relative risk from breast cancer in study and control populations in last three years of reported follow-up   79

15. Relative risk of death from breast cancer in study and control populations according to age   80

16. Relative risk of death from breast cancer in study and control populations after mean follow-up of 8·8 years   83

17. Centres selected for trial of early detection of breast cancer (TEDBC). Screening and comparison districts   88

18. Observed differences in mortality from breast cancer between screening and comparison centres (unadjusted and adjusted for pretrial mortality rates)   90

19. Observed differences in mortality from breast cancer according to year follow-up, adjusted for pretrial mortality rates   90

20. Relative risk of death from breast cancer in study and control populations   94

21. Relative risk of death from breast cancer in ever- versus never-screened women in Nijmegen (second study)   98

22. Relative risk of death from breast cancer in ever- versus never-screened women in Utrecht   99

23. Relative risk of death in ever- versus never-screened women in rural Florence adjusted for confounded variables   100

24. Cumulative relative survival rates for invasive breast cancers for BCDDP cases detected through screens and for cases in white females in the SEER programme   102

25. Summary of controlled randomised and
    comparative trials   105

26. Summary of case control studies. In Tables 25
    and 26 compliance figures in parenthesis are
    stable rates on repeat screens   106

27. All-cause mortality in controlled randomised
    trials   108

28. Mortality rates in general practices allocated to
    screening and control populations by socio-
    economic category   110

29. Comparison of all cause mortality, breast
    cancer detection rate and 10-year case
    survival in women attending and refusing
    screening in HIP trial   111

30. Examples of knowledge about breast cancer in
    Scottish women   114

31. Attendance in Edinburgh according to age and
    socio-economic status (highest and lowest of
    six categories)   114

32. Key messages in Edinburgh education
    campaign   115

33. Comparison of sensitivities of screening
    programmes   117

34. Stage II and more advanced cancers reported
    in controlled trials for HIP Two-Counties
    and Edinburgh data pathological 'staging' is
    given   122

35. Comparison of proportion of invasive cancers
    which are under 2 cm in size and node
    negative on pathological assessment   124

36. *In situ* (non-invasive) cancers in controlled
    randomised trials and one comparative study
    as per cent of all cancers detected   125

37. Contrasting stages in Sweden and other
    countries. Edinburgh and Malmo are for
    control populations in screening trials:
    percentages of invasive cancer   128

38. Attendance of invited women at screening
    clinic in Nijmegen   129

39. Comparison of detection of cancer on
    different mammographic views in 491
    patients with breast cancer   135

40. Results of study of single- versus two-view
    mammography in 169 patients with cancer
    and 194 healthy controls   135

41. Retrospective study of interpretation of single
    medio-lateral oblique and two-view
    mammography by the same radiologist in
    250 consecutive women   136

42. Overview of six studies in which practice of
    breast self-examination was related to the
    size and state of the axillary nodes of breast
    cancer   142

43. Clinical size and axillary node status (where
    known from histological report) in 616
    women related to practice of breast self-
    examination   143

44. Tumour size and histological node status 751
    cancers emerging in women offered
    instruction in breast self-examination
    compared to a consecutive series of 751
    historical controls   144

45. Surgical treatment of operable (Stages I and
    II) invasive cancer at Longmore Breast Unit,
    Edinburgh   149

46. Estimated prevalence of psychiatric disorder
    among interviewed women   151

47. General Health Questionnaire 'case rate' in
    269 women in interview and postal samples
    before and 6 months after screening   152

48. General Health Questionnaire scores of 5 or
    more in women attending screening clinic,
    at initial visit and 3 months later   152

49. Distribution of scores in subgroups before and
      3 months after screening   153

50. Work scheme for screening in Stockholm trial
      with actual numbers of women involved   155

51. Comparison of findings in patients referred to
      the screening clinic (where assessment was)
      and from hospital out-patient   160

52. Rates of biopsies (per 1000 women) and
      benign:malignant ratios reported in
      screening trials   161

53. Comparison biopsy rates (per 1000 women)
      and benign:malignant ratios in USA and
      Nijmegen over similar periods of screening   161

54. Predictive value of referral generated by a
      mammographic biopsy for diagnosis of
      cancer in Nijmegen programme of screening   162

55. Relationship age to benign:malignant ratio of
      biopsies generated by screening in BCDDP   162

56. Factors influencing risk of developing breast
      cancer   171

57. The application of risk factor analyses to
      selective screening   173

58. Comparison of costs per quality-adjusted life
      years gained from various health-care
      procedures   176

59. Incidence of contralateral breast cancer in
      controlled randomised trials of adjuvant
      therapy for primary breast cancer in which
      tamoxifen has been given in one arm alone   187

60. Controlled randomised trials under way in
      U.K. national breast cancer screening service   192

ACKNOWLEDGEMENTS

I am grateful to the publishers of the following books and periodicals for permission to incorporate graphic and tabular material in this monograph.

Journal of the National Cancer Institute, New England Journal of Medicine, Cancer (J. B. Lippincott Co), Johns Hopkins University Press, *International Journal of Cancer* (Wiley-Liss), *Breast Cancer Research and Treatment* (Klumar Academic Publishers), CA (American Cancer Society), Radiology (Radiological Society of North America), *American Journal of Roentgenology, International Union Against Cancer* (HAGREFE and HUBER), *Canadian Public Health Journal, International Journal of Epidemiology* (Oxford University Press), *European Journal of Cancer and Clinical Oncology* (Pergamon Journals Ltd), *Journal of the Royal College of Surgeons of Edinburgh* (Butterworth Scientific Ltd), *The Lancet, The British Medical Journal, British Journal of Cancer* (The Macmillan Press), *Journal of Epidemiology and Community Health* (British Medical Association), *Cancer Factsheet* (Cancer Research Campaign), Her Majesty's Stationery Office, *British Journal of Surgery, Social Science and Medicine*, Professor MAURICE TUBIANA

A. P. M. FORREST

PROLOGUE

On 25 February 1987, the Secretary of State for Health and Social Security included in a statement to the House of Commons the following:

'The Government attaches particular importance to reducing deaths from breast cancer . . .

'In July 1985 the Government appointed a working group . . . to consider the position. The report has concluded that screening by mammography . . . will enable us to reduce deaths from breast cancer.

'The Government accept the proposals made in the report and accordingly have decided to implement a national breast cancer screening service . . . throughout the United Kingdom.

(with) 'all necessary back-up facilities . . . assessment . . . diagnostic . . . (and) treatment facilities, counselling and after-care and training for key groups of staff (2,3).'

I was privileged to have been invited to chair the Working Group, and now to have been asked by the Nuffield Provincial Hospital Trust to answer the question 'why did Britain screen?'. This Queen Elizabeth, the Queen Mother, Monograph attempts to do so by presenting to health professionals the facts as we now know them. But it is the reader who must decide, on the basis of these facts, whether the decision to implement mass population screening for breast cancer was, for the United Kingdom, a correct one.

1

RECOMMENDATIONS

SCREENING

THE COMMISSION OF CHRONIC ILLNESS IN THE UNITED
States, in 1957, defined screening as 'the presumptive
identification of unrecogised disease . . . by the application of
tests, examinations or other procedures which can be applied rapidly' (4). Presumptive is the key word, because a
screening test, unless specific for the disease in question, is
not diagnostic. It only divides the population into those who
are test-positive, and who are likely to have the disease in
question, and those who are test-negative, and probably
without it. Those with positive tests require to be further
assessed by a series of diagnostic investigations from which a
conclusion about the presence or absence of the disease can
be reached. Those who are test-negative should not require
to be further investigated. The ability of a screening test to
define those with a disease is expressed by its sensitivity, and
to exclude those without the disease, its specificity.

Programmes of screening initially concentrated on the
detection, prevention, and control of communicable diseases; recently again emphasised by the screening of blood
donors, haemophiliacs, and pregnant women for antibodies
to human immunodeficiency virus (AIDS). Such diseases still
may pose, from time to time, an important health problem,
but programmes of screening now also have great relevance
for the detection of chronic disease. Then the objective is to
discover its presence at an earlier stage when treatment is
more effective and can prevent what otherwise would be
incapactitating or mortal (5).

The performance of routine checks in select groups of
persons, health profiles, is not relevant to this discussion,
which concerns itself only with the screening of a *population*

of 'normal' asymptomatic persons for the detection of occult disease—in this instance, breast cancer.

REMIT AND CONCLUSIONS

The terms of reference of the Working Group were:

(i) To consider the information now available on breast cancer screening by mammography; the extent to which this suggests necessary changes in U.K. policy on the provision of mammographic facilities and the screening of symptomless women; and

(ii) To suggest a range of policy options and assess the benefits and costs associated with them; and set out the service planning, manpower, and financial and other implications of implementing such options (3).

The principles which required to be met to justify screening for any disease had been formulated for the World Health Organisation by Wilson and Jungner in 1968 (6) and raised the following questions concerning breast cancer in the U.K.:

(i) It is an important health problem?

(ii) Is the natural history of the disease well understood and is there an early pre-clinical phase during which the disease can be recognised by a suitable test?

(iii) Is a suitable test available and, if so, is it acceptable to the general population, knowing that it must be applied not once, but at defined intervals?

(iv) Does treatment of breast cancer during its pre-clinical detectable phase, compared to treatment when it is symptomatic, prolong life?

(v) Can adequate facilities be provided for the diagnosis and treatment of those abnormalities detected in those who are test-positive?

(vi) Does the cost, in terms of expenditure of resources and potential physical and psychological harm justify the benefit provided?

In their Report, the Working Group concluded that these

questions had been answered in the affirmative, and recommended that there was need for a change of policy on the provision of mammographic facilities in the U.K. Further, they were convinced that the introduction of a programme of screening well women by mammography was justified as a national need. Their recommendations were fully supported by Government, which decided that they should be implemented by the National Health Service; and this is now well under way.

BACKGROUND

The Working Group had little difficulty in appreciating that breast cancer posed a formidable health problem in western women. It was recognised also that treatment of the disease at the time a woman presented symptomatically with a breast mass failed in the majority to provide long-term control. It was apparent that our understanding of the natural history of breast cancer had greatly increased over the past few decades; that by the time invasive breast cancer had become symptomatic it was most likely already to be a systemic and, by current methods of treatment, an incurable disease; but that there was an early pre-clinical stage during which such dissemination was less likely. Critical was evidence that the disease could be detected at this pre-clinical stage by mammographic imaging of the breast, and that when treated at this stage outlook was improved. When mammographic screening had been applied on a population basis, as in Sweden, mortality from the disease had been substantially reduced.

This critical evidence was provided by two large randomised controlled trials in which mammographic (in one plus clinical) examination had been offered on a random basis to large numbers of women. Non-invited women were controls (7–8). Further, there were two reports of case-control studies from cities into which screening by mammography had been introduced some years previously (9,10). In women who had died from breast cancer, the history of having never been screen exceeded that of age-matched healthy controls. The results of all four studies were consistent with a conclusion that mammographic screening was 'good news' (Table 1).

TABLE 1. *Critical evidence available to Working Group*

	Invited Population	1st Screen	Method of Screen	Date Last Published Report	Mortality Reduction
CONTROLLED RANDOMISED TRIALS					
Health Insurance Plan (New York)	62,000 40–64 yr	1963–66	Clinical and 2-view mammography	1982	30% (10 yr)
Two-Counties (Sweden)	163,000 40–74 yr	1977–81	Single-oblique mammography	1985	30% (9 yr)
CASE-CONTROL STUDIES					
Nijmegen (Netherlands)	30,000 35–64 yr	1975–82	Single-oblique mammography	1984	50%
Utrecht (Netherlands)	20,500 50–64 yr	1974–77	Clinical and 2-view mammography	1984	70%

Only the Nijmegen data failed (barely) to reach significant levels.
For HIP study, final results available from report of meeting.

Costs, in terms of all resource, were considered. It was appreciated that the introduction of mass population screening by mammography was expensive; although not excessively so compared to other established health needs. But, its priority within the health care system was not a matter we were asked to consider, nor, indeed, could we have done so. The ultimate decision was that of Government.

IMPLEMENTATION

The Working Group's recommendations were not to introduce screening mammography on a 'free-service' basis, but to establish a comprehensive service for screening. The target population was five million women aged 50–64 years who would personally be invited to attend for a single oblique-view radiography of each breast each three years. Steps had to be taken not only to provide the necessary facilities for mammography, but to identify those women who were to be offered screening, to arrange the best form of invitation, to interpret the mammograms, and to notify the results. But even this was but the first stage. Back-up facilities had to be provided for the evaluation, by diagnostic tests, of those abnormalities detected on the screening mammogram; also for the biopsy of those lesions suspicious for cancer, and finally for their treatment. All of this required the institution of organisational and management services, which were largely new. The screening process, as envisaged by the Working Group, is shown in Figure 1.

Basic Screen

It was recommended that the basic mammographic screen should be performed either in a static screening unit within an urban community or for rural populations in a custom-built mobile unit, both equipped with dedicated mammography units. Each unit would serve the needs of approximately 10,000 women in the target population each year, this taking account of a likely response rate of 70 per cent, the need to screen a few self-referred women over the age of 64

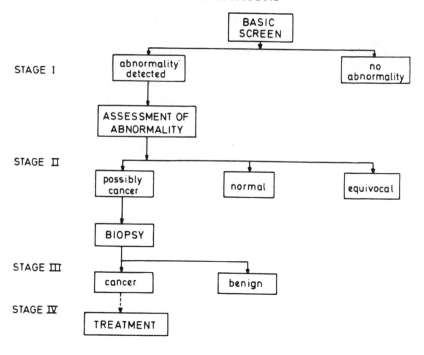

1. The screening process (3).

years, and in about 10 per cent to arrange for additional views on account of unsatisfactory or inconclusive films. The identification and invitation of women in the target population was an essential first step, which required an accurate and updated population register and encouragement to attend. Failure of response, from whatever cause, clearly mitigated against the success of a screening programme, as was only too evident from the results of screening by cervical cytology.

A basic screen can only separate out those women who are test-positive (with a mammographic abnormality) from those who were test-negative (and without an abnormality). A small proportion of women would have inadequate films. The standard of mammography and of interpretation of the films was critical to the success of the programme. It was recommended that guidelines were established to ensure that the taking, processing, and reading of films were kept under strict scrutiny. So also had the dose of radiation to be monitored. Recommendations for training of radiographic and radiological staff were of prime concern.

The decision to recommend single-view mammography as the basic screening method was based on the results of the trials carried out in Sweden and in the Netherlands. From their experience, it was reasonable to expect that not more than 10 per cent of women would be recalled for additional views; which would best be taken in the screening unit.

Assessment

The next stage in the screening process was the assessment by diagnostic tests of those abnormalities that were detected on the basic screening mammogram, the end-point being a decision on the need for a surgical biopsy. Abnormalities that indicated a positive test were of two main types: those which were discrete (opacity, area of altered architecture, cluster of micro-calcifications) and those which produced diffuse change (asymmetric increase in density, scattered micro-calcifications). Any alteration in appearance on successive mammograms also required evaluation.

The diagnostic methods which were required included clinical (physical) examination of the breasts; sophisticated mammography (e.g. magnification views to study the contour of an opacity or the size and shape of calcifications); ultrasonography (to determine if an opacity was solid or cystic); and fine-needle aspiration cytology (to aspirate a cyst or, if the lesion was solid, to obtain a specimen for cytology). In those countries with independent mammography clinics (as in the private sector in Britain), women in whom a mammographic abnormality was detected were referred to their family practitioner, to a radiologist or to a surgeon for further investigation; and this was an option which a general practitioner in the U.K. might wish to exert. However, the Working Group, noting the multi-disciplinary nature of these investigations, recommended that it would be better that a multi-disciplinary team consisting of radiologist, clinician (surgeon), and cytologist should develop the necessary expertise and experience to perform this function. Not only would this approach limit the number of women requiring biopsy, but it would facilitate monitoring of the assessment procedure. As this team would be hospital-based, they would also be available for the assessment of similar abnormalities detected in symptomatic women attending hospital out-patient clinics.

In general this alternative was preferred, largely due to the wish of the family doctors that their patients be assessed by an expert team. Experience has supported this view, particularly in the light of the development of stereotactic radiological methods by which a needle can be guided accurately into a non-palpable lesion for cytological sampl-ing. This technique, properly applied, can replace the need for biopsy of many benign lesions (11–13).

Biopsy

The third stage in the screening process was the biopsy. This implies the removal of tissue for diagnostic purposes; but with high quality assesment, this third stage could become, in many women, management rather than diagnosis. This was particularly important for the patient with cancer, in whom positive cytology could avoid the need for two oper-ations, one of which was diagnostic, the other therapeutic.

If a mammographic abnormality was palpable and benign or if the diagnosis was in doubt, its excision with a cuff of surrounding breast tissue was a simple procedure, most conveniently performed under local anaesthesia as a day-case. For the removal of an impalpable lesion, some form of localisation procedure was required, and this required radi-ological as well as surgical skills. Some surgeons preferred the use of a marker wire, which was both visible on x-ray and to the eye of the surgeon (14). Others preferred to inject a radio-opaque or visible dye, e.g., a suspension of carbon particle or mixture of contrast medium and methylene blue (15). In either case, the introduction of the marker was a radiological responsibility.

But it was the surgeon's responsibility to ensure that the radiological lesion has been removed. For this he required immediate radiology of the specimen, most conveniently performed in dedicated equipment in the operating suite. The surgeon was also responsible for ensuring that the pathologist received the specimen fresh, so that it could be sliced and each slice x-rayed to define the lesion requiring detailed attention. A histochemical assay for oestrogen receptor could also be performed. Immediate fixation of the specimen or hasty interpretation by rapid-section techniques had no part to play in a well-organised programme of screening (16–19).

Treatment

The Working Group believed that, if the assessment and biopsy stages of the screening process were well conducted, the patient should expect expert advice about treatment. A woman whose cancer was detected through screening would hope to avoid mastectomy, and she must be informed if there are alternatives that can safely be offered. Difficulty could arise in the management of the small screen-detected cancers, particularly those that were non-invasive and for which treatment policies were not clearly defined. Frankness and encouragement to participate in controlled randomised trials was the best way to proceed.

Numbers

It was relevant to know the likely proportion of women coming through each stage of the screening process. Those figures given in Table 2 and Figure 2 were 'best guesses' from experience in Sweden, Edinburgh, and Guildford. It was important that the skills of trained personnel were used economically and to the best advantage, not only for women generated by the screening service but also those referred from symptomatic diagnostic clinics. This was why the development of skilled teams for the diagnosis and treatment of breast disease, irrespective of the source of referred women, was considered to be a desirable development.

TABLE 2. *Estimated annual number of women undergoing different stages of the screening process (7–10)*

	Number of Women
Women to be invited each year	13,716
Accept invitation (70%)	9,600 ⎱ 10,800
Self-referrals (>64 yr)	1,200 ⎰
(Repeat films)	1,200
(Total screens)	12,000
Referred for assessment (10%)	1,080
Referred for biopsy (1·5%)	162
Breast cancer detected (0·55%)	59

Represented is a population of 471,000 women served by one basic screening unit capable of performing mammography on 12,000 women each year (3).

2. Proportion of women expected to attend each stage of the screening procedure.

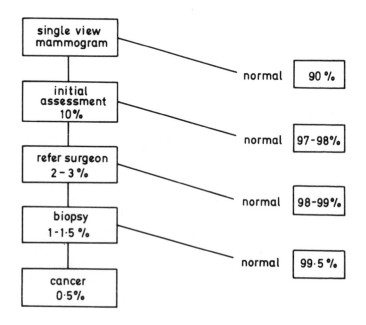

2

DISSENT

THE ACCEPTANCE BY GOVERNMENT OF THE RECOMMEND-
ations of the Working Group and their decision to implement these without delay was welcomed by many people, not
least by women's movements. Nor was Britain alone;
Sweden, the Netherlands, Finland, Canada, and now New
Zealand are also now in the process of introducing a service
for mammographic screening into their health-care system.
However, there have been a few dissenters who, although in
a minority, doubtless represent a body of opinion of which
account must be taken (20–30). And, as their comments are
seized on avidly by the press, they can but discourage women
from participating in the screening programme. In which
event it is doomed to fail.

The current programme of advertising screening mammography in the United States within a free-enterprise
health-care system may be seen to be commercially orientated; but it reflects a positive attitude of a nation towards
health, which, regretfully, we do not yet sustain, despite the
many opportunities freely provided by our health service.

The areas of dissent expressed by those who oppose the
introduction of screening can be summarised as follows:

1. Breast cancer is a disease for which there is no effective
treatment. There is no guarantee that its detection at an
earlier stage will improve the outlook for an individual
woman. Yet, this is what screening purports to offer.

2. Mammography is not a suitable test. Its sensitivity for
the detection of pre-clinical breast cancer is inadequate
(cases are missed); its specificity is poor (there are many
false-positive tests); and the predictive value of a positive
diagnosis for the diagnosis of cancer is low, requiring some
women to have unnecessary investigations or even surgery

11

with their adverse psychological effects. Through radiation exposure, mammography can induce cancer and may cause loss of more lives than are saved.

3. The conclusions of the Working Group were premature. They acted with undue urgency and haste, and should have awaited the results of the U.K. Trial of Early Detection of Breast Cancer (TEDBC) and the Edinburgh randomised trial. These trials, with that reported from Malmo, do not now show a statistically signficant benefit, and this cannot be ignored. Insufficient attention was paid to the very small gain in breast cancer mortality and its lack of effect on mortality due to all causes.

4. Detailed recommendations were inappropriate. Basic screening should use two-view not single-view mammography, and there should be double-reading of the films; the interval between screens would be two not three years; younger women should have been offered some form of screening.

5. The programme was expensive and the money used to fund it would better have been spent either in improving diagnostic services or health education or to support basic science, leading to true prevention or effective treatment of the disease.

6. Screening should be selective, and confined to high-risk groups.

In the chapters that follow, the facts that bear on these various areas of dissent will be presented, not with any intention of reaching a conclusion on their validity, but to allow the reader to consider the evidence and make up their own mind on what he or she would now recommend. It is of particular importance that it is women who should decide what they want to see achieved; for breast cancer is a disease which predominently affects the female sex. Men only rarely are affected.

3

BIOLOGY OF BREAST CANCER

ORIGIN

BREAST CANCER STARTS IN THE TERMINAL-DUCT LOBULAR units of the female breast that form the primary secreting units. They are composed of tiny terminal ductules with dilated sac-like ends (the acini or alveoli) embedded in fine connective tissue (Fig. 3). Readily visible on microscopy, the lobules are themselves embedded in the coarse connective tissue and fat that make up the supporting stroma of the breast and give it its characteristic shape (31–3). A system of ducts convey the breast fluid to the exterior. Ductules draining the lobules join with others to form larger ducts, which coalesce as they run towards the nipple, to form some 6–10 main lactiferous ducts that open onto its surface. Once

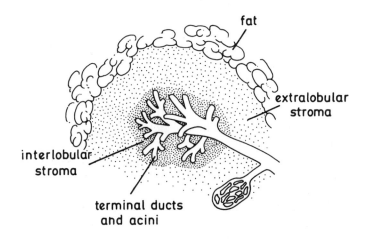

3. Terminal duct-lobular unit of the breast.

13

outside the lobules, the ductules and ducts are clothed by a layer of elastic tissue which maintains their shape. Should this degenerate, the ducts dilate and become filled with dried-up secretions—the condition of duct ectasia seen in the ageing breast. With the exception of a small portion of the laciferous ducts close to the nipple, the ducts are lined throughout their length with epithelial cells of secreting and absorptive type. In the resting breast these form and absorb a watery fluid, which is rich in electrolytes, steroid hormones, and immunoglobulins (34–7). Only during pregnancy does the breast lobule fully develop and secrete milk. At other times breast fluid can be obtained only by applying suction to the nipple, a method that has been used to study its composition in health and disease.

A second layer of cells surrounds the epithelium. These are the myo-epithelial cells, which are contractile, with processes intermingling between the epithelial cells. They are under hormonal control, and during lactation are stimulated by pituitary hormones released by the suckling reflex, compressing the ductal system to drive the milk towards the nipple. They also may be concerned with maintaining the intensity of the basement membrane.

It is now believed that breast cancer starts in the epithelium that lines the ductules and acini within the breast lobule (32–3). The presence of actively functioning lobules is regarded as a necessary pre-requisite for the development of the disease. Breast lobules normally involute following the menopause, but can regularly be found in breasts involved by cancer, even in post-menopausal women (38).

Hyperplasia of the lobular epithelium is the earliest sign of proliferative change. The epithelial cells lining the terminal ductules and acini enlarge, become more numerous and several layers thick. This change does not necessarily progress; but in some women the epithelial hyperplasia becomes excessive and the cells develop abnormal features with an irregular pattern of growth. This stage is termed 'atypical hyperplasia'. Although this change only rarely will proceed to malignancy, it would appear to be a step in that direction. However, first the cells must become 'transformed' to acquire the properties of unrestrained division and growth that characterise malignant cells. This is a fundamental change of genetic constitution.

Once transformation to malignant phenotype has occurred, the stage is set for the development of a non-invasive or 'in-situ' cancer. By definition, such malignant cells cannot invade or penetrate the basement membrane that maintains the integrity of the epithelial layer. Nor can they gain access to the capillary network of the lymphatic or venous systems. They are confined to the breast lobule growing only into the lumen of its hollow structures. For invasion to occur, a second series of fundamental changes are believed to be necessary, these allowing the expression of proteins that can 'unstick' neighbouring cells, degrade the extracellular matrix (basement membrane) and promote migration (39–41).

When endowed with invasive properties, the malignant cells can penetrate normal tissue barriers, to infiltrate into the surrounding breast tissues and to gain access to lymphatic and venous channels. Once within these channels, they are carried with lymph or blood to be deposited in regional lymph nodes, liver, lungs, brain, bone marrow, and other sites.

At this stage these clumps of cells are but micro-metastases; but potentially they are the fore-runners of gross metastatic deposits of tumour which eventually cause clinical relapse of disease and death. It is not known whether these disseminated cells immediately start to replicate in their new metastatic sites, or whether they may lie dormant for periods of time. What is clear is that *clinical* relapse may be delayed for many years, a fact which in earlier times gave false assurance concerning the curability of the disease.

As oft stated by Brinkley and Haybittle, following reporting the results of their long-term follow-up study, 'breast cancer is a disease which disseminates early, but recurs late' (42). It is this 'new biology' of breast cancer that has led to the present emphasis on the role of systemic therapy for invasive disease, and to recognition of the prime objective of screening: the detection of the disease at a stage before dissemination has occurred.

A DIFFUSE DISEASE
From this somewhat simplistic account of the step-by-step process leading to the development of invasive breast cancer, it would appear that it is the potential endpoint of a diffuse hyperplastic change in the breast. And, although hyperplasia only infrequently leads to cancer, it does seem to be permissive—a necessary step—in its later development. It has long been recognised that in breasts that contain invasive cancer, areas of epithelial hyperplasia that may be atypical are frequently found, as are areas of *in situ* malignant change (43–4). As indicated in the title of a recent study from Guildford, in which whole breast sections indicated that 71 per cent of 127 invasive cancers had associated carcinoma-in-situ, 'invasive breast cancer is but the tip of the iceberg' (45).

The frequency of these changes in normal breasts can be ascertained only by the detailed study of breasts, removed post-mortem, from women who have died without evidence of symptomatic breast disease. Few such studies are available; most include sparse information on the relationship of proliferation of the breast epithelium to cancer (46–7).

In a recent study from Denmark, in which the breasts of 110 young women dying from accidental or other medico-legal causes were cut into 5 mm slices which were then examined by x-ray and by microscopy (involving over 60,000 separate blocks of tissue), foci of occult malignancy were reported in 22 of which 20 (18 per cent) were non-invasive. In all but one woman with cancer (a lobular carcinoma-in-situ) there was concomitant atypical hyperplasia of the ductal epithelium, a change that was recorded in 29 of all 110 women (48) (Table 3). By contrast, the number of occult cancers reported from a study of 519 similar autopsy specimens in New Mexico, in which radiologically suspicious areas in 5 mm slices of breast were sectioned, was only 11 (6 invasive and 5 in-situ) (49). It should be noted that post-mortem material may have artefacts which make interpretation difficult.

Estimates of the frequency of hyperplastic epithelial change have also been made from examination of specimens of tissue surgically removed from the breasts of women with

TABLE 3. *Incidence of atypical hyperplasia and* in situ *and invasive cancer*

Age	Number of Women	Number (%) with Atypical hyperplasia alone	Number (%) with Cancer In situ	Invasive
20–29	23	1	0	—
30–39	36	2	3 (8%)	—
40–49	33	4	13 (39%)	—
50–59	18	1	4 (22%)	2 (11%)
TOTAL	110	8 (7%)	20 (18%)	2 (2%)

Incidence of atypical hyperplasia and *in situ* and invasive cancer in the breasts of 110 women examined following accidental death. Four of nineteen non-invasive cancers were of lobular type; 21 of 22 breasts involved by cancer also had atypical hyperplasia (48).

benign disease. The most exhaustive study is that of Page and his colleagues from Nashville, Tennessee, who reported on 10,366 biopsies from women aged over 20 years (50). The incidence of epithelial hyperplasia and atypia is given in Table 4.

All women in this series have been followed up to determine the relevance of these changes, believed to be a marker of instability of the epithelium (51), to the later development of symptomatic cancer. For those with hyperplasia of mild, moderate or severe degree, this approximated twice that of women with normal epithelium; when the hyperplasia was atypical, the relative risk was 5·3. A history of cancer in a first-

TABLE 4. *Frequency of diagnosis of proliferative disease and carcinoma* in situ

Histology	Number	%
Benign specimens		
non-proliferative lesions	7221	68·5
proliferative lesions without atypia	2768	26·2
atypical hyperplasia	377	3·6
Carcinoma–*in situ*	176	1·7

Frequency of diagnosis of proliferative disease and carcinoma *in situ* in 10,542 women having a biopsy for suspected benign breast disease. Invasive cancers are excluded. (50). SOURCE: *New England Journal of Medicine*, with permission.

degree relative markedly increased the relative risk associated with atypical hyperplasia to $\times 11 \cdot 0$. It must be noted that these risks are relative to those with normal epithelium; they cannot be construed as actual risk of developing breast cancer compared to the general population.

It has been known for many years that invasive breast cancer can be multi-focal. One of the earliest observations was made in 1891 by Harold Stiles in Edinburgh, many years before the classic description by Qualheim and Gall and studies that Helen Stewart carried out in Cardiff (52–4).

So also is non-invasive cancer described as multi-focal (32–3). In Edinburgh, Anderson recently combined radiology and microscopy to ascertain the incidence of multi-focal deposits in 100 breasts removed for cancers detected by screening. Additional and separate deposits of tumour were found in 34 per cent of 83 invasive and 30 per cent of 17 non-invasive cancers. Although most frequent in the sector of the breast containing the dominant tumour, deposits were also identified in other quadrants (multi-centric) (55).

The changes that lead to breast cancer apparently affect both breasts. A woman with cancer of one breast is at greater risk of a cancer in the contra-lateral breast than is a normal woman; and in any woman treated for breast cancer, careful follow-up of the opposite breast, with regular mammography, is essential. When a generous biopsy has been taken of the opposite breast at the time of treating an invasive breast cancer, malignant changes have been reported in from $7 \cdot 5$ to $18 \cdot 0$ per cent (56–8).

It does appear that the epithelial abnormality that leads to invasive breast cancer is diffuse, and likely to be evidence of an abnormal stimulus affecting both breasts (e.g., of hormonal origin). Using a monoclonal antibody prepared against a membrane-enriched fraction of breast cancer cells, which showed differential re-activity between benign and malignant lesions, Onuchi and his colleagues found that atypical hyperplasia as well as *in situ* cancers demonstrated significantly higher reactivity than benign lesions; further evidence to support a gradation of change from hyperplasia to malignancy (59). Other markers of proliferative activity are being explored (60).

NON-INVASIVE BREAST CANCER

It is important to appreciate at this stage that there are two types of non-invasive cancer (61–2). One is lobular carcinoma *in situ* (LCIS), a rare disease (only 1000 cases are described in the world literature) diagnosed only by histopathology. There are no clinical or mammographic features, so that a finding of LCIS in a biopsy specimen is fortuitous. Even when a tissue biopsy found to contain LCIS is indicated by a mammographic abnormality (e.g., micro-calcifications), this is invariably due to a separate and benign cause. LCIS is identified only in pre-menopausal women, usually 40–47 years of age. Histologically, one or two breast lobules are packed with uniform but frankly malignant cells, which spread along the ductules. Evidence of coincidental invasion is rare and lymph-node metastases have been described in less than 2 per cent of all cases.

The other form of carcinoma *in situ*, ductal (DCIS), is not only a histopathological but also a clinical and mammographic entity. Before the availability of mammography it was diagnosed on clinical grounds following the appearance of a breast mass (75 per cent) or a bloody discharge from the nipple. Now the most common method of diagnosis is by mammography, either performed as a routine in the symptomatic clinic or on mammographic screening. Mammographic signs include distortion of the breast architecture, an asymmetrical increase in density, and micro-calcifications, either of linear and branching intraductal type or of clusters of fine punctate granules, which may be localised or diffuse.

Histologically DCIS may be: (i) solid, in which the lumen of the ductule is packed with malignant cells, which if they necrose in the centre (so that 'worms' of white tissue can be expressed from the specimen) is termed a carcinoma of comdeo type; and (ii) cribiform or macropapillary, in which small cells grow either in a lace-like pattern into the duct lumen (cribiform or sieve-like) or as delicate fronds (micropapillary). DCIS is more likely to have areas of micro-invasion (particularly when large in size) and lymph node metastases are more common (5 per cent) than in LCIS, which most now consider to be but a marker of instability of the lobular epithelium.

The incidence of carcinoma *in situ* is increased in those women who attend for screening. In the large Breast Cancer Detection Demonstration Project in the USA, 614 (17 per cent) of 3548 cancers detected by screening were of this type (63). Similar incidences have been reported from other programmes.

As the discovery of an *in situ* cancer leads to its removal, either by mastectomy or local excision, the natural history of untreated disease is unknown. From follow-up studies of patients treated by local excision, it is clear that a breast that has been involved by non-invasive cancer is at increased risk from the later development of invasive disease. This is important when considering treatment (see page 180).

A THRESHOLD

It is an essential principle of screening for any disease that there is an early stage that can be detected by the screening test, and that treatment of the disease at that early stage confers greater benefit than if delayed until the disease is symptomatic. For breast cancer this is the stage before dissemination has occurred to form micro-metastases. True non-invasive breast cancer is at such a stage; and although a small proportion of non-invasive cancers have evidence of dissemination to the axillary nodes, this is believed to be due to undetected foci of micro-invasive cancer within the tumour. This occurrence is more common, if not limited to, those with non-invasive tumours of clinically detectable size (64).

Even if undetected, the timespan of an *in situ* cancer is likely to be long, and its early detection will have little immediate effect on mortality. The immediate success of screening is more dependent upon whether there is an early stage of invasive cancer, during which dissemination is unlikely to have occurred. Studies supporting this concept have concentrated on the size of the primary tumour, which has been related either to the presence of axillary node metastases at the time of surgical treatment or to the development of clinical metastatic disease on long-term follow-up.

In 1971 Gallagher and Martin, from the M. D. Anderson Hospital in Houston, reported a classic study of the mammographic and histopathological findings in 209 breasts removed by radical mastectomy for the treatment of invasive cancer (65). The objective of the study was to determine factors that might improve the accuracy of mammography. But they were also concerned to know whether there was an upper limit of *radiological* size at which local treatments might still be curative, as indicated by the frequency of metastases in the axillary nodes. When the volume of the tumour mass was 0·125 ml or less (equivalent to a maximum diameter of 0·5 cm), the incidence of nodal metastases did not exceed 10 per cent. They applied the term 'minimal' to those cancers that were non-invasive, or if invasive were of 0·5 cm or less in size, predicting that they would prove to have an uncommonly good prognosis.

This prediction proved to be correct. In a retrospective follow-up of 415 women with such 'minimal' tumours, conducted in four centres, relapse-free survival over a median time of five years (1–26 yrs) was 97 per cent (66). As a result of the findings of the large Breast Cancer Detection Demonstration Project (BCDDP) in the United States, this definition of 'minimal' cancer was extended to include not only non-invasive cancers but invasive cancers of 1 cm in diameter or less (67). In the most recent report of the BCDDP, by this definition, 893 of 3548 (25 per cent) screen-detected cases were 'minimal' (63). Axillary lymph node metastases were identified in only 9 per cent and survival rates at five years exceeded 95 per cent.

A recent analysis of 24,740 women with breast cancer included in the Surveillance, Epidemiology and End Results (SEER) programme of the National Cancer Institute has confirmed these relationships (68). As the size of the primary tumour increased, so also did the incidence and extent of axillary node involvement, while five-year survival declined (Fig. 4). A multi-variate analysis indicated that size and axillary node status were independent and additive variables, size having greatest relevance in node-positive patients. Of the 24,750 women, 1335 had tumours less than 1 cm in size. Their five-year survival was on average over 95 per cent. Also identified in this study was a small subset of small tumours (82 in number) which showed unusual aggression; a finding of relevance to the appearance of clinically detectable cancers soon after a negative screen: so-called interval cases.

The state of involvement of the axillary nodes is only one indicator of prognosis. Women without node involvement may still have rapidly progressing disseminated disease; those with metastases may still survive for many years. In one long-term follow-up study, at least 21 of 81 20-year survivors had involved axillary nodes at the time of primary local treatment (69).

4. Relationship of tumour size to node involvement in 24,740 women with primary breast cancer (68).

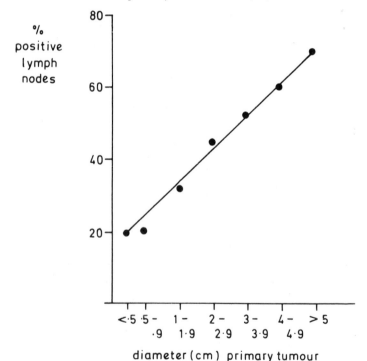

SOURCE: Carter et al, 1989: Cancer: J. B. Lippincott Co., with permission.

That the significant relationship between size and node status is retained in cases detected by screening has been confirmed in the Swedish Two-Countries study (70) (Fig. 5).

In the study reported by Kolsciesny and Tubiana, the index used to determine whether dissemination had taken place at the time of primary treatment was the development of clinical metastatic disease during follow-up to 25 years (71–2). Their series included 2648 women with breast cancer in whom clinical measurement of tumour size were made at primary treatment and related to later proof dissemination. The distribution was linear (Fig. 6). The median volume at which 50 per cent of tumour had disseminated was 23·6 ml (equivalent to a diameter of 3·56 cm). The larger the tumour, the shorter the time interval between initial treatment and relapse. When the volume of the tumour mass was 1 ml or less (diameter 1 cm), the likelihood of dissemination did not exceed 20 per cent.

5. Relationship of tumour diameter to the histology of the axillary lymph nodes in screen-detected and symptomatic cancers (70).

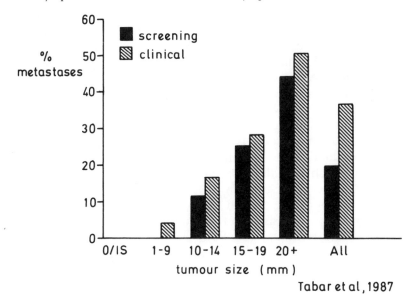

Tabar et al, 1987

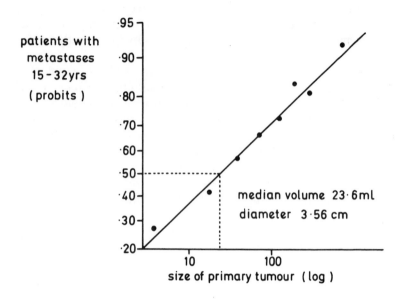

6. Relationship between tumour diameter at primary treatment and the subsequent development of metastatic disease (71). SOURCE: IV International Conference on Senology, with permission.

Within each size of tumour there was a great variation in the likelihood of dissemination, confirming the importance of factors other than size in determining the natural history of the disease. These include its degree of differentiation, as assessed by a number of techniques, ranging through simple histopathology, nuclear and cell grade, thymidine-labelling index, cytometric analysis of DNA content to expression of tumour-derived products. For example, tumours of well-differentiated type (cribiform, tubular, lobular), of low grade, which are diploid, have a long S-phase, express oestrogen-receptor protein or cathepsin-C (P52) or do not express epidermal growth factor receptor, have a more favourable prognosis than those which by these indices are poorly differentiated (73–81). The expression of human oncogenes, for example c-erb B2 and c-myc in the primary tumour is also now being related to prognosis, and may provide a useful guide to appropriate therapy, particularly in those patients in whom nodes are free from involvement, and the aggressiveness of the disease therefore unknown (78–81). Studies investigating these factors in screen-detected cancers are now in progress.

These various findings suggest that the natural history of invasive breast cancer is one of steady progression from a relatively non-aggressive tumour of small size. A 1·0 cm tumour, however, contains one billion cells, which with estimated doubling times of human breast cancers of 2–5 months would take 5–15 years to replicate from a single cell, assuming that its growth was exponential. Therefore, there must be a long period of time during which the tumour is biologically present yet not detectable as a clinical mass.

Tumours of 1 cm in size are palpable on clinical examination only if superficially placed in the breast. But contained within the pre-clinical growth phase of a cancer is a period when it can be detected by a suitable screening test—the pre-clinical detectable phase or, as termed by Walter and Day, the 'sojourn time'. The point at which a screening test detects the cancer divides this sojourn time into delay time and lead time. For a good test lead time will exceed that of delay (Fig. 7) (82).

7. Model to illustrate the principle of screen-detection of cancer during its 'sojourn' phase.

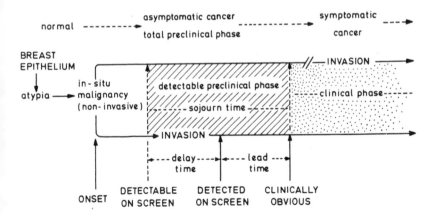

4

INVASIVE BREAST CANCER

A HEALTH PROBLEM

THE REPORT OF THE WORKING GROUP INDICATED THAT each year in the United Kingdom there were approximately 24,000 new cases of breast cancer and 15,000 deaths from the disease. This figure has not changed (83). During their lifetime, 6 per cent of our female population will develop the disease. There are some 150,000 living women in the U.K. who have been treated for breast cancer, of whom one dies each 30 minutes. In the United States one woman dies from breast cancer each 13 minutes. From USA it is reported that during the 10 years of the Vietnam war there were 57,000 deaths from combat, while 330,000 women died from breast cancer at home (84). And there are reports from all developed countries that the incidence of the disease is rising, particularly in younger women, even when the impact of earlier diagnosis and better cancer registration are taken into account (85–8). Were breast cancer a communicable or an acute disease, an epidemic would be declared. Yet, unlike communicable diseases of the past, it is not even registrable by law.

There is a marked variation in the incidence and mortality of breast cancer between countries, and this is further discussed in Chapter 9. Suffice it to say that, for age-adjusted mortality rates, England and Wales is still top of the league (Fig. 8) (89).

The risk of presenting with symptomatic breast cancer increases with age. Rare before the age of 25, its incidence increases up to the time of the menopause. Following a slight downward trend during the menopausal years [the menopausal hook of Clemmenson (90)] its incidence again continues to rise with advancing years, although at a

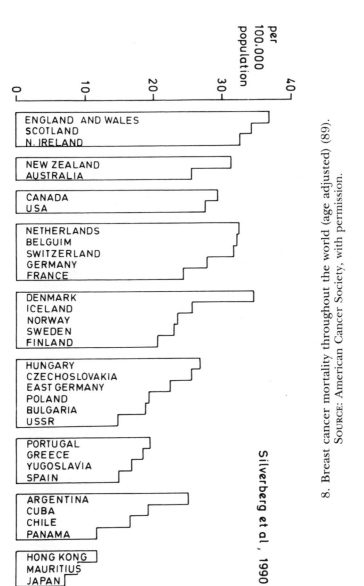

8. Breast cancer mortality throughout the world (age adjusted) (89).
SOURCE: American Cancer Society, with permission.

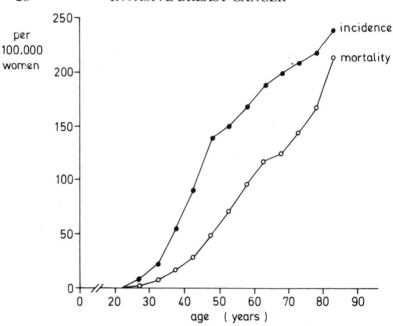

9. Age specific incidence (1982) and mortality rate (1985) rates for breast cancer in UK (3).

reduced rate (Fig. 9). It has greatest prevalence at the age of 55 years.

Breast cancer accounts for 20 per cent of all cancer deaths. But, because of variations in the age distribution of different cancers, the proportion of deaths from breast cancer to those to all causes varies by age (Fig. 10).

This proportion is greatest between the ages of 44 and 50 years, following which it steadily declines. For this reason, reduction in the number of deaths from breast cancer in older women cannot be expected to cause a *significant* reduction in all-cause mortality.

AN INCURABLE DISEASE?

The curability of breast cancer can be defined in a number of ways (91).

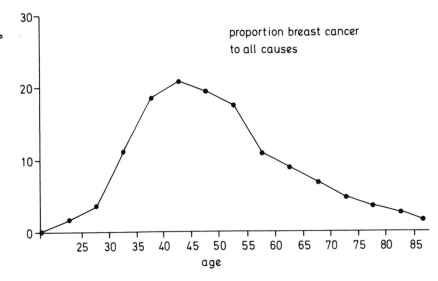

10. Deaths in females: UK 1985 (3).

Mortality Rates

Firstly, the gap between cumulative annual incidence and death rates is taken by some to indicate a 'cured' group (in this country, of around 35 per cent) who do not die from their disease (Fig. 9). But this is not necessarily so. In U.K., cancer incidence is based on non-compulsory notification of clinical cases to Cancer Registries, which also receive copies of death certificates in their area that include mention of cancer. Although inaccuracies do occur, those for cancer of the breast, which is easily diagnosed, are believed to be relatively small.

Mortality rates are based on death certification with the Office of Population Censuses and Surveys (OPCS) in England and the Central Registry Office (CRO) in Scotland and North Ireland. A death is encoded as being due to breast cancer only if this is recorded in Part I of the certificate as the primary underlying cause of death. Overt signs of breast cancer, which are present at death but not believed to be its direct cause, are recorded in Part II of the certificate. But this does not contribute to published mortality statistics.

The errors that exist between the recorded primary cause of death, as recorded on the death certificate, and that discovered at post-mortem examination are known overall to be in the order of 20 to 40 per cent (92–94). However the error for death due to breast cancer is much smaller, and in one study reported to be 6 per cent (95).

A recent detailed study of the validity of death certification in breast cancer cases has been reported from Cambridge (96). This was of 193 deaths in women known to have breast cancer in whom the entries on death certificates were compared with clinical, cancer registration, and post-mortem records. The under-estimate in certifying breast cancer as the *primary* or underlying case of death was only 4 per cent. However, the error in recording breast cancer as a *secondary* cause was much greater. Thus there was no entry of 'breast cancer' on the death certificate of 21 of 58 women known, from their clinical records, to have overt signs of the disease at death. It was concluded that the difference between national statistics for registration and deaths from breast cancer represented a considerable over-estimate of women who remain free from symptoms of breast cancer before dying, apparently but not certainly from some other cause, and cannot be regarded as indicating a group who have been cured of their disease.

Definitions of Cure

Life is a personal matter, and most people would regard freedom from relapse of breast cancer for the remainder of their lifetime following its treatment as 'cure'. This definition of 'personal cure' does not consider the possibility that the disease is present in asymptomatic form. The woman who, following treatment of her breast cancer, dies in a car accident on her way home from hospital is, by this definition, cured.

A second definition is 'clinical cure', which implies complete eradication of the disease. This is the desirable end-point of treatment; but success can be measured only by a complete pathological search for asymptomatic deposits of disease on death, which is not practicable.

The third definition of cure is 'statistical'. As described by Marion Russell, 'We may speak of cure of a disease when there remains a group of disease-free survivors, probably a decade or two after treatment, whose annual death rate from all causes is similar to that of a normal population group of similar sex and age distribution.' (97)

The determination of such a cured group requires long-term follow-up studies of women treated for breast cancer by local means alone. A number of such studies have now been reported, several from Britain, including the classic study from East Anglia of Brinkley and Haybittle (69,98) (Fig. 11). These investigators initially believed that there was a small sub-group of women, representing 20 per cent of those treated, whose annual death rate, after periods varying from 15 to 25 years, was no greater than that of age-matched normal controls, and who therefore could be regarded as being statistically 'cured'. However, extension of the period of follow-up to over 30 years indicated that the ratio of observed to expected deaths continues to exceed

11. Long-term survival of 704 patients with breast cancer treated by local surgery or radiotherapy (98).

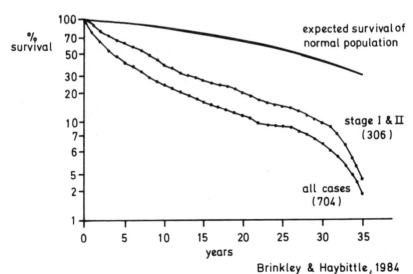

Brinkley & Haybittle, 1984

1:0. Detailed studies of the cause of death have confirmed an excess mortality from metastatic disease. Similar studies from other countries are confirmatory, including one from Sweden in which, in young women, excess mortality from breast cancer has persisted for 40 years (99–103).

These results confirm that symptomatic invasive breast cancer is most often a systemic disease that cannot be cured by local treatment alone. But, some women will not experience further problems during their lifetime. In Brinkley and Haybittle's series this proportion was only 26 per cent.

THE PROBLEM

To understand the problem of invasive breast cancer it is necessary to understand the disease as it has presented to surgeons in our hospitals over the past century. But also to appreciate how a false premise could lead to faulty management, with concentration on radical local ablative therapy as the best means of cure. Although there were some who did not accept that the theory underlying this approach represented the truth.

The new biology of the disease—which emphasises early dissemination—described in Chapter 1 allows only two approaches to improving what is a daunting situation. Firstly to recognise, as stated by Geoffrey Keynes, that 'the invaders are bound to gain the upper hand in the end unless they are repelled by systemic treatment'; and secondly that detection before such invasion has occurred offers the only serious hope of control. One needs only to look at the unchanged mortality from the disease during the past 50 years to recognise that something must be done (Fig. 12); which is why the screening of normal women by mammography is now being implemented in many countries.

Clinical Presentation

Typically, invasive breast cancer forms a mass of tumour tissue in the female breast that is hard and irregular and is integrated into the surrounding breast tissue. It distorts the breast, first noticed by a flattening of its normal smooth contour when this is put on stretch by raising the arms, but

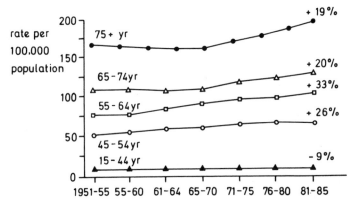

12. Breast cancer mortality: England and Wales, 1951–85 (83).
Source: CRC Factsheet, 1988: Cancer Research Campaign.

later by obvious asymmetry. Distortion and contraction of
the supporting fibrous bands lead to tethering of the skin
over the tumour, and that of the ducts to asymmetrical
retraction of the nipple.

If the cancer is superficially placed, the skin becomes
adherent to it and cannot be moved freely over the breast
mass. If deep in the breast, it may become attached to the
fascia that lies on the pectoral muscles or to the muscles
themselves, interfering with free movement of the breast on
the chest wall. The lymph nodes in the axilla may be palpably
enlarged, but only 70 per cent of the palpable nodes contain
deposits of metastatic tumour. The remainder show only
benign re-active change. Conversely, metastases are present
in 30 per cent of nodes that are not palpable.

These typical features are well illustrated on a diagnostic
mammogram, which in the majority of cases will confirm the
diagnosis. There is a dense opacity of irregular shape, often
containing central clumps of calcifications. Its border is
spiculated, due to columns of cancer cells and reactionary
fibrous tissue projecting circumferentially into the surrounding breast tissue.

Secondary mammographic features include asymmetry of
the breast, distortion of the trabeculae, prominence of the

ductal system, increased vascularity and thickening of the overlying skin. On fine-needle aspiration, cancer is most commonly hard and gritty and the apsirate contains clumps of obviously malignant cells.

These are the signs of an established cancer, but one that is still regarded as operable. Should it not be diagnosed at this stage, but continue to increase in size, it may invade the skin, forming a plaque of firm tumour tissue that may ulcerate, or, having penetrated the skin, project from its surface as a fungating growth. Invasion of the lymphatics in the skin gives rise to skin oedema and satellite nodules; invasion of the skin capillaries to redness—the so called 'inflammatory cancer'.

Should the tumour extend deeply to penetrate the muscle it will become fixed to the chest wall with erosion of ribs. Lymph nodes in the axilla become larger and, owing to extension of tumour, fixed to one another and surrounding structures. Extension of lymph-node involvement to the neck and to the internal mammary nodes also occurs.

But, for most patients advancing local disease is not the most fearful clinical problem. This is the systemic spread of the disease, which, as has been indicated, occurs early, although clinical relapse may be long delayed. Common sites for metastases are the bone marrow, lungs, liver, brain, and pleural and peritoneal cavities; but no site is exempt. Deposits of tumour cause the upsets of function, which eventually lead to organ failure and death. Symptoms can be severe—breathlessness from deposits in the lung or pleura, pain from those in bone, headache, and neurological deficits from those in brain or spinal column—coupled with general debility from visceral metastases.

On microscopic examination of an invasive cancer the pattern is one of disorder. Groups of large irregular and obviously malignant cells infiltrate a fibrous stroma with variable attempts to form granular or tubular structures. There is increased formation of collagen, streaks of elastica and infiltrate of lymphocytes. Within the breast there may be evidence of lymphatic or ductal invasion. This is the typical ductal cancer of no special type that accounts for 70 to 80 per cent of cancers.

The remaining 20 to 30 per cent of invasive cancers form a number of specialised types. Most common is the lobular, typified by the regular pattern of its small cells, and believed to be the invasive form of lobular carcinoma *in situ*. Other are the medullary cancer, a well circumscribed tumour with sheets of undifferentiated cells and prominent lymphocytic infiltration; mucoid cancer, in which cancer cells appear to float in a lake of mucinous material; tubular cancer, with small irregular tubules infiltrating into a dense fibrous stroma; and cribiform cancer, in which cyst-like spaces are lined by a honeycomb arrangement of the cells. These differentiated forms of cancer are not to be disregarded for two reasons: When compared to the nondescript ductal cancer, they have a disproportionately good prognosis; and there is some evidence that they may be more common in screen-detected cases (73,104–5).

Staging

It was the need to aid the clinician in the planning of treatment, to give some indication of prognosis, to evaluate the results of treatment and to facilitate exchange of information that prompted the Union Internationale Contre Cancre to take steps in 1953 to introduce an international system for classifying breast and other cancers, based on that developed in Villejuif, France, by Pierre Denoix. The TNM system is now accepted throughout the world as standard. TNM stands for Tumour, Nodes, and Metastases, each of which is classified according to extent of involvement. T defines the local extent of a breast tumour by its size and the presence or absence of involvement of neighbouring tissues; N whether axillary and other regional lymph nodes are infiltrated by metastases or not; and M whether distant metastases are present or not. Assessment of extent is by careful clinical measurements and, wherever possible, by histological confirmation.

From TNM categories the stage of the disease is determined. In general, Stage I disease is a small tumour limited to the breast; Stage II either a tumour of larger size (>2 cm) or one associated with axillary node involvement; Stage III locally advanced disease involving skin or chest wall; and

Stage IV that which clinically has disseminated to sites outside the local area.

Revisions of the TNM staging have taken place regularly, the most recent in 1987. The 1987 classification has now been internationally agreed by both the International Union against Cancer and the American Joint Committee on Cancer. There are some differences in detail between the 1978 IUCC classification (as has been used in the Swedish trials and is summarised in Table 5) and the revised version. For example the distinction whereby axillary nodes were classified on clinical grounds as being likely involved or not has been abandoned. Large tumours (>5 cm) without evidence of skin or chest wall involvement—the so-called 'operable stage III' have been downstaged to stage II while involvement of supraclavicular nodes has been upstaged by from III to IV and therefore regarded as evidence of disseminated disease. These changes do not affect comparisons between trials, in which the 1978 classification has generally been used (106–8).

TABLE 5. *Summary table of TNM clinical classification of breast cancer (from 1978 classification) as used in screening trials. In pathological TNM, size is as measured on the gross specimen and node involvement by histological examination*

Stage	T	N	M
I	0–2 cm (T_1)	Not palpable (N_0)	None (M_0)
II	Over 2–5 cm (T_2)	Palpable axillary (N_1)	None (M_0)
III	Over 5 cm (T_3)	Axillary fixed to each other or to adjacent tissues (N_2)	None (M_0)
	Infiltrating skin or chest wall (T_4)	Other regional nodes (N_3)	None (M_0)
IV	Any	Any	Distant metastases (M_1)

It should be noted that classification by stage (I–IV) as shown in Table 5 is by clinical findings; and that contrary to what is done by some, pathological findings contribute to pTNM category only.

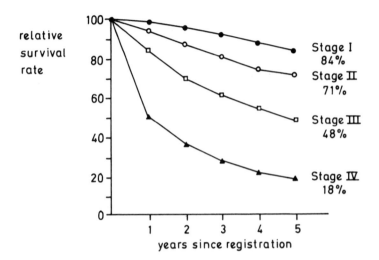

13. Breast cancer in England and Wales: effect of stage on CRC Factsheet, 1988: Cancer Research Campaign prognosis (83).

The influence of stage on prognosis is shown in Figure 13 (83).

Radical Local Treatment: A False Premise

The surgical treatment for breast cancer 'took off' late last century. Prior to the introduction of anaesthesia and of antisepsis, only operations of necessity (e.g., for the removal of ulcerating and fungating breast disease) were attempted. Often, as vividly portrayed by John Brown in 'Rab and His Friends', with fatal results. There was then no expectation of cure (109).

With the development of painless and safe surgery, operations could be designed on anatomical and pathological principles and have clear objectives. For breast cancer these were eradication of the visible and palpable tumour in the breast and axilla. The first such 'radical' operation was probably performed by Lister in Glasgow, just two months after he had first used his 'carbolic treatment' for a clean surgical (as opposed to a traumatic or infected) wound. The patient was his sister, Isabella Pim. She recovered quickly and without complication, and was well for three years before she died from a 'tumour in the liver', no doubt metastatic in origin (110).

Similar operations were soon practised by others in Europe; but on account of the late stage of the disease, local relapse of disease was common. This high recurrence rate, seen on a tour of European clinics, prompted Halsted to design the 'radical mastectomy' which still bears his name (although the more commonly used technique was that of Meyer) (111–2). Although this operation, which removed the muscles clothing the chest wall, is not now practised in Britain, there are surgeons world-wide who continue to use it, believing that they have nothing better to offer.

It seems that Halsted's main objective was to achieve local control of what we would regard as advanced local disease. Mistakenly, he came to believe that he was also achieving cure: for he wrote 'If three years had passed without detecting either local recurrence or symptoms of internal disease, one could feel sure that cure had been achieved.' By convention this three-year period was later extended to five, which, considering the natural history of the disease, was equally irrelevant. Belief in the efficacy of local therapy was further consolidated by Sampson Handley, who belittled the spread of breast cancer by embolisation of lymphatic and blood streams (113). He believed that breast cancer spread by a wavelike permeation of columns of cells along the lymphatic pathways towards the regional lymph nodes. Only when they were breached did 'secondary spread' to viscera occur. This erroneous belief, coupled with suggestions stemming from Virchow's work that the regional lymph nodes 'filtered out' embolised cells, established breast cancer as a loco-regional disease, best cured by radical local therapy (114). The scope of the radical operation was extended, by supra-radical operations—removing lymph nodes in the neck and from within the chest—and even amputating the whole forequarter, and by the introduction of radical post-operative radiotherapy to 'sterilise' the region of residual cancer cells.

It has taken almost a century to prove that both theory and practice were wrong. Firstly by experimental evidence of the primary role of embolisation, both by the lymphatics and bloodstream in the spread of cancer; and secondly by the results of a large number of controlled randomised trials indicating that such extensions of treatment did not improve the rate of cure. A recent overview of trials of postoperative radiotherapy has indicated that, in the long term, radiotherapy (of the type then given) may even do harm (115–17).

The Unorthodox

Not all surgeons or radiologists accepted the logic of radical surgery. In London, Patey doubted the necessity of resecting the chest-wall muscles, and his 'modified radical' operation is now accepted surgical practice when removal of the breast and axillary lymph nodes is indicated (118). In Edinburgh, McWhirter believed it illogical to treat the axillary nodes surgically and other nodal areas by irradiation, and asked surgeons to limit their operation to removal of the breast alone (so-called 'simple' mastectomy), allowing him to irradiate the 'primary field' of lymphatic spread en block (119). In Cardiff we were concerned to spare the morbidity of radiotherapy to those not requiring it, and introduced 'sampling' of the lower axillary lymph nodes as a means of selecting those patients in whom mastectomy by itself was adequate treatment (120).

But the big step had already been taken. In 1920, Geoffrey (later Sir Geoffrey) Keynes was 'entrusted' by his professor, George Gask, to carry out a 'clinical trial of treating breast cancer with intense irradiation', at that time with radium. Observing 'astonishingly good results' in 50 patients with inoperable disease, he extended his treatment, combined with local removal of the tumour, to operable cases; and by 1936 reported that the results did not differ from those of the radical operation (121–3).

Keynes suggested that radical surgery was both illogical and mutilating, and that systematic, not radical, treatment gave the only hope of cure. Others followed his example and discarded radical surgery (110), action now fully vindicated by the results of several controlled randomised trials that have indicated that local excision of the tumour followed by radiotherapy is, at any rate for the treatment of small tumours, a viable alternative to mastectomy (124–6). This change of emphasis on the extent of primary treatment did not improve survival, but was a remarkable advance in understanding the objectives of treating the disease. The objective of local treatment is to achieve local control, which does not require multilating surgery.

Psychosexual Morbidity

During this period of change, great advances also were being made in our understanding of the psychiatric morbidity of treatment for breast cancer.

The pioneering studies of Tina Morris, Greer and Maguire indicated that following mastectomy one in five women develop anxiety or depression of moderate or severe degree (127–8). Tense and on edge, they had difficulty in dealing with day-to-day problems, some even afraid to leave home on their own. Everything became an effort, they lost interest in work and family, slept and ate badly, and lost their sexual desire.

It was initially believed that these effects were due to loss of the breast; and there is no doubt that mastectomy has its own psychosexual morbidity. This can be offset by reconstructing the breast mound, a procedure that we now offer at the time of primary surgery to all patients requiring a mastectomy (129). But it is not only the mastectomy which causes morbidity; similar effects can follow treatment with preservation of the breast (130). Other factors come to bear, including fear of the disease, lack of confidence in their doctor, guilt that faulty personality or lifestyle has caused the cancer, withdrawal of support by husbands and friends.

Certain women are more prone to react adversely: Those failing to adapt to the presence of the disease, who are divorced or unhappily married, have low self-esteem or previous psychiatric problems are more at risk.

It is as a result of this new knowledge that we have seen the development of counselling, by trained health professionals, of women with breast cancer. It is easier for a woman to express her fears and worries to another woman, who is less hierarchical than her surgeon and is prepared to listen. In many centres, including Edinburgh, the nurse counsellor is an indispensable member of the therapeutic team. Early recognition of those women who are destined to develop severe psychiatric problems with reference for appropriate treatment is an important preventive role.

ONE SOLUTION

Systemic Treatment

As invasive breast cancer is potentially a systemic disease, effective treatment for micro-metastatic spread is one way to improve rates of cure.

For Palliation. Systemic treatment for breast cancer by removal of the ovaries was introduced in 1895 for the control of recurrent disease following mastectomy by George (later Sir George) Beatson, then in Glasgow. His observation of remission of disease was the first direct evidence of a relationship between the ovarian hormones oestrogen and progesterone and cancer of the breast (131). Interestingly, the first evidence that these hormones regulated normal breast development was also made by a surgeon, Percival (later Sir Percival) Pott, in 1775 (132).

Recognition that the beneficial effect of oophorectomy on advanced disease was limited to pre-menopausal women led to the later introduction of removal of the adrenal and removal or destruction of the pituitary glands (133–6).

We now know that the effect of these operations is to deprive the tumour of oestrogen, either in the young woman by removing their main source (the ovaries), or for those past the menopause by removing or inhibiting the source of the precursor steroids that are utilised by liver, muscle, and fat for the synthesis of oestrogens (the adrenals) (137). It is also now well established that it is only, but not all of, those tumours that express a high-affinity binding protein for oestrogen (the oestrogen receptor) that are sensitive to oestrogen deprivation.

During this period of endocrine surgery, pharmacological agents capable of antagonising the effects of oestrogen were also being used for the palliation of advanced disease

(138–40). The agents then available, androgens or synthetic oestrogens, were given in high dose and caused serious side effects. Knowledge of the mechanism of oestrogen synthesis and action has stimulated the development of non-toxic yet potent agents which have now ended the era of endocrine surgery. These include the gonadotrophin-releasing hormone analogues (e.g., goserelin), which cause a profound inhibition of ovarian function; the aromatase inhibitors (e.g., aminoglutethimide and 4-hydroxyandrostenedione), which inhibits the enzymes responsible for the peripheral synthesis of oestrogens; and tamoxifen, which binds to the oestrogen receptor to form an ineffective complex. The discovery of the biological effects of tamoxifen by Harper and Walpole in 1966 was a huge step forward in the therapy of breast cancer (141). Tamoxifen, with its absence of side effects, is now first-line treatment world-wide for relapsed disease.

The other form of systemic treatment that is available is cytotoxic chemotherapy, which can achieve rapid regression of locally advanced and disseminated disease. Because of this rapid effect, chemotherapy is used preferentially for the management of life-threatening conditions, e.g., impending organ failure from liver or pulmonary or bone-marrow metastases. But, otherwise, in the U.K. chemotherapy is generally reserved for those not responding to tamoxifen.

As an Adjuvant. Systemic therapy for advanced disease is not given with expectations of cure. Systemic therapy for early disease has, as its objective, the elimination of micro-metastatic disease. Insufficient time has elapsed to know whether this objective can be achieved; but there is no doubt that the administration of systemic therapy, as part of the primary treatment of invasive breast cancer, does prolong life. This evidence has come from a series of controlled randomised trials in which systemic treatment has been given as an 'adjuvant' to local treatment, usually mastectomy.

The first such trial, was of suppression of ovarian function, this by radiation. It was initiated in 1953 by Ralston Paterson in Manchester (142). More recent studies have concentrated on the effects of tamoxifen and of chemotherapy; and there is now unequivocal evidence that both give benefit. This comes from the report of the Early Breast Cancer Trialists Co-operative Group, which, under the leadership of Richard Peto in Oxford, carried out an overview analysis of the mortality results of all randomised trials, world-wide, of adjuvant tamoxifen and chemotherapy; these included over 30,000 women (143).

There were 28 trials of tamoxifen including 16,000 women. Its administration over a period of one to two years led to a highly significant reduction in annual mortality of 16 ± 3 per cent overall, which in women of 50 years of age or more was 20 ± 3 per cent. Although in absolute terms the increase in five-year cumulative survival was only from 68 to 73 per cent, this effect was highly significant (Fig. 14).

There were 31 trials of chemotherapy including 9069 women. Again, a significant reduction in overall annual mortality was observed (14 ± 4 per cent). This effect was more

14. Result of overview of randomised trials of tamoxifen as adjuvant therapy in 8142 women over 49 years of age (143). SOURCE: *New England Journal of Medicine*, with permission.

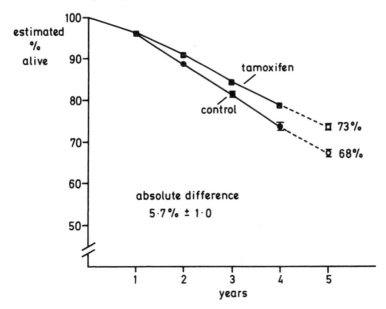

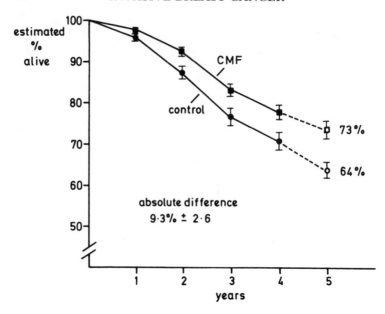

15. Result of overview of randomised trials of chemotherapy as adjuvant treatment in 1692 women under 50 years of age (143).
Source: *New England Journal of Medicine*, with permission.

prominent in young women (less than 50 years) and when combinations of chemotherapeutic agents were used. In absolute terms this amounted to a significant increase in five-year cumulative survival from 64 to 73 per cent (Fig. 15).

In the trials of tamoxifen the drug was given only for one to two years. In that which we reported from the Scottish Cancer Trials Office, tamoxifen was given, in the immediate treatment arm, for five years (144). A significant overall reduction in mortality was again observed, which in a subset of patients, separately randomised, all of whom have received tamoxifen for five years, has proved to be substantial. When one considers that not all tumours are sensitive to tamoxifen, the effect in those which are may be great.

There are still many questions to be answered about the role of primary endocrine therapy and chemotherapy in the management of invasive breast cancer, and these are being actively explored in many centres. To imply, even at the present state of knowledge, that it does not constitute an advance is nonsensical, for it has opened up the potential for cure of what, to date, has been an incurable disease.

ANOTHER SOLUTION

The alternative solution to 'repelling the invading cells' by systemic treatment is to remove the primary tumour before dissemination has occurred. For this, it must be detected while it is sojourning in its pre-clinical detectable phase. From the information presented in Chapter 3, it is apparent that this must be when the tumour is non-invasive or, if invasive small, not palpable and without axillary node metastases. This approach depends on whether there is such a method available. This will be discussed in the next chapter.

5

THE METHOD

KNOWLEDGE THAT THE PRIME OBJECTIVE OF SUCCESSFUL screening is to detect breast cancer at its pre-clinical stage, i.e., before it has become detectable by clinical examination, clarifies the requirements for a suitable test. Physical examination, whether by breast self-examination (BSE) or routine clinical (physical) examination of the breasts by a doctor or nurse, may detect cancer at an earlier stage than that noticed accidentally in the shower or bath, but it still can only detect a tumour that is palpable. It is the nonpalpable tumour that one seeks to discover, which at this time can be achieved reliably only by soft-tissue imaging of the breast by mammography.

EVOLUTION OF MAMMOGRAPHY

Following the discovery of x-ray imaging by Roentgen in 1895, it could be expected that soft-tissue imaging of the breast would soon be explored. It was a German pathologist, Salomon, who in 1913 first imaged the breast, this to enable him to study the pattern of spread in mastectomy specimens. Correlating radiological and pathological features, he recognised that 'small black spots' were a feature of cancer (subsequently shown by Leborgne to be calcifications) and also that imaging had potential value in recognising occult cancer (145–7). Following the first world war, attempts were being made to x-ray the breast in the living. Probably the first radiological picture of a breast was published by Kleinschmidt in a textbook of radiology in 1927 (147). In 1929 Warren, from Rochester, New York State, reported the first large series of mammograms in 119 women, 58 with

46

cancer (148). He took antero-lateral stereoscopic films of both breasts with the patient's arm above her head, a position that he had found to display the breast while imaging the thoracic aorta! His radiological studies of post-mortem and pathological material enabled him to define criteria by which a pre-operative diagnosis could be made in 54 of 58 cancers.

Others in South America and Europe were also exploring the potential of this technique but, although a number of papers were published in the 1930s, interest in the procedure waned. According to Egan, this was due to a failure to grasp the principles of the techniques and the lack of a co-ordinated effort to conduct well-designed studies. However, there were pioneers—Gros in France, Gershon-Cohen and Egan in the United States, and Leborgne in South America—whose careful studies correlating clinical, radiological, and pathological findings eventually put mammography on a sound basis (147,149–54).

While it is difficult to unravel their independent contributions, there is no doubt that the technological developments leading to modern high-quality mammography stem from Gros and Egan. A new technology was required, the essentials being to provide a system that allowed radiological visualisation of the smallest structures within the breast with a resolution of one-tenth that normally regarded as the minimum (0·05 mm). The need to contrast the fibrous and glandular components of the breast and to detect the smallest micro-calcifications demanded a particular spectrum of x-ray photons of low kV, which in 1960 Gros reported could better be generated by a molydenum rather than tungsten anode. This gave optimum conditions for imaging the thin and fatty breast, and is now standard on all dedicated mammography units. The size and composition of the breast scatters the x-ray photons, which blurs the image; but this can be reduced by vigorous compression of the breast so that it is spread out as an even 'slice', some 4·5 cm thick, onto the x-ray plate. In developing the first dedicated mammography unit with the Compagnie Generale L'Electrique (CGR—senography), Gros incorporated a compression device that is independent from the x-ray tube, and this also now is standard (155). It is the need for compression that makes mammography uncomfortable and even painful for some women, but its role of separating the tissues of the breast and preventing movement is essential for good mammography.

The requirements for modern film-screen mammography are well documented (156–61) (Table 6). The resolution to detect the smallest micro-calcifications is achieved by a tube with a small focal spot that is fixed at a distance of about 45 cm from the breast. The image-recording system must be highly sensitive and have a large density range. The fine-grain industrial film of high silver content, which initially was used, had the correct characteristics, but, because exposure time was long, the radiation dose was high and the cost excessive. Films of low silver content were developed with a single coating of emulsion, which when used with high-intensity screens gave satisfactory results with a greatly reduced dose. These screens, manufactured of rare earths, convert x-ray to light photons which expose the film. To ensure intimate contact between screen and film, they are packed in a sealed black polythene envelope from which the air has been excluded.

TABLE 6. *Requirements for modern mammography* (161)

IMAGE CONTRAST
    Anode material: radiation spectrum
    Filtration
    Scatter: size and composition of breast
    Characteristics of film-screen
    Processing: development

IMAGE SHARPNESS
    Size focal spot
    Magnification: focus: object-film distance
    Resolution of image-recording system

NOISE
    Grain of film
    X-ray quantum 'mottle'
    Structure-intensifying screens

It is necessary to process the films under carefully controlled conditions of temperature, composition and depletion state of the developing fluid and of time. Dedicated processors are now available. Good viewing conditions, automatic roll-on film cabinets and magnification aids are essential aids.

While modern units give mammograms of excellent quality in the fatty breast, the examination of the dense breast can still cause problems. However, because of the low radiation dose required with modern film-screen systems, it is possible to use fine fibre-spaced grids that further reduce scatter and improve contrast. Many radiologists now use grid films routinely for all screening mammograms; increasingly of moving (reciprocating) type (162).

Magnification of a normal-sized image on the film can be achieved by a magnifying glass or electronic equipment. For finer discrimination it is much better to magnify the initial image by increasing the distance between the breast and the film (163). Modern machines with a very small focal spot and adjustable breast-film distance produce excellent magnification views. These are essential for the closer study of small lesions.

Initially, two standard projections, medio-lateral and cranio-caudal, were employed, to which was added an axillary view to demonstrate the axillary tail and axillary nodes. The medio-lateral oblique projection was seldom used, until Lundgren reported that, as it contained a greater proportion of the breast tissue than either the lateral or craniocaudal views, it might be used as a sole screening test (164–6). And in Sweden, in Nijmegen, in Holland, and now in U.K. this was put into practice; although not without misgiving from some.

There were also pioneers in Britain who were exploring and developing the new technology, without whose efforts the U.K. trial of breast screening could not have taken place (167–176). However, one should note that, in 1985 half of the 219 Health Districts and Boards in U.K. were without any mammographic facilities, while many others had equipment that was regarded as obsolete (3).

RADIATION RISK

A serious disadvantage of the early techniques for mammography was that, although good images could be produced, the dose of radiation to the breast was excessive, and might be 20–30 mGy (2–3 rads) for each exposure. In the HIP study, using the Egan technique, the skin dose averaged 77 mGy (7·7 rad) per examination (177). This was due to the need to compensate the low kV of the x-ray photon beam with the relative insensitivity of the fine-grain industrial film, resulting in a long exposure time.

In 1976, much concern was being aired at the potential risk of mammography in *causing* cancer (20). This was justified; as indicated above, the dose of radiation given in a 'complete' mammographic examination (which included repeat films) could extend to many rads.

At the time of concern there was good evidence that radiation was a risk factor for breast cancer in humans. But this involved exposure of the breast to higher doses of radiation than mammography, even in these early days. That which was received for irradiation of the breast therapeutically, from multiple fluoroscopic examinations for tuberculosis or from an atomic exposure, was substantial (178–81). For example that given to 28 surviving schoolgirls who were 14–15 years of age at the time of the atomic explosion in Hiroshima, six of whom have developed breast cancer varied between 1·5 and 6·0 Gy. Their relative risk of the disease, compared to age matched controls, was 23·1 (12·9–42·2) (182).

These reports indicated that the susceptability to breast cancer risk from irradiation was greatest when less than 20 years of age, following which it steadily declines. A recent report from Israel indicates that a small dose of 16 mGy (1–6 rads) to the breast of young (5–9 years) girls significantly increases their risk of later development of breast cancer (183). But after the menopause the risk appears to be small. A long latent period also occurred between exposure to radiation and the development of a cancer, mostly 10 to 15 years, with a minimum latent period of 5 to 10 years. Risk was limited to females.

At high levels of radiation, the relationship between dose and effect was linear. To determine whether there was a risk associated with the range of doses then used for mammography, it was necessary to extrapolate the dose-effect curve and also to consider the results of animal experiments; justification for which depended upon whether the linear relationship between dose and effect was maintained at low levels of radiation and if there was a threshold below which radiation was harmless. On the assumption that cancer arose from a single transformed cell, a linear-quadratic model was developed, from which lifetime risk from low doses of radiation could be calculated. This suggests that if two million women over the age of 50 were to receive a low-dose single-view mammogram (mean breast dose 1·5 mGy), there would be, after a latent period of 10 years, one excess cancer per year. Compared to an incidence of breast cancer at age 60 that approaches 2000 per million women, this risk is of no consequence.

But risk is not only determined by dose. The quality of the radiations, fractionation, exposure time, sensitisation, and host factors are relevant. With the development of low-dose

16. Radiation dose received by breast related to later risk of breast cancer (180).

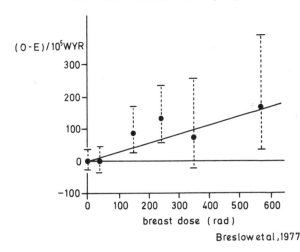

Breslow et al, 1977

mammography the risk is reduced to insignificant proportions, provided high standards of quality are maintained.

Measurement of the dose of radiation delivered by mammography is usually of that received by the skin from which an absorbed dose to breast tissue is calculated. This is often referred to as the mid-breast or average dose. It is the average dose to the glandular tissue of the breast which is relevant to radiation risk. This would appear to be satisfactorily low (184–6) (Table 7). But continual monitoring of the dose of radiation delivered on mammography is an essential precaution.

TABLE 7. *Dose of radiation to each breast for two-view mammography in the Canadian National trial* (186).

Mammography unit	Film	Dose (mGy)
CGR		
seno-1	MRF 31 (Du Pont)	1·9–2·6
500 T	OM (Kodak)	1·2–2.0
Fx	OM	1·8–2.0
Elscint		
mam-1	OM-1	1·3
Philips	MRF 31	1·7
Picker	NMB (Kodak)	2·0
Siemens	OM	1·3–1.8

SOURCE: *Can. J. Pub. Hlth.*, with permission.

XEROMAMMOGRAPHY

This alternative method of imaging the breast with x-ray photons uses an electrostatic receptor instead of film (187). This consists of a plate of selenium which carries a positive charge. When exposed to x-ray photons the particles of selenium lose their charge in proportion to the amount of radiation received. A latent image is produced which corresponds to the pattern of absorption of the photon beams as they pass through the breast.

This image is 'developed' by spraying negatively charged particles of blue talc onto the plate. These heap up particularly where photons have been absorbed by dense breast tissue, forming a stronger image against the lighter background of the areas of complete discharge. It is this heaping-up effect that enhances the edges of areas of contrasting x-ray photon absorption within the breast (e.g., calcifications). The 'developed' image is copied onto paper as a permanent record.

Xeromammography uses standard x-ray equipment with a tungsten anode. The dose of radiation required to discharge the plate is higher than for film-screen combinations, and is in the order of (1–2 rad) 10–20 mGy per exposure. Reversing the charge so that the image is converted to the negative mode reduces the dose, but not to the levels now possible with modern film screen combinations. A liquid toner has now been developed which improves film quality and reduces dose.

Although initially the preferred technique in Utrecht, xeromammography is not used for any national screening programmes.

WHAT DOES THE RADIOLOGIST SEE?

Once the breasts are fully developed they remain symmetrical in most women. This symmetry is not only of shape, but of the glandular structures. A mammogram of one breast is the mirror image of the contralateral breast; a fact of great convenience to those who have to read some 70 pairs of films in one hour. Right and left films of the same projection are mounted side-by-side on the viewing screen; one the mirror image of the other.

First the radiologist must decide if the examination is of satisfactory quality, this including not only density and contrast but also whether the whole of the breast has been included on the film. It is the deep aspect of the breasts that is liable to be excluded on the film, particularly inferiorly in the breasts of thin women.

Secondly, he must determine whether symmetry is maintained, looking in turn at the skin, the subcutaneous fat, the glandular structures, ducts, fibrous septa and vasculature. The glandular tissue is normally orientated towards the nipple; the fibrous ligaments traverse the fat. Ill-defined and diffuse asymmetry may be due to overlapping glandular tissues, but this can readily be ascertained by a second view. When medio-lateral oblique mammography is the sole method of screening, the investigation of such 'composite' shadows is the most common reason for requesting a cranio-caudal view.

Thirdly, the radiologist will look for abnormalities caused by focal lesions. These are a localised distortion of the breast tissue, a small opacity, a cluster of calcifications, or diffuse calcifications throughout a segment of the breast. These he will wish to investigate further by additional films and magnification views. Calcifications are usually present in normal breasts; most characteristically benign. The smooth round calcifications of lobular origin, the 'blobs' of calcification within a fibroadenoma, the crescent—shaped calcifications in the wall of a cyst or the casts of ducts in duct ectasia are typical and do not require further investigation. Those that may be associated with malignancy are micro-calcifications, which may be linear or branching within a duct, or discrete clusters of small, irregular, jagged, sharp, and punctate granules. They are obviously polymorphic. A line drawn around the periphery of the calcifications reveals an irregular shape—described variably as trapezoid, rectangular, bottle-shaped, propellor and kite—the long axis of which lies in the direction of the nipple (161).

Punctate micro-calcifications extending diffusely through a segment of the breast may also be a sign of cancer.

It was initially considered that micro-calcifications were specific for malignancy; this is not so. But one-half of all occult cancers present as micro-calcifications. The number of micro-calcifications present is the most helpful diagnostic guide. In general, less than five does not raise a suspicion of cancer. With malignant calcifications, the more one looks at the film the greater is the number one sees. They come out from the dark (188–92).

EVALUATION

In considering the suitability of any investigative test, it is necessary to define its effectiveness in detecting the disease in question. For screening mammography, this is the identification of those with breast cancer. Three standard measures are used: sensitivity, specificity, and predictive value, all of which have been applied to mammographic screening (193–4).

It must be emphasised that one cannot extrapolate data on the accuracy of mammography as a *diagnostic* test to the *screening* situation. In the diagnostic symptomatic clinic, mammography is complementary to knowledge of the presence or absence of a breast mass, its clinical characteristics, and the results of fine-needle aspiration and cytology; it is of value in guiding the diagnostic process and is interpreted in relatively relaxed circumstances. Not so with screening mammography, the interpretation of which is carried out with no other knowledge than the appearance on the film. Screening mammography has one objective: to determine whether the films are normal (test-negative), abnormal (test-positive), or are insufficient to allow a decision, which is why concentrated effort and precise decisions are of the essence. In U.K. the Pritchard Committee recommended that radiologists participating in screening should read the films of 6000 cases per year (195).

Sensitivity

The sensitivity of screening mammography defines the proportion of women who have a cancer of the breast in whom a positive test has been recorded. To calculate sensitivity, one requires to know the number of women who are test-positive (a) and also those who are falsely test-negative (c), so that the total number of breast cancer cases can be calculated (a+c) (Table 8). This number (c) can be determined with precision only if all women with a negative test are fully investigated for the presence or absence of breast cancer, which ideally would include complete histopathological examination of both breasts. This is an impossible mandate, and one cannot estimate sensitivity with precision.

For this reason, the number of cancers that 'surface' spontaneously during a defined period after a negative screening test (conventionally 1 year) are taken to represent the number missed by the screening test. The denominator

TABLE 8. *Sensitivity, specificity and predictive value*

		True Disease State	
		Breast Cancer Present	*Healthy (Breast Cancer Absent)*
Screening test	Positive	a	b
	Negative	c	d

$$\text{Sensitivity} = \frac{a}{a+c} \left[\frac{\text{positive test in those with cancer}}{\text{all who have cancer}} \right]$$

$$\text{Specificity} = \frac{d}{b+d} \left[\frac{\text{negative test in healthy}}{\text{all who are healthy}} \right]$$

$$\text{Positive predictive value} = \frac{a}{a+b} \left[\frac{\text{positive test indicative of cancer}}{\text{all who have a positive test}} \right]$$

a = true positive   c = false negative
b = false positive   d = true negative

of the sensitivity equation is then the number of test-positive cases plus these so-called 'interval' cases. This conventional method of defining sensitivity has great disadvantages.

Specificity

The specificity of a screening test defines the likelihood that a positive test is recorded in a person without the disease. It is represented by the proportion of all women who do not have breast cancer in the population which is screened who are test-negative, i.e., who have a normal mammogram. The reciprocal of specificity is the false-positive rate.

As all women with positive mammograms are further investigated by diagnostic tests, the number of false-positive mammograms (b) is known. As on a first screen the prevalence of breast cancer in the population will not exceed 6 cases per 1000 (0·6 per cent), the number of women without breast cancer (b+d) approximates the total population screened. The definition of specificity is more accurate than that of sensitivity.

The 'Trade-Off'

Sensitivity and specificity are inversely related and have to be 'traded off' against each other. This relationship depends on the threshold which the radiologist applies when deciding the need for further investigation of an abnormality on the screening mammogram. Should his/her threshold of suspicion be set high so that he does not miss cancer, the test will have high sensitivity, but a large number of normal women will be brought back needlessly, so the specificity will be low. Conversely, if he/she sets the threshold of suspicion to ensure that few normal women are recalled (high specificity), he/she will miss more cancers and the test therefore will have low sensitivity.

These values reflect the efficiency of the test. An ideal test would have 100 per cent sensitivity and specificity, so that all positive tests would include, and all negative tests exclude, breast cancer. But, as seen from the figures available to the working party, this is not an ideal world (Table 9).

TABLE 9. *Mean and range of sensitivities and specificities available to working group* (3)

	Sensitivity (%)		Specificity (%)	
	1st Round	Later Rounds	1st Round	Later Rounds
Clinical only	47	62 (50–78)	94	—
Clinical +mammography	91 (81–96)	79 (69–91)	93 (87–97)	97 (94–99)
Mammography only	86 (78–94)	78 (77–78)	97 (96–97)	99 (97–99)

The relationship between sensitivity and specificity can be represented by calculating relative operating characteristic (ROC) curves (196) (Fig. 17). In the medical setting, relative operating characteristics are subjectively determined symptoms, signs and laboratory values, which are used to make a diagnosis that leads to treatment. They are termed *relative* because the weight of the level of diagnostic criteria—or thresholds of suspicion—vary. Rombach and his colleagues in Nijmegen have applied the ROC theory to mammogra-

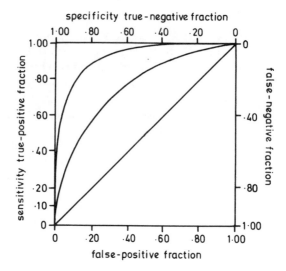

17. Hypothetical ROC curves to illustrate the principle of 'trade-off'
of sensitivity and specificity.

phic screening, and have constructed ROC curves relating
sensitivity and specificity to different thresholds of decision-
making, based on data from 50,102 successive examinations
in 14,400 women. They suggest that they may be used to
determine optimal values for new screening programmes.
By necessity there is a large grey area between a *normal* and
abnormal mammogram with which the radiologist has to
contend, and this makes the definition of 'optimal' difficult.

Predictive Value

The sensitivity and specificity of a screening test are
measures of its validity. A third variable is the predictive
value. The positive predictive value represents the proportion of those with a positive test who, on further investigation, are shown to have breast cancer. This is calculated by
dividing the number of women with a positive test (a)
subsequently proven to have breast cancer by the total
number who are test positive (a+b): (Table 8).

The positive predictive value not only reflects the sensitivity and specificity of the test but the prevalence of the

disease in the population which is screened. This dependence on prevalence increases as the prevalence decreases. Thus the larger the proportion of healthy women, the greater is the number of false positive tests and the larger the denominator in the equation. Methods of taking prevalence into account are available (197–8).

It follows therefore that positive predictive value is not a measure of the validity of the screening test but that the frame of reference is the whole screening programme. As the prevalence of breast cancer in the population is low so also will be the predictive value of a positive test.

Despite this principle positive predictive value is applied in a number of reports as a measure of the efficiency of the test itself. As the majority of abnormalities detected on mammography have a benign cause, 'positive predictive value', used in this way, is dependent on the quality of the mammography and its radiological interpretation.

The predictive value of a negative test cannot be calculated—and in any case is of little interest.

The relationship between sensitivity, specificity and predictive value is demonstrated in Figure 18.

Alternative Methods of Calculating Sensitivity

It has been indicated that the conventional method of defining sensitivity is to regard those cases that 'surface' within 12 months of a negative screen as representing those that have been 'missed' by the screening mammogram. This can only be an approximation, for some are missed on account of faulty reading; some are 'new' cancers that, because of their fast growth rate and aggressiveness, have a very short pre-clinical phase and truly were not detected at the screen. There are also those that, although missed on the initial screen, are so slow growing that they are not likely to surface within 12 months, and would not be regarded as interval cases.

As the number of interval cancers depends upon the prevalence of the disease in the population, it is better to express interval cancers as a rate or the expected incidence (proportional interval rate), which in a controlled trial is that of the control population (82). Other methods of calculating

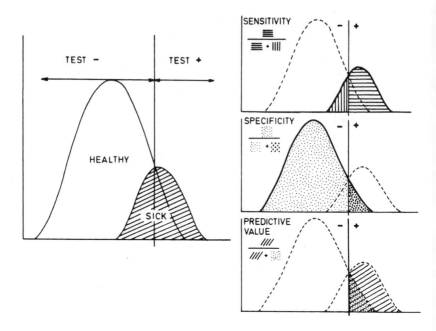

18. Model of estimates of efficiency. Sensitivity and specificity are applied to populations: predictive value to the test.

sensitivity of breast cancer screening programmes, based on prevalence and incidence rates have been proposed, and will be further discussed in Chapter 8 (199).

ALTERNATIVES

Alternative methods of detecting breast cancer in its pre-clinical phase have been actively pursued. These include thermography, microwave densitometry, light transillumination, ultrasonography, computerised axial tomography (CT) and magnetic resonance imaging (MRI) (200). To date none of these have approached the sensitivity of mammography for the detection of the non-palpable lesion. Regretfully, even in Britain, some of these (for example, 'light-scanning') are being applied indiscriminately to the so-called 'screening' of young women, despite clear evidence of their lack of value (201–2). The indiscriminate use of unproven methodology by those ill-equipped to understand validity is quite unethical.

The role of regular clinical examination of the breast by a skilled examiner, either alone or in combination with mammography, is still controversial. There is no evidence that periodic clinical examination of the breasts on a population basis reduces mortality from breast cancer. Nor is there such evidence on the role of breast self-examination. But both are good habits, which health-aware women adopt. They are considered further in Chapter 8.

6

THE EVIDENCE

IN DEFINING CRITERIA TO DETERMINE THE APPROPRIATE-
ness of screening for a disease, the U.S. Preventive Services
Task Force and Canadian Task Force on the Periodic Health
Examination classified three grades of supportive evidence
(203). Grade I was that derived from at least one properly
controlled randomised trial; Grade II from either (i) well-
designed controlled trials without randomisation, (ii) cohort
or case-control analytical studies, or (iii) multiple time-series
studies with or without intervention; Grade III the opinions
of respected authorities, descriptive studies, or reports of
expert committees. All three grades of evidence are available for breast screening.

Obviously the most satisfactory evidence is that comparing
the mortality of breast cancer in two populations of women,
one of whom has been invited to be screened, the other not.
The two populations can be selected in a number of ways: the
same population before and after the introduction of the
screening programme; two different neighbouring populations one offered screening, the other not; or random
allocation of women within one large population to form a
study group (invited to be screened) and a control group.
Clearly the third method is the ideal. The alternative method to
test the efficacy of screening is the case-control study, in which
a history of having been 'ever' or 'never' screened in women
dying from breast cancer (the cases) is compared with that of
healthy living women (the controls). Such studies are carried
out in populations into which, some time previously, programmes of screening have been introduced (204).

EVALUATION

The detection of breast cancer earlier in its natural history

62

has three effects. Firstly there is a shift of stage, towards more tumours being non-invasive, smaller in size and to have a reduced incidence of axillary node metastases. Secondly, the survival time of those with breast cancer is prolonged, and thirdly, the mortality from breast cancer in the population of women who have been screened is reduced. However, only the third can be taken as evidence of success. Three biases affect the first two: lead-time, length, and selection bias (193–4).

Lead-Time Bias

Successful screening advances the time at which breast cancer is diagnosed, pulling this back into its sojourn phase. The disease must present at an earlier stage than when symptomatic (Fig. 7).

Survival is measured from the date of diagnosis to death, a time that automatically has been lengthened by earlier diagnosis, even if the date of death remains the same. The time by which the diagnosis is advanced by screening is the 'lead-time', the duration of which reflects the efficiency of the test. Various mathematical models can be used to estimate this (see Chapter 7).

Length Bias

A second bias is the length bias. Breast cancers vary greatly in their rate of growth, this affecting not only their clinical course but also the time they 'sojourn' in the pre-clinical phase. An episode of screening is likely to detect a disproportionate proportion of slow-growing tumours, automatically reducing the distribution of stage and increasing case-survival times (Fig. 19).

Selection Bias

It is known that women who accept an invitation to be screened are more likely to be health-aware than those who refuse to participate. They have higher educational attainment and better socio-economic status. All-cause mortality is influenced by social status and it is suggested also that

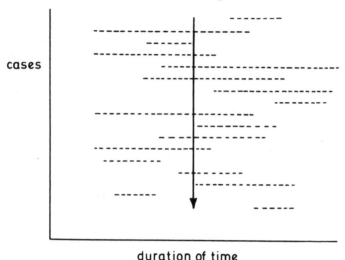

19. Length bias: horizontal lines represent different durations of sojourn time, vertical line an episode of screening.

mortality from breast cancer may be lower in the better-off; women attending for screening being likely to survive longer than those who refuse to participate. Evidence to support this suggestion has come from two recent studies in USA relating breast cancer mortality to socio-economic factors (205–6).

Elimination of Bias

These biases can be eliminated by comparing the mortality from breast cancer in the whole of the population of women invited to participate in a screening programme with control women who have not. By measuring the mortality against person-years of risk from date of entry to the study and not of diagnosis, one eliminates lead-time bias; by including all breast cancers in the study population (and not just those detected by screening), one eliminates length-bias; and by considering all women (both screened and unscreened) in the control group, one eliminates selection bias. As case-control studies consider only those women who have taken up the offer of screening, they are prone to selection bias, and over-estimate the effect of making screening available to a population a proportion of which will not wish to accept.

Critical Evidence

At the time the Working Group made its recommendations, the critical evidence in support stemmed from the results of two controlled randomised trials carried out in New York and Sweden and two case-control studies from Holland (7–10). They all indicated that the mortality from breast cancer could be reduced significantly by periodic mammography (Table 1). Since then, the final report of the New York study has been published, the results of the Swedish trial have been updated, and a further three case-control studies reported, all of which support the original conclusion (177,207–210). However, there are also reports of other trials, with less convincing results. These are the randomised trial in Malmo, Sweden, the U.K. Trial of Early Detection of Breast Cancer (TEDBC) and, as an integral part of the study, the Edinburgh randomised trial (211–3).

In this chapter the design of each of these trials (and three ongoing trials in Sweden and Canada) is described in detail, and relevant results summarised. For in the next chapter we will consider how they compare. Mention is also made of two studies—the population screening programme in Gävleborg, Sweden (152,154), and the large Breast Cancer Detection Demonstration Project in the United States (208,209) —to complete a report of large screening projects. These have been summarised in Table 10.

U.S. STUDY:HEALTH INSURANCE PLAN (HIP)

Considering the general lack of interest in the use of mammography, the initiation of the HIP trial in December 1963, by Shapiro and colleagues in the National Cancer Institute, was remarkable (214). Its objective was to determine whether, by detecting breast cancer at an earlier stage by periodic breast screening using physical examination and

TABLE 10A. *Prospective trials from which mortality data have been reported*

	Invited Population	Age (yr)	Recruit-ment	Method	No. of Rounds	Interval (mo)	Mean Follow-up (yr)
CONTROLLED RANDOMISED TRIALS							
Health Insurance Plan (New York)	S 30,131 C 30,565	40–64	1963–66	Clinical + 2-view mammo.	4	12	18 (all)
Two-Counties (Sweden)	S 77,080 C 55,985	40–74	1977–80	1-view mammo.	2	<50 24 ≥50 33	7·9
Malmo (Sweden)	S 21,088 C 21,195	40–70	1978–86	2-view mammo. ×2 then 1- or 2-view	6	18–24	8·8
Edinburgh (Scotland)	S 23,226 C 21,904	45–64	1979–81	Clinical 2-view mammo. ×1 then 1-view	7 4	24 48	6·2
COMPARATIVE STUDIES							
TEDBC (U.K.)	S 45,088 C 127,117	45–64	1979–81	Clinical 1-view mammo. (Ed 2-view ×1)	7 4	24 48	6·6
BCDDP (U.S.)	283,222 (participants)	35–74	1973–75	Clinical + 2-view mammo.	5	12	11 (all)

TABLE 10B. *Case-control studies from which mortality data have been reported*

	Population Offered Screening (Participated)	Age	Recruit-ment	Method	No. of Rounds	Interval (mo)	Dates Case-Control
Nijmegen (Netherlands)	23,210 (19,702)	35–64	1975–76	1-view mammo.	4	24	(1) 1975–81 (2) 1975–82
Utrecht (Netherlands)	20,555 (14,796)	50–64	1974–76	Clinical + 2-view mammo.	3	12, 13, 24	1973–81
Florence (Italy)	24,313 (14,899)	40–70	1970–81	2-view mammo.	2	30	(1) 1977–84 (2) 1977–87

TABLE 10C. *Ongoing trials not reported*

	Population Offered Screening (Participated)	Age	Recruitment	Method	No. of Rounds	Interval (mo)
Canada	S 44,958 C 44,877	40–59	1980–85	Clinical + 2-view mammo.	5	12
Stockholm	S 40,318 C 19,943	40–64	1976–83	1-view mammo.	2	24
Gotëborg	S 22,000 C 30,000	50–59	1982–	2-view mammo.	—	18

In Canadian trial, controls 40–49 have initial clinical examination, 50–59 annual clinical examination.

mammography, one could alter its natural history and reduce its mortality.

Experience from clinical practice and from a few individual programmes of screening gave some expectation of benefit. There was increasing acceptance that mammography could detect breast cancer when still occult, and a multicentre study had demonstrated that the technique developed by Egan was accurate and reproducible (215).

Organisation

Under the leadership of Michael Shimkin, director of the biometry branch at the National Cancer Institute, a site was sought for conducting a trial. That chosen was greater New York, where a prepaid comprehensive medical care plan with about 700,000 members in 31 affiliated groups was in operation. This was the Health Insurance Plan. It was equipped with a computerised record system; it had previously participated in epidemiological and other research studies; and it had, in one of its groups, an enthusiastic radiologist, Philip Strax, who had adapted Egan's technique for screening purposes.

Following a pilot study that demonstrated that a project of this magnitude could be conducted successfully, the controlled randomised trial was launched in December 1963. Twenty-three medical groups were chosen, these containing 80,300 women of 40–64 years of age. They were stratified into five-year age cohorts, within which every nth woman was allocated for an invitation to be screened (study group) and each n+1 woman as a control (control group). Study and control pairs were randomly listed in sequence for the initial invitation to be screened, the date of entry to the trial for both study and control women being that of the initial invitation. This date was adhered to, even if an invited women had failed to keep her appointment. Active steps were taken to encourage women in the study group to attend for screening. Only 42 per cent of women replied to their original invitation. Those who did not received a further letter, and if still non-responsive were contacted by telephone. Women who failed to keep an appointment were also telephoned. It was estimated that without such active encouragement only 45 to 50 per cent of the study group would have attended for screening. As it was, 20,200 women, 67 per cent of the study group, had an initial screen, recruitment for which ended in June 1986. Those not participating in the initial screen were not contacted further.

Comparability between study (30,130) and control (30,165) groups was assessed by sampling each population, and, in the case of the study group, participants and 'refusers'. Study and control women were closely comparable other than a lower proportion in the study population reporting ever to have had a lump in the breast (Appendix 1, p. 194.)

Screening

Screening was by a clinical examination (performed by a clinician) and two-view film mammography (medio-lateral and cranio-caudal), using the Egan technique of low kv, high m.amp-sec exposures and non-screened industrial film (M type). Radiation dose was high: on average 77 mGy (7·7 rad) to the skin, and 20 mGy (2 rad) to the mid-breast. All films were read independently by two of the three project radiologists, differences being resolved by the third. A 10 per cent sample of all films were reviewed by Egan for quality and interpretation.

Clinical and radiological findings were separately recorded, but combined to determine whether the examination was negative; a biopsy or aspiration was recommended; or the woman should be re-examined in 6 months. Those in whom biopsy or aspiration was advised were referred to their group surgeon. Identification of breast biopsies, and cancers diagnosed, were made from HIP records and hospital insurance claims and verified from hospital charts and pathological reports. Deaths were identified by intensive follow-up of all breast cancer cases, personal communication with family physician and next of kin, and from death certificates. At 5, 10, and 15 years, mail surveys of all study and control cases not known to have breast cancer or to have died were carried out; a tracer organisation was used to track down changes of name or address. Finally, arrangements were made to access the cancer registry of the New York State Department of Health and the National Death Index of the National Cancer For Health Statistics to match samples of project and central records.

Thus there is confidence of a very high level of identification of cancers diagnosed within the first 10 years after entry to the study, and of deaths in these women over an 18-year period. No identifiable breast cancer case was lost to follow-up for mortality. To counter inaccuracies in death certification, an extensive verification procedure was used, with review of all questionable causes of death. Breast cancer deaths were defined as those that were attributable to breast cancer as the underlying cause.

Results

These are reported in a series of recent papers (7,177,216). The response to an invitation to be screened was not great: 67 per cent of women attended. But only 25 per cent of those participating missed more than one screen. In all, 40 per cent of the invited population attended all four screening sessions.

The immediate effect was the detection of an increased number of cancers in the study compared to the control population. But by five years after entry to the study (18 months after screening ended) the number of breast cancers in the study and control groups was almost equal, and at 10 years identical (Fig. 20). Within five years 304 cancers had been detected in the study population and 295 in the controls (Appendix 2, p. 194). As clinical and mammographic findings had been assessed separately, it was possible to determine the effect of both. Had clinical examination not been included, 45 per cent of cancer detected during the first five years of the study would have been missed (Appendix 3, p. 195).

The stage distribution of cancers were retrospectively classified from hospital records. Compared to controls, tumours in the study population were smaller with reduced lymph-node involvement. There was a greater incidence of *in situ* disease (Appendix 4, p. 195). In 69 per cent of cases tumour size had been accurately measured and was less than 2 cm in 40 per cent of all breast cancers detected in the

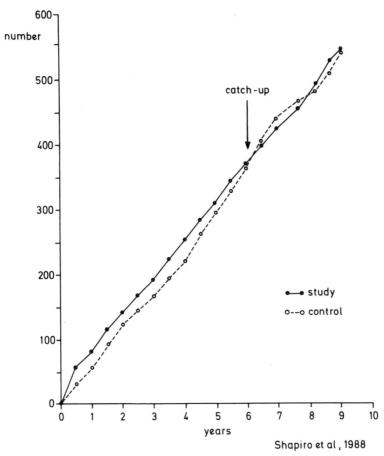

Shapiro et al , 1988

20. Cumulative numbers of cancers detected in study and control populations in HIP trial. Catch-up is at 5–6 years after entry for 4 annual episodes of screening (177). SOURCE: Johns Hopkins University Press, with permission.

study population and 30 per cent of controls. In a subset of cases in which five nodes were available for histological examination, 19 per cent of study and 34 per cent of control cancers had four or more nodes involved. This difference in the stage of cancers in study and control populations were present at all ages, but less marked in women under

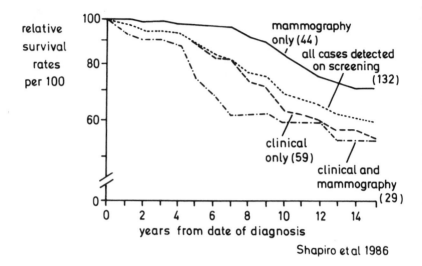

21. Survival of women with breast cancer diagnosed within 5 years of entry to HIP trial from date of diagnosis (177) (adjusted for lead time). SOURCE: Johns Hopkins University Press, with permission.

50 years of age. Distribution by stage is given in Appendix 5, p. 195.

As might be expected, the cumulative survival rates of women whose breast cancer was diagnosed in the study population during the first five years of the trial were more favourable than those of controls, particularly those diagnosed by screening (Fig. 21). In screen-detected cases, one year of lead-time was deducted from the duration of survival. Greatest long-term benefit was observed in those whose cancers were detected at incident screens.

Annual mortality statistics available for 18 years of follow-up indicate that at 10 years there were 30 per cent fewer deaths from breast cancer in the study than control population, a difference that persisted at 23 per cent to 18 years (Table 11; Fig. 22). This reduction in mortality emerged four years after screening started and did not start to decrease until year seven. A second statistic, person-years of life lost (PHYLL), which takes account of both the numbers

TABLE 11. *Deaths from breast cancer at 5–18 years among women with breast cancer diagnosed within five years of entry to trial* (177)

Population	Number of Cases	Breast Cancer Deaths (number)		
		5 Years	10 Years	18 Years
Study	307	39	95	126
Control	301	63	133	163
% Difference	—	38·1	28·6	22·7
95% Confidence Intervals	—	8·9–59·5	7·4–45·5	2·7–39·0

Differences are significant on formal testing. For 879 cancers diagnosed within seven years of entry (after catch-up point), 10- and 18-year mortality differences were 29·3 and 23·7%. SOURCE: Johns Hopkins University Press, with permission.

22. Cumulative mortality from breast cancer in study and control populations in HIP trial. Cases within 5 years of entry from date of diagnosis (177).

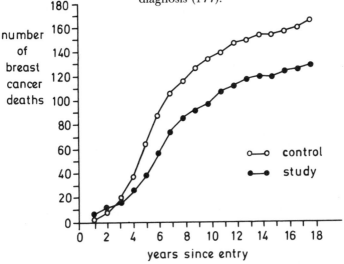

Shapiro et al , 1988

SOURCE: Johns Hopkins University Press, with permission.

and timing of death, was also calculated. Differences of similar magnitude were observed (Table 12). In 1977, the results of the trial were validated by an expert committee (168) and more recently by the performance of additional analyses for which the original statistical tapes were made available (217–8).

TABLE 12. *Person-years of life lost (PYLL) from breast cancer deaths at 5–18 years amongst women whose breast cancer was diagnosed within five years of entry. PYLL takes account of both number and timing of deaths* (177)

Population	PYLL (years)		
	5 Years	10 Years	18 Years
Study	77·5	444·5	1365·0
Control	98·5	632·5	1830·5
% Difference	21·3	29·7	25·4

SOURCE: Johns Hopkins University Press, with permission.

Additional Analyses

In the original analysis of the data, mortality was expressed as rates proportional to the population at risk from the time of entry to the study, this serving as the denominator. On the grounds that it is mortality from breast cancer that is under scrutiny, and that one first has to contract a disease before dying from it, these further analyses have been restricted to those women whose breast cancer was diagnosed at the time when screening could expect to be effective. To eliminate lead-time bias, case-fatality has been measured from date of entry to the study, not date of diagnosis. To achieve comparability between study and control groups, account was taken of the likelihood that during the initial period of screening, those with slow-growing cancers would be diagnosed to a greater extent than those with aggressive disease (lead-time bias). This was achieved by considering all breast cancer cases diagnosed in study and control populations from entry to the study to the 'catch-up point' at which the cumulative number of cases in the controls equalled those in the study population. In one

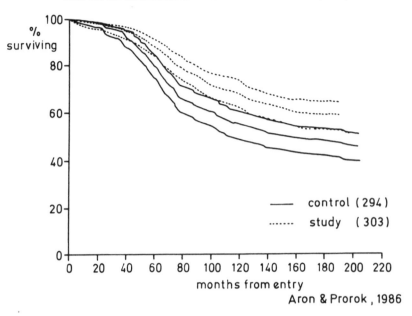

23. Cumulative probability of survival from breast cancer diagnosed within 5 years from time of entry to HIP trial: calculated from date of entry into trial (217).

study this was taken at between five and six, in the other seven years.

Both these analyses, which allow statistical evaluation by Fisher exact and log-rank tests, have confirmed that a mortality reduction has occurred that, in the words of one author, is 'beyond doubt' (Fig. 23), with even, in some, 'elimination of the risk of mortality' (217).

The Prorok model underlying these analyses was used by Shapiro himself to calculate probabilities of death at 18 years (Table 13). The results are in keeping with the findings of the other two analyses.

Mortality rates from causes other than breast cancer were classified by age of entry and by cause of death. They were identical in study and control populations, providing further evidence of the comparability of the populations as well as indicating that deaths due to breast cancer had not been lost (Appendix 6, p. 196).

TABLE 13. *Probability of death from breast cancer amongst women diagnosed within five years of entry, determined from date of entry to trial* (177)

Population	Mean % Probability ± Standard Error	
	10 Years	*18 Years*
Study	31·8 ± 2·7	43·6 ± 3·0
Control	45·3 ± 2·9	56·4 ± 2·9
% Difference	29·8	22·7

SOURCE: Johns Hopkins University Press, with permission.

SWEDISH TRIALS

Two-Counties

Under the auspices of the National Board of Health and Welfare, a controlled randomised trial of screening by single medio-lateral view mammography was initiated by Tabar and his colleagues in two counties of Sweden, Kopparberg in the midwest (starting October 1977), and Ostergotland in the southeast (starting May 1978). Enrolled were 162,891 women aged 40 years or more (8,207).

To preserve homogeneity of study and control populations, the population to be invited was stratified into 19 blocks according to area of residence, 7 in Kopparberg and 12 in Ostergotland. To ensure that few women had moved from the district or had developed breast cancer between the times of allocation and invitation to be screened, and that women in a given block would be called at the same time, study and control women within individual blocks were identified 2–3 weeks before screening started from the Swedish central population register, which is updated each month. In Kopparberg, each block was divided into three groups for randomisation, two being allocated to the study population for an invitation to be screened and one as controls. In Ostergotland, the blocks were equally randomised. The date of entry for both study and control women was the date of randomisation.

Invitation was by personal letter, which was sent to all women for the first two screening rounds. As women over 74 years of age responded poorly (50 per cent to first, 30 per cent to second screen), they were not invited to subsequent rounds; nor have they been included in the analysis of results.

Screening was by single medio-lateral oblique mammogram of each breast. Radiation dose to skin was 5·7 mGy (0·57 rad) and absorbed 1·1 mGy (0·11 rad). For women of 40–49 years of age, the average interval between the first and second screen was 24 months; for those of 50 years or more 33 months. The interval for subsequent screens was 22–24 months.

Films were read by project radiologists. Were there suspicion of an abnormality, the woman was recalled for a complete three-view mammographic examination; only if suspicion remained was she further investigated by clinical examination, fine-needle aspiration and cytology. Radiologists were responsible for the assessment procedure, with reference to a surgeon only if biopsy was indicated.

In Sweden, nationwide cancer registration permits identification of breast cancer cases, including those who have moved residence to other counties. Deaths were identified through the National Bureau of Statistics, and included all cases in which breast cancer was certified as the primary or a contributing cause. However, a death was classified as being due to breast cancer only after full review of clinical and pathological records, as detailed in the appendix to a recent report (207).

Results. The first report of the results, to December 1984, has been updated on two occasions, the most recent for a mean follow-up of 7·9 years, this to December 1986 in Kopparberg and to December 1987 in Ostergotland. Notable is compliance: 89 per cent of women aged 40–47 years attending the first and, of them, 83 per cent the second screen (207,219–20). As in the HIP study, an excess of breast cancers was detected in the early years of the study (prevalence screen 5·56 per 1000 women screened), twice as many cancers as in the HIP first screen (Appendix 7, p. 196.) Unlike the HIP study, the 'catch-up point' has not yet been reached. The number of breast cancers detected in the study population has remained consistently higher than in the controls.

There has been a marked shift to cancers of a more favourable stage in the study population (Appendix 8, p. 197). This has been apparent particularly by the detection in the study group of invasive cancers of smaller size and reduced axillary node involvement compared to controls, a finding confirmed by a detailed pathological study of cases in Kopparberg that also has shown that tumours are of a more favourable histological grade (221–2). Compared to other studies, the proportion of *in situ* cancers is low (8 per cent in study population).

To assess the effect of screening on stage, Tabar has introduced the cumulative incidence of 'stage II and more advanced cases' as assessed by IUCC TNM 1978 criteria (page 36). Pathological staging of tumour size and of lymph-node status was used, so that represented are tumours greater than 2 cm in size, all node-positive cases and

24. Cumulative rates of stage II and more advanced cancers in Two-Counties trial (264).

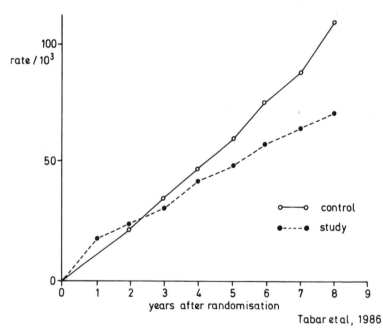

Tabar et al, 1986

all that are locally or systemically clinically advanced (200). These have been reported both as numbers and rates. The rates for study and control populations are shown in Figure 24. There was an initial excess in the study population, presumably due to the 'mopping-up' effect of the prevalent screen; but this rate crossed over with the control population at two years, and overall was significantly reduced at 31 per cent.

There have been three analyses of mortality, now covering an average follow-up of 7·9 years (207). For the most recent, a small number of cases of breast cancer diagnosed between randomisation and initial screen and also of women who have left Sweden have been excluded. Full details of the method of classifying deaths have been reported. Mortality was expressed by Poisson log-linear modelling using person-years of risk as the offset. Significance was tested by deviance chi-squared statistics adjusted for age at randomisation and county of residence.

The numbers of breast cancer deaths and the relative risk of death from breast cancer in study and control groups are given in Table 14. There has been a steady increase in the reduction of mortality in each county, which has now reached significance in both. The combined mortality reduction of 31 per cent, first reported in 1984, has been maintained. Analysis by age group revealed significant differences only for those over 50 years of age (Table 15). A reduction in mortality from breast cancer in the study group

TABLE 14. *Relative risk of death from breast cancer in study and control populations in last three years of reported follow-up* (207)

Year	No. of Breast Cancer Deaths		Relative Risk of Death (95% confidence limits)	(%)
	Study	Control		
1984	87	86 (125)	0·68 (0·50–0·93)	0·01
1985	124	119 (171)	0·71 (0·54–0·92)	0·009
1986	150	167 (225)	0·70 (0·55–0·87)	0·001

Significant differences were not affected by adjustment for age and county. Numbers of deaths in control population have been adjusted in parentheses to take account of 2:1 randomisation in Kopparberg.

became apparent at about four years after the start of screening, and has persisted at 30 per cent for eight years (Fig. 25).

TABLE 15. *Relative risk of death from breast cancer in study and control populations according to age (207)*

Age	No. of Breast Cancer Deaths Study	Control	Relative Risk of Death (95% confidence limits)	(%)
40–49	28	24 (33)	0·92 (0·52–1·60)	0·8
50–59	45	54 (74)	0·60 (0·40–0·90)	0·01
60–69	52	58 (74)	0·65 (0·44–0·95)	0·03
70–74	35	31 (44)	0·77 (0·47–1·27)	0·3

Numbers of deaths in control population have been adjusted in parentheses to take account of 2:1 randomisation in Kopparberg.

25. Cumulative mortality rates in Two-Counties trial (264).

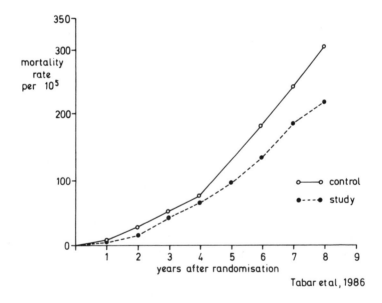

Tabar et al, 1986

Overall, one death has been saved each year for each 9600 women invited to be screened. Among women aged 50–74 years during the four- to nine-year period when screening was exerting its effect, one death was saved each year per 4000 invited women, or one death per 1400 mammographies, per 13·5 biopsies and per 7·4 cases of breast cancer detected. These are not insignificant benefits.

All-cause mortality did not differ significantly between study and control groups, the slight excess of deaths in the controls being eliminated by adjustment for age and county of residence. Among those with breast cancer there was an excess of deaths from intercurrent disease in study as compared to control populations, but when adjusted for person-years at risk this difference was, to quote, 'quite emphatically non-significant.' (Appendix 9, p. 197.)

Screening of the control population started in 1985. During the trial, it was estimated that 13 per cent of controls had at least one mammogram (223).

Malmo

A controlled randomised trial was initiated in the Swedish town of Malmo by Andersson and colleagues in October 1976 (211,223). Women aged 40–70 years of age were identified from the city population register and divided into 25 birth-year cohorts, within which they were randomised to study (invited for screening) or control populations. Invitation was by personal letter, the date of entry being defined as the date of invitation. Women who refused the first invitation were invited to subsequent screens only if they lived in Malmo.

Screening was by film-screen mammography. Two views (medio-lateral oblique and cranio-caudal) were used for the first two rounds; thereafter one or two views, depending upon the mammographic density of the breast.

The first round of screening was complete by September 1978. Further screens were planned at intervals of between 18 and 24 months. All participants had completed five rounds and most six by the end of the trial on 31 December 1986. The mean duration of follow-up in each group was 8·8 years.

In Malmo there is one general hospital where a specialist team treats, by standard protocols of management, almost all breast cancers in the city. Those in whom biopsy was indicated were referred to that team, which treated over 98 per cent of the patients with breast cancer in both study and control groups. The remaining 2 per cent of cases were identified through the National Cancer Registry. The number and causes of death were identified from national statistics and included women who had left Sweden.

Deaths were verified by an 'end-point committee' of an oncologist and pathologist, who, following a full review of clinical, pathological, and post-mortem findings, independently determined the cause of death. A third member was available to resolve disagreements. Seventy-six per cent of recorded breast cancer deaths in both study and control populations had post-mortem examinations performed; a remarkable rate compared to that in the U.K. (85). Verification of the cause of death was stringent, only 129 of 193 certified deaths from breast cancer (63 study, 66 control) being accepted as due to that cause.

Results. Compliance was less than in the Two-Counties Study, 74 per cent of women attending the first and 70 per cent subsequent screens. An excess of breast cancers was again detected in the first screening round, this persisting until the end of the study (588 study, 477 control) (Appendix 10, p. 198). More non-invasive cancers were detected in study than control populations (16 vs 11 per cent) and the cumulative rate of Stage II and more advanced cancers (presumably as defined by Tabar) followed the Two-Counties pattern, the cross-over point being at three years (Fig. 26; Appendix 11, p. 198). Breast cancers detected in the study population were of smaller mean size (1·0 vs 1·9 cm).

Despite this shift in stage, there was no significant reduction in breast cancer mortality in the study population. In fact, it exceeded that of controls during the first six years of the trial (Table 16). These excess deaths occurred in women less than 55 years of age (29 per cent more in study cases). For older women, the trend was reversed, 21 per cent fewer women in the study group dying of breast cancer. If deaths

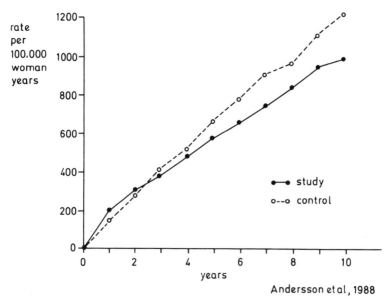

26. Cumulative rates of stage II and more advanced cancers in Malmo trial (211).

are considered only after six years (1983–86) there was a 30 per cent reduction of mortality in the study population, which on a preliminary analysis reached 42 per cent in year seven (Fig. 27). It is notable that 51 of the 63 breast cancer deaths in the study group did not occur in screen-detected cases.

The numbers of death from all causes in the study population equalled those of controls; death certification

TABLE 16. *Relative risk of death from breast cancer in study and control populations after mean follow-up of 8·8 years* (211)

Age (yr)	No. of Breast Cancer Deaths Study	Control	Relative Risk of Deaths (95% confidence limits)	(%)
<55	28	22	1·29 (0·74–2·25)	0·3
≥55	35	44	0·79 (0·51–1·24)	0·4
Total	63	66	0·96 (0·68–1·35)	—

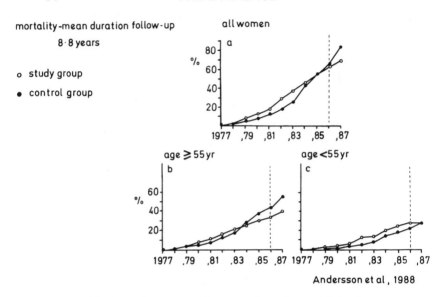

27. Cumulative mortality rates in Malmo trial (211).

was based on post-mortem findings in 58 per cent and 57 per cent of cases, respectively, and specific causes of death were similar (Appendix 12, p. 199).

A confounding influence in the Malmo trial was the policy of free access to breast screening, then on offer in that city. Survey of a random sample of 500 women in the control population revealed that 24 per cent had at least one mammogram (35 per cent in those 45–49 years of age). Twenty per cent of cancers in the control population were detected by mammography; 11 per cent were non-invasive. Women in the study population, even when participating in the trial, also had access to mammography between screens. This may explain the high incidence of interval cancers in the study population (24 per cent of all cancers diagnosed) and of non-invasive cancer in interval cases (26 per cent).

Stockholm

In March 1981, 60,261 women aged 40–64 years of age, living in south-east Stockholm, were individually randomised, two-thirds for inclusion in a study population who were invited to be screened, one-third as controls. Randomisation was by birth date, women born between days 1–10 and 21–31 of the month forming the study population, and those between days 11–20 the controls. There were 40,318 and 19,943 women in these two populations. Invitation was by personal letter; screening by single oblique mammography (224–6).

Two rounds of screening at an interval of two years were planned, following which the control population were to be screened.

All screening mammograms were performed in a single unit and interpreted by an experienced radiologist. Abnormalities detected on the initial mammogram were first evaluated by conventional 3-view mammography, which if suspicion remained was followed by clinical examination and fine-needle aspiration cytology, using stereotaxic localisation for all non-palpable lesions.

The two rounds of screening were complete by October 1985; the control population has now also been screened (1986–7).

Attendance rates have exceeded 80 per cent in both first and second screens with little variation between age groups. Numbers of cancers detected and stage are given in Appendix 13, p. 199. The rate of breast cancers in the study population rose sharply during the two rounds of screening and has remained higher than in the controls. At five years the cumulative rate exceeded that of controls by 44 per cent (Fig. 28). The numbers of Stage II and more advanced cancers (presumably determined pathologically) showed the expected shift to a more favourable stage with a cross-over point at 3·5 years. In the study population 29 per cent of cancers detected at first screen were of this type (Fig. 28).

It is pointed out by the Stockholm group that the early excess of 'advanced' cancers in the study population observed in all Swedish studies is partly due to the 'hiding' of these cases among the unscreened controls. The screening of the control population has allowed an estimate of the 'hidden' numbers; when this was added to the incidence of 'advanced' cases in the control population, the difference

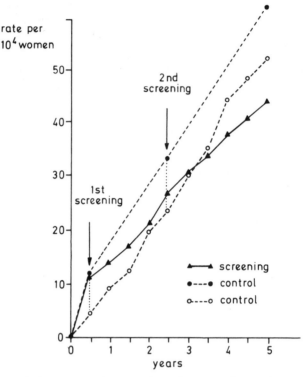

28. Cumulative rates of stage II and more advanced cancers in Stockholm trial. Third rate includes 'hidden' cases in control popula-tion (225). SOURCE: Frisell et al, 1989: Breast Cancer Research and Treatment. Klumar Academic Publishers, with permission.

between study and control populations was significant after four years.

The proportion of women in the control group who had a mammogram prior to their official screen is not stated; but 25–30 per cent of the study population had had a mammo-gram within the three years previous to their invitation. No mortality figures are yet available.

Göteborg Trial

A controlled randomised trial was started in the city of Göteborg in December 1982. It included all women aged

50–59 years, who were invited for screening by two-view mammography every 18 months (227). There are approximately 22,000 women in the study and 30,000 in the control populations.

Assessment is by standard Swedish procedure: a first-stage extension of screening by supplementary mammography followed, if suspicion remained, by clinical examination and fine-needle aspiration stereotactic localisation for the impalpable lesion.

No published reports of the results of this trial are yet available in English other than in abstract. Compliance has been high: 88 per cent of women aged 50–9 years attending the first round, 76 per cent the second. Interval cancer rates are low (0·02 per 100 women per year), indicating high sensitivity (208) (209).

U.K. TRIALS

TEDBC

In the 1970s in U.K. a few pilot studies of screening for breast cancer had been reported, and four centres had been designated to determine the feasibility of mammographic screening of the population (228). The need to evaluate breast cancer screening within the National Health Service was recognised; and a Working Group, under the chairmanship of Sir Richard Doll, knowing that the option to repeat the HIP trial had been excluded, planned a comparative study of the mortality of breast cancer in health districts offered different services for the diagnosis and early detection of breast cancer. It was further decided that this study should consider the effect not only of screening by mammography and clinical examination, but also of instruction in breast self-examination (BSE). The study was named the Trial of Early Detection of Breast Cancer (TEDBC).

Following a request for submissions, four health districts were chosen, two as screening disticts (Edinburgh and Guildford) and two for BSE. Four comparison districts were identified as controls: Dundee, Oxford, Southmead and Stoke-on-Trent. In the screening districts, registers were compiled for all women of 45–64 years of age from the lists of general practitioners, including those who would reach the lower age during the seven years of the project. Invitation was by personal letter, its date being the date of entry into the study. In comparison districts, all women were given the same date of entry, midway through the two years of recruitment for the screening centres (Table 17).

TABLE 17. *Centres selected for trial of early detection of breast cancer (TEDBC): Screening and comparison districts* (212)

	Number of Women in Initial Population	Follow-Up Mean Year/Woman to December 31 1986
SCREENING CENTRES		
Edinburgh	23,194	6·2
Guildford	22,647	6·5
COMPARISON DISTRICTS		
Dundee	22,626	
Oxford	31,474	6·8
Southmead	24,693	
Stoke	48,324	

Breast self-examination districts, Huddersfield and Nottingham, not included.

Between 1979 and 1981, 45,841 women were invited to attend for screening, with 127,117 listed women of similar age in the comparison districts. Those refusing the initial invitation to be screened were not further invited.

The programme of screening lasted seven years. This consisted of a clinical examination annually, with mammography in years one, three, five and seven. Details of screening in Edinburgh and Guildford varied only slightly. In Edinburgh the initial mammographic screen was by two views, medio-lateral oblique and cranio-caudal; subsequent screens by a single oblique view. In Guildford a single oblique view was used for all screens. Agfa medichrome film with intensifying screens was used in both centres. The dose of radiation to the midplane of the breast was 2 mGy (0·2 rad) (228–30).

Breast cancers diagnosed were identified from registers of histopathological findings of all benign and malignant biopsies maintained by trial pathologists. Methods of treatment are recorded and the status of all women with a diagnosis of breast cancer checked each year. The records of all women have been 'flagged' in the NHS central registries in Southport and Edinburgh to identify those leaving their districts.

For the initial analysis of mortality, deaths in the study and comparison districts were compiled from central registers of deaths (OPCS in London and GRO in Edinburgh). Only those in which breast cancer has been certified as the primary cause (part I of the certificate) have been considered as breast cancer deaths. It was intended for later reports to verify all deaths by a case-note search, but this was not done for the first analysis, which was to 31 December 1986 or seven years from date of entry, whichever was the earlier (212).

Results. The response to the initial round of screening was low (60 per cent in Edinburgh, 70 per cent in Guildford); for the fifth round it was 53 per cent and 65 per cent. However, despite doubts on the quality of mammography, detection rates on prevalent screen were, by comparison with other studies, reasonable (5·5 in Edinburgh, 4·8 in Guildford) (Appendix 14, p. 200). In all, 748 breast cancers were detected in the study population and 1472 in the comparison districts. Rates in the two screening centres over the follow-up period of 5–7 years was 2·57 per 1000 women-years compared to 1·70 in the comparison districts. Apparently the 'catch-up point' has not yet been reached.

No significant reduction in mortality has emerged between the study and comparison districts. When stratified for age at death and duration in the trial, the mortality from breast cancer in the two screening districts combined was reduced only by only 14 per cent.

As it was uncertain whether, in the absence of screening, the mortality of all eight districts would be the same, a second analysis was carried out in which data on the mortality from breast cancer during the nine years before the trial started was used to calculate a standardised mortality ratio for each district, which could be applied as a correction factor. This increased the mortality reduction to 20 per cent, also not reaching significant levels (Table 18).

TABLE 18. *Observed differences in mortality from breast cancer between screening and comparison centres (unadjusted and adjusted for pre-trial mortality rates) (212)*

	Screening Centres	Comparison Districts	Relative Risk of Death (95% confidence limits)	(%)
Unadjusted	102	362 (129)	0·86 (0·69–1·08)	0·23
Adjusted	—	—	0·80 (0·64–1·01)	0·06

Deaths in comparison districts have been adjusted for population differences (by a factor of 2·8) in parentheses.

A difference in mortality emerged only after the fifth year of screening. For years six–seven, a reduction of 46 per cent was observed, and this was significant at the 1 per cent level All-cause mortality rates are not reported (Table 19; Fig. 29).

TABLE 19. *Observed differences in mortality from breast cancer according to year of follow-up, adjusted for pre-trial mortality rates (212)*

Years Since Entry	Deaths from Breast Cancer		Relative Risk of Death (95% confidence limits)	(%)
	Screening Centres	Comparison Districts		
1–3	29	68 (24)	1·10 (0·71–1·71)	NS
4–5	45	119 (43)	0·97 (0·68–1·38)	NS
6–7	28	177 (63)	0·54 (0·36–0·81)	<0·01

Deaths in comparison districts have been adjusted for population differences (by a factor of 2·8) in parentheses.

Edinburgh

Edinburgh was one of four centres initially designated to test the feasibility of screening for breast cancer for the

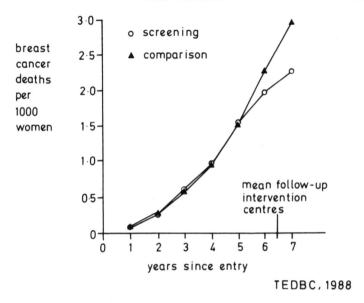

29. Cumulative mortality rates in TEDBC (212).

National Health Service. On the initiative of Professor Eric Samuel a custom-built screening unit was built on the grounds of a community health centre, and, with the co-operation of a group of 11 general practitioners, 5321 women of 45–69 years of age were invited to attend for clinical examination and mammography; 82 per cent did (231). As, unlike the other clinics testing feasibility, that in Edinburgh did not provide access to self-referred women, it was eligible to participate in TEDBC, and was selected as one of two screening centres, the other being Guildford.

Immediately discussions were initiated to examine the possibility that Edinburgh might extend its responsibility to TEDBC by conducting a controlled randomised trial within the city, and this was supported by the Cancer Research Campaign and by the Chief Scientist's Office of the Scottish Home and Health Department (232). All but three of the 348 general practitioners in the city agreed to co-operate. At that time, an extensive campaign of health education for women had started in Edinburgh, this including instruction in breast self-examination. Thus the objective of the Edinburgh trial was to determine the value of clinical examination and mammography in reducing the mortality of breast cancer in well-informed women; a euphemism when one considers that 35 per cent of women in the control group were to present with locally advanced cancer!

For a number of reasons it was considered better were all women from one practice to belong either to study or control populations. Randomisation was therefore between practices and not individual women. Age-sex registers were drawn up for all women aged 38 to 64 years in 85 practices, which, once indexed, were stratified for size and randomised. For the screening practices the eligibility of each woman for screening was checked (a previous diagnosis of breast cancer or having moved out of the district excluded), and personal invitations were issued, the date of entry to the trial for survey purposes being the date of that invitation. For control practices, the date of entry to the study was the same for all women in each practice, being the date on which it was indexed and randomised. Eligibility, as for the study population, was subsequently checked and ineligible women excluded.

The procedure for screening was that for TEDBC. Clinical examinaton was by doctors or nurses. Two mammographic views (medio-lateral oblique and cranio-caudal) were taken at the first screen; thereafter, single view. The average skin dose for two exposures was 6 mGy (0·6 rad) to each breast, but this has since been reduced.

Films were read by trained clinic doctors with review by two radiologists who also read a 5 per cent sample of all films. Suspicion on either clinical or mammographic grounds led to recall for further examination and review at the screening clinic, following which those in whom biopsy was considered advisable were seen with a specialist surgeon. All clinic staff regularly attended a symptomatic breast clinic for continued training.

For the identification of breast cancer, a pathology register of all benign and malignant biopsies was set up in liaison with the local cancer registry. Deaths were notified from the General Registry Office in Edinburgh and follow-up of all breast cancer cases carried out. The records of both study and control populations were 'flagged' in the NHS central registry. It was intended to verify all breast cancer deaths from hospital records, but, for the purposes of the first report, these have been defined as those in which breast cancer has been recorded on the death certificate as a primary or secondary (i.e., underlying or contributory) cause. However, it was confirmed that a diagnosis of breast cancer had been made after the entry date.

Results. Sixty-one per cent of the study population attended for their initial examination; 53 per cent for their third (213). Over the seven years of the study there were 395 women with breast cancer detected in the study population and 268 amongst controls (Appendix 15, p. 201). Cancer detection rate was highest at initial screen (6·15 per 1000), thereafter varying between 1·0 and 3·0 per 1000 person-years, depending on whether the screen was by clinical-only or clinical-plus mammography. Rates for controls were 1·9.

The stage of the disease was assessed by UICC clinical stage, and in those of stages I and II by pathological size and by node status. There was a shift towards a greater proportion of *in situ* disease (10 per cent in study population; 17 per cent in prevalence screen and 2·6 per cent in controls) and a reduction in the proportion of women with locally advanced and disseminated disease (16 per cent versus 35 per cent) (Appendix 16, p. 201). When only those with tumours of clinical stages I and II were considered, the tumours in the control group were smaller and, where node status was known, less likely to be associated with involved nodes (Appendix 17, p. 202). However, calculation of stage as in the Two-Counties study (stage II plus more advanced) revealed a pattern very different from that in Sweden, there being no divergence between study and control populations (Fig. 30). This is believed to be due to a greater proportion of node-positive cases even in those with small tumours.

The distribution of cancer stage according to method of detection is shown in Appendix 18, p. 203. The advanced stage of the disease in non-attenders is notable

There were 68 breast cancer deaths in the study group and 76 in the controls, mortality rates of 4·0 and 5·0,

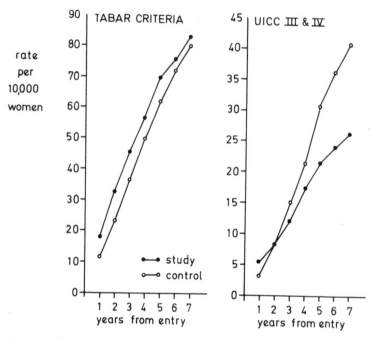

30. Cumulative rates of stage II and more advanced cancers in
Edinburgh trial (213).

respectively. The difference in mortality of 16 per cent (age-
adjusted 17 per cent) was not significant. In those over 50
years of age, however, it reached 20 per cent (Table 20; Fig.
31).

TABLE 20. *Relative risk of death from breast cancer in study and
control populations* (213)

Mortality	*Relative Risk of Death (95% confidence limits)*
Adjusted for age	0·83 (0·58–1·18)
Adjusted for socio-economic status	0·81 (0·55–1·18)
Over 50 yrs of age (not adjusted for socio-economic status)	0·80 (0·54–1·17)

There were, respectively, 68 and 76 deaths accountable to women
diagnosed since entry date, mortality rates per 10,000 women-years of
4·31 and 5·14. None of the differences reached significance.

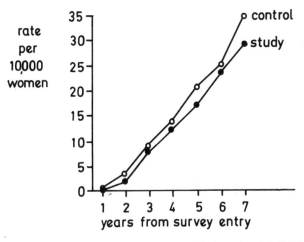

31. Cumulative mortality rates in Edinburgh trial (213).

As a study of a 20 per cent sample of women for comparability between practices had revealed significant and related differences between all-cause mortality and socio-economic status, a second analysis was carried out in which a correction factor was applied for this variable. This increased the reduction in mortality to 19 per cent; again, not significant. The effect of socio-economic status on all-cause mortality was mainly due to an increase in cardio-vascular deaths (Appendix 19, p. 204).

It is not surprising that the results of the Edinburgh trial are almost identical to those of TEDBC. Only the control population and the method of accounting for deaths from breast cancer differed. Although breast cancer deaths included those in which the death certificate indicated breast cancer as a primary or secondary cause, they were not verified from clinical records. The difference in all-cause mortality between study and control populations is a matter for concern. This is further discussed in Chapter 7.

CANADIAN TRIAL

In January 1980, a controlled randomised trial was instituted in Canada (233–4). It had two objectives: first, to determine if annual screening by clinical examination and mammography reduced the mortality from breast cancer in women aged 40 through 49 years; and second, whether in older women (50–59 years), the addition of mammography to annual clinical examination conferred benefit. Five annual screening examinations were planned, women being invited to participate by public advertisement, radio, TV, and the press.

Unlike other trials, women were allocated to study and control groups only after they had attended the screening clinic and given their consent. As it was considered unjustifiable not to offer some form of screening to all who had volunteered, all women had an initial clinical examination, irrespective of their subsequent allocation, as soon as they had signed the consent form. They were also taught breast self-examination. Therefore the trial will compare, in those aged 40–49 years, annual clinical and mammographic examination with an initial clinical examination, and in those over 50 annual clinical examination alone or clinical examination plus mammography. As there is no invited population, no response rates will be available.

By March 1985 the fifteen centres involved had recruited 88,968 women for the trial. Clinical examination was mostly performed by nurses, but in some centres by doctors. Two-view film-screen mammography was used, the average dose to each breast being 1·1–2·2 mGy (0·11–0·22 rads) per examination. Those in whom abnormalities were detected are referred to their personal physician.

Reports on factors influencing recruitment and on the sensitivity of screening have appeared, but as yet not on cancer detection rates, staging or mortality (186,235–6).

CASE-CONTROL STUDIES

Case-control studies have been reported from two centres in the Netherlands and one in Italy. In two centres additional case-control studies were performed so that information is available from five separate analyses. All have shown an advantage in terms of mortality from breast cancer in women who have accepted an invitation for screening by mammography on at least one occasion. But, because of selection bias, the mortality advantage is an overestimate.

Nijmegen

On 1 January 1975, mammographic screening was introduced into the Dutch town of Nijmegen (population 150,000). In the first screening round all women born between 1910 and 1939 (aged 35–64) received a personal invitation, subsequently extended to all women born before 1944 (9).

Screening was by single-view mammography, initially medio-lateral, but since 1981, medio-lateral oblique. The interval between screens, which were carried out in a municipal health centre, was 24 months.

Films were processed immediately, and examined by the radiographer. If quality was poor or if there was a suspicion of an abnormality, a second view was taken. All mammograms were read the following day by the project radiologist. Should he decide that further investigations were required, the woman was referred through her general practitioner to one of two hospitals in Nijmegen, where a diagnostic team of radiologists, surgeon and pathologist decided on further action.

A report of the results of six screening rounds has recently been published in which compliance, detection rates and sensitivity are detailed (237).

The existence of this programme has allowed the performance of two case-control studies. The first was based on 46 deaths from breast cancer between 1975–81, identified by death certification and verified as having been diagnosed since the commencement of screening. For each five-year age group, five living controls matched by birth year were selected at random from statistical records. The screening history of both groups were ascertained, and the relative risk of dying from breast cancer in ever- and never-screened women calculated. This was equivalent to a reduction of mortality from breast cancer in screened woman of 52 per cent.

As a check on selection bias, the underlying incidence and mortality of breast cancer in unscreened women was compared with those in the neighbouring town of Arnheim, where no screening had taken place, and which before 1974 had identical rates to those in Nijmegen. They were still exactly as expected.

In the second study, reported in 1985, 16 additional deaths from breast cancer were included (208). A new group of control women was selected, five for each case, and it was confirmed that the date of diagnosis of the case was after their first screening invitation. The relative risk of dying from breast cancer in those who had never been screened was identical to that in the previous study. Given that two-thirds of women could be expected to attend for screening, this represented a 33 per cent reduction in deaths from breast cancer in the population overall. Successive screens further reduced the relative risk of death from breast cancer; no reduction was observed in those under 50 years of age (Table 21).

TABLE 21. *Relative risk of death from breast cancer in ever–versus never-screened women in Nijmegen (second study) (208)*

Age at First Invitation (yr)	Number of Cases	Relative Risk of death
35–49	19	1·23 (0·31–4·81)
50–64	27	0·26 (0·10–0·67)
65+	16	0·81 (0·23–2·75)
All	62	0·51 (0·26–0·99)

There were 62 cases and 310 controls. Except for age group 35–49, ratios are significant (from Verbeek *et al.*, 189).

Utrecht

In 1974, as part of the Diagnostisck Mammacarcinoom (DOM) project, screening by clinical examination and mammography (initially xeromammography) was introduced into the city of Utrecht. Women of 50 to 64 years of age (20,555) were invited to attend for screening on five occasions, at an interval of 12, 18, 24 and 48 months. Seventy-two per cent attended the first screen; 42 per cent the fifth screen. As a cancer registry had been opened in the city the previous year, all cases of breast cancer diagnosed in the city could be monitored.

Subsequently, the project was extended to include younger women, and, at the time of the most recent report, over 55,000 women over 40 years of age have been screened at least once. Response and breast cancer detection rates, the distribution of stage of the disease on detection, and estimates of the efficiency of screening have been reported in detail (238–9).

In 1984 a report of a case-control study was published (10). Through the Central Bureau of Statistics, 56 deaths from breast cancer during the period 1973–1981 were identified in women born between 1911 and 1925, of which 46 were verified from hospital records. For each case, three age-matched control women were selected at random from local authority lists and the relative risk of dying from breast cancer in ever– and never–screened women were calculated. This was equivalent to a significant reduction in mortality of 70 per cent (Table 22). Significant differences were observed only for women over 50 years of age.

TABLE 22. *Relative risk of death from breast cancer in ever–versus never-screened women in Utrecht* (10)

| | Relative Risk of Death | |
Age (years)	Age at Invitation for Screen	Age at Diagnosis
50–54	0·82	1·13
55–59	0·31	0·31
60–64	0·05	0
All	0·30 (0·13–0·70)	

There were 46 cases and 138 controls.

Florence

Two case-control studies have recently been reported from Florence in Italy (209–10). In 1970 mammographic screening was introduced to 25 surrounding rural communities and personal invitations sent to 24,813 women of 40–70 years of age to attend a mobile screening unit. Screening was by two-view mammography, repeated at an interval of 2·5 years. Sixty per cent of invited women participated.

Between 1977 and 1984, 153 deaths were certified as due to breast cancer, of which 57 were eligible for inclusion in the study on account of age and date of diagnosis. For each case, five living women matched for date of birth were randomly selected from the residential lists of the same municipality. The relative risk of death from breast cancer in ever– versus never–screened women was significantly reduced, indicating a reduction in mortality of 40 per cent in screened women. With successive screens the risk was further reduced, but there was no mortality reduction in women under 50 years of age.

A second case-control study has recently been carried out in which the history of having ever or never attended for screening has been compared in 103 women dying of breast cancer between 1977–87 and 515 living age-matched controls. The findings confirm those of the initial study (Table 23). For women over 50 years of age with at least one screening test in the previous $2\frac{1}{2}$ years the reduction of risk was 50% (0·49: (0·25–0·95))

TABLE 23. *Relative risk of death in ever-versus never-screened women in rural Florence adjusted for confounding variables* (210)

	Number of Cases	Number of Screening Rounds 1+	2+	Ever-versus never-screened
40–49	28	0·51 (0·18–1·42)	1·18 (0·31–4·47)	0·63 (0·24–1·64)
50+	75	0·62 (0·32–1·19)	0·40 (0·19–0·82)	0·51 (0·24–0·89)
Total	103			0·53 (0·33–0·85)

OTHER STUDIES

Although not controlled trials, mention should be made of two other studies: the first population trial of single and medio-lateral oblique-view mammography as the sole method of screening, in Sweden; and the huge Breast Cancer Detection Demonstration Project in the United States.

Gavlëborg

Single oblique-view mammography was first introduced by Lundgren and Jakobsson for breast screening on a population basis in the Swedish town of Sandviken, in the county of Gavlëborg. In March 1974, 6845 women were invited to attend a mobile unit; films being processed centrally and read the following day. A suspicious finding led to complete three-view mammography, and if suspicion still remained to reference to a breast unit. In 1975 the programme was extended throughout the county so that, by the end of 1979, all women over 39 years of age had been invited, of which 63,918 had been examined, 25,304 twice.

Reports of this experience with recall and detection rates, distribution of stage, and interval cancer rates provided evidence that this method of screening in expert hands was both acceptable and efficient, and led to the detection of a high proportion of invasive cancers when still small. It provided a 'gold standard' for successful mammographic screening by single-view mammography (164–6,240).

BCDDP

In 1973, the benefits shown in the HIP study inspired the American Cancer Society, in association with the National Cancer Institute, to initiate a large demonstration project to determine the feasibility of introducing mammographic screening on a nationwide basis. This was named the Breast Cancer Detection Demonstration Project (BCDDP). By 1975, 29 centres were functioning in 27 locations widely distributed throughout the United States. Each enrolled some 10,000 women for annual screening by clinical examination and mammography, and initially thermography, over five years. Recruitment was by compiling lists of eligible women who were to be personally contacted by volunteers and, as a group, through announcements on radio, television and the press. All women who attended were taught breast self-examination (BSE) and were to be followed up for five years after screening ended. Those in whom an abnormality was detected were referred to their personal physician.

Initially women of 35–74 years of age were eligible for full screening, but in later years mammography was restricted to those of 50 years of age and over. By September 1981 there were screening documents available on 283,222 women, over half of whom had attended all five screens. Almost 4500 breast cancers were diagnosed in 4200 women; there were 24,000 benign biopsies; and a further 9000 women had been referred for an opinion that they did not seek.

Women with cancer have been traced through to 1986. Two major reports have been published, one in 1982, the other in 1987 (63,241). The most recent report includes 4485 breast cancers in 4257 women, of which 3548 were detected on screening, half at the first screen; 744 were interval cancers, 142 within one year of a negative screen.

Most striking was the improved detection by mammography compared to the HIP study. Only 257 of 3437 cancers (7 per cent) would have been missed had a physical examination not been performed (Appendix 20, p. 204). There was a high incidence of *in situ* cancer (17 per cent) and of invasive cancers less than 1 cm in size (8 per cent). Axillary lymph node involvement in these cases was low (1·9 and 14·3 per cent) (Appendix 21, p. 204).

To assess survival, comparisons were made between 2934 invasive cancers detected in BCDDP and 46,849 cases included in the National Cancer Institute's Surveillance, Epidemiology, and End Results (SEER) programme. A correction for lead-time of one year was applied to screen-detected cases. A marked survival advantage was reported at five and eight years of follow-up (Table 24). Stage by stage,

TABLE 24. *Cumulative relative survival rates for invasive breast cancers for BCDDP cases detected through screens and for cases in white females in the SEER programme* (63)

	Number of Cancers	Survival Rates (%)	
		5 yr	8 yr
BCDDP	2,934	87	81
SEER	46,849	74	65

SOURCE: American Cancer Society, with permission.

survival rates were similar (Appendix 22, p. 205). It is the larger proportion of small and node negative cancers in BCDDP which has improved overall survival (for example of <2 cm tumours 30 v 11 per cent of total).

In 1988 annual cumulative incidence and mortality rates of breast cancer in 55,053 white women aged 35–74 years of age on entry to the project was calculated, using total population at risk as the denominator (242). Data from the SEER programme was used to determine expected rates. For the first nine years of entry the cumulative incidence was 1·34 times that expected. For 3585 women with breast cancer diagnosed within five years of entry, cumulative mortality was reduced, over that expected, by 20 per cent less. Case-fatality (without lead-time adjustment) was reduced by 50 per cent in cases detected by screening.

But those enrolling in BCDDP were a very select group of women; 88 per cent were white, 79 per cent married, 20 per cent had a previous mammogram, and 93 per cent a previous breast examination by their physician.

7

SOME COMPARISONS

IN THE LAST CHAPTER, THE VARIOUS TRIALS HAVE BEEN described in considerable detail so that the reader can be assured of their validity. In Table 25 and 26 the main findings are listed for comparison. Most notable are the differences in breast cancer mortality between the five controlled trials and four case-control studies. This is not surprising, for, as already pointed out, a case-control study compares screened, not-invited-to-be-screened and non-screened women and is strongly biased by only well-motivated and health-aware women attending.

Although the reductions in mortality observed in Malmo and in U.K. did not reach statistical significance, the change in each trial is in the same direction. Had screening no effect, the observed changes in mortality would be distributed equally on either side of the 'null' line (Fig. 32). It is important to recognise that many of these trials included women under 50 years of age, in whom a significant benefit of screening has not yet been demonstrated. When only women of 50 years or more are considered, the reduction in mortality is greater.

There can be no doubt that screening by mammography benefits women who develop breast cancer. But, the reasons for these variable results require to be explored. These have been summarised as (i) weakness in trial design leading to artifactual bias, (ii) poor compliance, (iii) inefficient screening (212).

TRIAL WEAKNESSES
Design
When designing any experiment one cannot forecast unexpected events which may introduce bias. Studies involving

TABLE 25. *Summary of controlled randomised and comparative trials*

Trial	Population	Compliance	Prevalence Detection Rate/1000	Diagnosed	Breast Cancers % Screen Detected	Deaths	Mean Follow-up	Mortality Reduction Total	Mortality Reduction >50 yr
HIP	60,696	67 (58)	2·7	S 307 C 301	43·4	S 96 C 133	10	30	32
Two-counties	133,065	89 (86)	5·6 (invasive)	S 1295 C 768	89·3	S 160 C 167	7·9	30	40
Malmo	42,283	74 (70)	7·6	S 558 C 447	64·6	S 63 C 66	8·8	4	21
TEDBC	172,205	66 (55)	4·8 and 5·5	S 748 C 1472	—	S 102 C 362	6·6	20	—
Edinburgh	45,130	61 (54)	6·2	S 395 C 268	61·5	S 68 C 78	6·2	17	20

TABLE 26. *Summary of case-control studies. In Tables 25 and 26 compliance figures in parenthesis are stable rates on repeat screens.*

		Population	Compliance %	Prevalence detection /1000	Matched case (Cs)/controls (C)	Mortality total	Reduction % > 50 yr
Nijmegen	1	150,000	85 (50)	5·6	Cs 46 / C 230	52	—
	2	—			Cs 62 / C 310	49	74
Utrecht		20,555	72 (42)	7·2	Cs 46 / C 138	70	69
Florence	1	24,313	60 (45)	—	Cs 57 / C 285	43	51
	2	33 075			Cs 103 / C 514	47	49

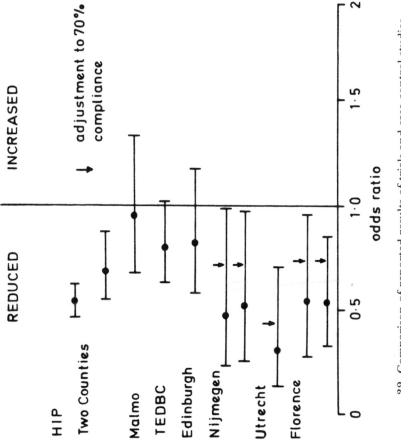

32. Comparison of reported results of trials and case-control studies.

tens of thousands of women would be expected to be free from such artefacts, but this is not necessarily so.

A trial may have insufficient power to give a statistically valid answer to the question asked. The power of a trial depends upon having a sufficiently large number of end-points for comparison: In trials of screening for breast cancer, the endpoint is the number of deaths from breast cancer. This, in turn, depends on the number of cases of breast cancer diagnosed in trial and control populations, which reflects compliance and the sensitivity of the test (243).

In the HIP trial, where breast cancer deaths have been followed for 18 years, significant differences in mortality were observed within five years of entry to the trial. This also was the case in the Two-Counties trial; but not so with either Malmo or Edinburgh. The power of both these trials has been questioned (213,244).

TABLE 27. *All-cause mortality in controlled randomised trials* (177,207,211,213)

| | Deaths from All Causes | |
	Study (%)	Control (%)
Health Insurance Plan	73·7	75·4
Two-Counties	71·4	70·9
Malmo	8·42	8·54
Edinburgh	80·7	109·8

Rates per 10,000 women-years (Malmo percentage).

The purpose of random allocation is to ensure that study and control groups are comparable. This can be tested by surveying social and demographic features in samples of the two populations. This was done in the HIP study. Concordance was excellent (Appendix 1, p. 194). Study and control populations can also be compared by estimates of mortality from all causes other than breast cancer. In the HIP trial, this was identical up to ten years from entry dates. There is also good agreement of all-cause mortality between study and control populations in the Swedish trials (Table 27).

But not in those from Britain. The TEDBC was not a randomised trial and it could not be assumed that mortality rates in each of the six different health districts would be the same. A standardised mortality ratio noted on the mortality in each district during the ten years before the start of the comparative study was applied to each. This altered the expected mortality in the two screening districts by 4 and 9 per cent and in the comparison districts from 0 to 16 per cent.

As in the Edinburgh controlled randomised trials, mortality from all causes differed between study and control populations, it is far from certain that the standardised mortality ratio applied to Edinburgh, which was based on pre-screening mortality rates for the whole city, is valid (213).

In Edinburgh, randomisation of the populations was not individual, but by cluster, the general practice to which a woman belonged being the unit randomised. Individual randomisation was not practicable, as no adequate lists were available, either at health board or general practice level, to use as a sampling frame (245). As all the women in one practice would belong to the same population within the trial, randomisation by practice was also more acceptable to the general practitioners concerned. Practices were stratified before randomisation, but only for size.

Early on in the study it was appreciated that the socio-economic status of women in different practices affected attendance. It was well known that socio-economic status affected mortality from all causes, and a survey of 78 participating practices by Alexander and her colleagues had shown that mortality rates differed considerably between practices (246–7). In a 20 per cent random sample of women of age 46–64 socio-economic status was also determined using post-codes to identify enumeration district for the 1981 census, from which car ownership, room occupancy, and social class of the head of the household were extracted. Standardised mortality ratios for individual practices correlated highly with these variables (Table 28).

The extent to which these differences might affect comparisons of mortality between the study and control populations in the Edinburgh trial was subsequently determined

TABLE 28. *Mortality rates in general practices allocated to screening and control populations by socio-economic category* (247)

	Mortality/1000 Woman-Years			
	All-Cause General Practices		Cardiovascular Disease General Practices	
Socio-Economic Category	Screening	Control	Screening	Control
Highest	5·99	7·85	2·14	3·18
Medium	7·97	8·84	3·03	3·14
Lowest	9·12	10·04	3·67	4·34

(245). Mortality from all causes in the controls exceeded that of the study population by 20 per cent, this being due predominately to deaths from cardiovascular disease. When stratified by age these differences were highly significant. By applying a factor to correct for socio-economic status between practices, this difference in mortality, although still present, became insignificant. This method of adjustment was subsequently used in the Edinburgh screening trial, but differences in all-cause mortality between study and control populations were still evident. This can only be regarded as a serious confounding factor.

In the U.K. trials it can safely be assumed that screening mammography was rare in the control populations. In the HIP trial also mammography was 'extremely infrequent' in the controls (177). In the Two-Counties trial 13 per cent of control women had at least one mammogram, which will have reduced its effectiveness; but not to the extent to which free access to mammography could have influenced the results of the Malmo trial. Almost one-quarter of women (35 per cent of 40–49 year olds) in a sample of the control population had at least one mammogram. A similar figure can be assumed in Stockholm: 25–30 per cent of the invited population had a mammogram within the previous three years of entering the trial.

Selection bias has a profound effect on the results of a case-control study. Women accepting an offer of screening such as in BCDDP and the Canadian national trial centres were shown to be generally well educated and health aware. But it should not affect those of controlled trials in which an analysis of mortality is based on all deaths in the invited study population, irrespective of whether women attend for screening.

However, it can affect the proportion of women who accept the invitation to be screened. In the HIP trial, those who refused or were reluctant participants of screening were less health aware than those who promptly accepted their first invitation. They also had higher socio-economic and educational status (177).

This effect can be assessed by comparing breast cancer incidence and mortality and also all-cause mortality in those who accepted or refused an invitation for screening. This information is not generally available; but in the HIP study the incidence of breast cancer in the 'refused' group was, compared to the control population, low, while survival was more favourable. All-cause mortality, excluding breast cancer, was higher in the 'refused' group. This finding was taken by some to represent an under-reporting of breast cancer deaths, but, as the excess of deaths was due to cardiac and respiratory disease, this is unlikely (Table 29). Further, the total number of cases of breast cancer in study and control populations were equal at 10 years, and mortality from all causes other than breast cancer were identical.

TABLE 29. *Comparison of all-cause mortality, breast cancer detection rate and 10-year case survival in women attending for and refusing screening in HIP trial* (177)

| | Study Population | | |
	Screened	Refused	Controls
All cause mortality (excluding breast cancer) per 10,000 woman-years	56·8	93·0	68·9
Breast cancer detection within 5 years of entry (per 1000 woman-years)	2·26	1·61	1·95
10-Year case survival	64·4	49·4	46·4

SOURCE: Johns Hopkins University Press, with permission.

In the Two-Counties trial the incidence of breast cancer in the group who did not attend was higher than in controls, and the disease was more advanced. The suggestion that there was an increased mortality from intercurrent disease in women with breast cancer in the study population has not been supported by a detailed analysis of the causes of death.

It has been said that, because all-cause mortality has not been reduced in any of the populations offered screening, screening for breast cancer has no purpose; a criticism which was directed particularly at the Swedish study.

But, as has been pointed out by Tabar and his colleagues, in the age group invited to be screened in Sweden, breast cancer accounts only for 7 per cent of all deaths. A 30 per cent reduction in mortality from breast cancer, therefore would lead only to a 2 per cent reduction in mortality overall. Further, up to an average of 8 years of follow up, deaths from breast cancer diagnosed since the start of the trial are only one half those expected in the general population; so that the expected effect on all-cause mortality is only 1 per cent Tabar pointed out that very few public health or therapeutic measures in western countries could be expected to show a significant effect on all cause mortality: an outright ban on smoking might be the one example! (207).

Response

In the U.K. TEDBC, 51 per cent of the deaths in the study populations occurred in the 28 per cent of women who did not attend for screening: in the Two-Counties trial, respective figures were 30 and 10 per cent. In Table 25 the proportion of women 'stabilising' for screening in the invited populations are compared. Edinburgh is bottom of the league. Attendance rate is a key issue in determining the success of a programme. Only those women who attend for screening can hope to derive benefit from it.

One reason for non-response is listing under a wrong address. Although in an Edinburgh study this only accounted for 3 per cent of non-attenders, this was of a practice where lists were known to be more accurate than average. In the Edinburgh trial overall it approximated 5 per cent (232).

The number of women who promptly accepted a first invitation to be screened in the HIP study was only 42 per cent. Special steps were required to encourage another 25 per cent to attend. In most programmes a second invitation has been sent some months after a non-response to the first; but thereafter women not attending ('refusers') do not receive further invitations. The positive promotion of screening may increase attendance, but even in the U.S.A., where mammographic screening is strongly promoted, only 17 per cent of 50,000 women surveyed in 1987 had a mammogram during the previous 12 months. Sixteen per cent had never heard of mammography (248).

The reasons for non-compliance have been addressed. In the HIP study, a detailed examination of demographic characteristics of a sample of 'refusers' indicated that they were older, had lower educational attainment, were less likely to be Jewish, to have married or borne children or to have previously reported a lump in the breast than attenders. Their attitude towards preventive health measures was indifferent. Women who did not require extra efforts to accept the invitation and those who regularly attended the whole HIP programme had high socio-economic and educational attainment. But no such personal characteristic marked more than half the women who attended all four examinations.

In Britain, studies to determine whether attendance at a breast screening clinic is a problem of 'administration or attitudes' (249–50) have revealed that similar factors apply. Women of low socio-economic status, who are poorly educated and who are frightful of the outcome of screening are less likely to attend, as are those who are unmarried, separated, or divorced. But for many (60 per cent in one sample) the dominant reason for non-attendance was based on practical issues: away on holiday, work or family commitments, or simply lack of interest, regarding screening as irrelevant. Many just 'could not be bothered' to attend.

A critical factor influencing attendance is a woman's previous health behaviour. In Edinburgh, Roberts and her colleagues wished that the randomised trial should be carried out within a well-informed population. A survey by interview of 810 women, selected randomly from popula-

TABLE 30. *Examples of knowledge about breast cancer in Scottish women* (251)

About Breast Cancer	% Yes Answers
Can cause symptoms other than lump	18
Accounts for 1:10 of all lumps	18
Trauma may be a cause	28
Cannot or only sometimes can be detected at at early stage	42
Surgery is only treatment	40
Self-examination practised	57
regularly	19
Cure more likely if 'caught' early	87

tion registers in Aberdeen and Edinburgh, revealed that the level of knowledge concerning the nature of breast cancer was poor (Table 30) (251). Only 2 per cent of women recognised skin dimpling as a symptom of breast cancer; and 45 per cent that there was any treatment for the disease other than surgery. Although 87 per cent had heard of breast self-examination, only 57 per cent practised it, 19 per cent on a regular basis. Young women (39–49), those of better 'social class' and those with a history of a previous breast problem were more knowledgeable. The majority (87 per cent) understood that early diagnosis increases the chance of cure, but only 42 per cent believed it possible to detect the disease in its early stages. These are dreadful

TABLE 31. *Attendance in Edinburgh according to age and socio-economic status (highest and lowest of six categories)* (213)

	% Attending Annual Screens		
	1st	2nd	3rd
Age 45–49	63·8	56·8	55·9
60–64	56·5	47·7	47·6
Socio-economic status			
Highest	67·3	61·5	59·6
Lowest	53·9	47·2	45·0
All women	61·3	54·6	53·1

statistics. Older women were less likely to attend, either for their initial screen, or more-so for repeat screens. Age and socio-economic status were important determinants of attendance in the Edinburgh programme. (Table 31).

A campaign of health education, funded by the Cancer Research Campaign, coincided with the start of screening (252–3). It consisted of a standard talk with slides, and a leaflet. Key messages were aimed to reassure (Table 32). The advantages of early detection were stressed, including that of avoiding mastectomy; self-examination was encouraged and taught. Recruitment was through industrial medical officers, personnel managers, and church, social and political organisations, with some low-key publicity. 'Health shops' were opened temporarily to provide information on woman's health in several parts of the city, one of which, in a central location, remained open for 16 months. Over a 12-month period 12,000 women attended talks, and 70,000 leaflets were distributed. Contact of some type was made with 25 per cent of women in Edinburgh.

TABLE 32. *Key messages in Edinburgh education campaign* (252)

- Nine of ten breast lumps are harmless
- Risk of breast cancer increases with age—very rare in young women
- Early diagnosis leads to increased chance of cure
- Women can help themselves by self-examination
- If breasts change, see a doctor

Evaluation of the campaign was by questionnaire and by a further interview to assess knowledge about breast cancer in randomly selected women in Aberdeen and Edinburgh. When adjusted for age and socio-economic status, this demonstrated a small but significant improvement in general knowledge about the breast and in the techniques of breast examination in the Edinburgh sample. But, despite the delivery of leaflets to all women in the control population of the screening trial, the incidence of locally advanced disease was unchanged (254).

Maureen Roberts suggested that in Britain an intensive campaign of health education, backed up by self-referral diagnostic clinics, should take precedence over breast screening (29). No one can deny the importance of righting an appalling situation; but the introduction of screening should strengthen this objective, increasing awareness of the importance of early diagnosis and also of the need for high-quality diagnostic services. To deny the potential effectiveness of the only method proven to reduce the mortality from breast cancer could but weaken the importance of these other measures in the eyes of our female population. As indicated by Jocelyn Chamberlain, we 'cannot throw out the baby with the bath water!' (255)

It is salutory to consider that less than 10 per cent of women were motivated to attend BCDDP and the Canadian national trial screening centres on the advice of their physician. It is the responsibility of all health professionals to become aware of why women are being screened and, if they accept the potential for benefit, to encourage women to attend. This encouragement should start in the doctor's surgery. In practices participating in the pilot study for the Edinburgh programme, examination of the breasts was regularly practised; 82 per cent responded promptly to an invitation to be screened.

Efficiency

The only correct measure of efficiency of a screening programme for breast cancer is mortality. Comparisons of mortality as an endpoint are possible only within structured controlled trials or, to a lesser extent, case-control studies; and this takes years. Alternative methods to measure the efficiency of ongoing programmes are a necessary part of quality control.

Those used to evaluate mammography as a diagnostic method have already been referred to: sensitivity, specificity, and predictive value. Sensitivity: how often a mammogram yields a positive result when breast cancer is present; specificity: how often the mammogram is negative when breast cancer is not present; and positive predictive value: the frequency with which a positive test indicates the diagnosis of the disease.

Sensitivity. As indicated on page 55, the calculation of
sensitivity conventionally uses the number of interval cancers that emerge during the 12 months following a negative
screen to represent 'missed' cases, and these are added to
the number of positive tests to provide a denominator for
the sensitivity equation. Although the usual interval is 12
months, some have preferred 24 months, which obviously
lowers sensitivity (220). In an attempt to define interval
cancers more logically, Shapiro and colleagues counted as
interval cases not only those surfacing within 12 months of a
negative screen, but also those which at their first annual re-
screen were locally advanced. In programmes of biennial
screening the total numbers of interval cancers diagnosed
between screens are used to determine sensitivity. In Edin-

TABLE 33. *Comparison of sensitivities of screening Programmes*
(177, 229, 237, 225, 220, 213, 166)

	Number of Cancers		
	Detected on screening	Interval	Sensitivity %
PREVALENCE SCREEN: 12 MONTH INTERVAL CASES			
HIP	55	12	82·0
Gavlëborg	172	10	94·5
Nijmegen	52	4	92·9
Edinburgh	92	8	92·0
Guildford	93	6	93·9
PREVALENCE SCREEN: 24 MONTH INTERVAL CASES			
Gavlëborg	172	33	83·9
Stockholm	124	64	66·0
Nijmegen	52	14	78·8
Edinburgh	92	40	69·7
PROGRAMME			
Two-Counties (7 yr)	797	261	75·3
Stockholm (5 yr)	217	102	68·0
Nijmegen (14 yr)	203	67	75·2
Edinburgh (7 yr)	201	80	71·5
Guildford	186	77	70·7

burgh and Guildford mammography was a biennial event, so that those cases detected on the clinical-only intervening screen can be regarded as 'interval' to allow comparisons with other programmes. The sensitivity of the whole programme can also be calculated in this way. Comparative figures for these various estimates of sensitivity are given in Table 33. They indicate the difficulty of comparisons based on interval cases; but suggest that, compared to Nijmegen and the Two-counties studies, the efficiency of the British programme was in doubt.

Interval cancers include not only 'misses' but also highly aggressive cases which 'surface' within a few months of a truly negative screen.

To correct for this, the initial screening mammograms of interval cases can be reviewed, to determine with hindsight whether the lesion was detectable at that time, and therefore a true 'miss'. This was done in Malmo, where three of six interval cases surfacing within six months had demonstrable abnormalities on their screening mammogram, two of which were regarded as true false-negatives. On this basis, the sensitivity of the first screen in the Malmo trial was 94 per cent (204).

A similar method has been used to determine sensitivity in the Canadian trial. The screening mammograms of those cases detected by clinical examination alone at the initial screen, those emerging spontaneously as interval cases over the next 24 months, and those detected clinically at the first annual re-screen were reviewed and apportioned as true misses or true interval cases. The overall sensitivity of the first screen, calculated on this basis, was reported to average 75 per cent. In the 15 centres involved it varied from as low as 57 to a high of 100 per cent (236).

But, as Day constantly states, the calculation of sensitivity from the numbers of interval cancers is an uncertain exercise. Not that a comparison of interval cases is not helpful; but they must be expressed as a rate, proportional to the expected incidence of breast cancer in the absence of screening. This rate can be determined in the Two-Counties and Edinburgh trials from the control populations so that a comparison can be made. In the Two-Counties trial the proportional incidence of interval cancers was 19 per cent in the first and 32 per cent in the second 12 months after a negative screen. In Edinburgh, even when those cases detected at the first annual clinical screen were discounted, the corresponding rates were 28 per cent and 36 per cent; a very unfavourable comparison.

A simple mathematical method of calculating sensitivity from prevalence and incidence rates related to expected incidence has been devised by Day (183). The rate of detection of cancers in the screened population at first screen (prevalence rate) by itself gives a guide as to the efficiency of screening; but this depends not only on the efficiency of screening, but on the prevalence of breast cancer in the population that is screened. This rate also is therefore better expressed as a proportion of the expected incidence rate.

These different methods of calculating sensitivity have been applied to the HIP trial. That of the whole pro- gramme, based on 12-month interval cases was 73·7 per cent. If, following a negative first screen, those with non- localised disease detected at their first annual re-screen were included as interval cases, sensitivity was reduced to 72·4 per cent. If node positive cases at re-screen were included, sensitivity was correspondingly lower. Sensitivity calculated on the assumptions that the difference between the detection rate at annual re-screens and the underlying incidence rate represented missed cases was higher, at 76·1 per cent; while that calculated from application of the exponential model was 80 per cent! Sensitivity is a variable parameter.

Specificity. Different methods of calculating specificity have also been applied. Most commonly this is derived from the number of screens having a false positive recommendation for investigation. Over the whole course of the HIP pro- gramme this amounted to 6·1 per cent, giving a specificity of 93·9 per cent. Similar figures have been reported from other programmes.

The problem of false-positive interpretation of a screen- ing mammogram is considered in Chapter 9.

Lead-time. Ideally one wishes to know the time by which the diagnosis has been advanced by screening. Following an episode of screening there is a period of 'escape' when the incidence of breast cancer in those with a negative screen falls below that expected in the absence of screening. Cases then gradually start to emerge at periods of time proportional to their agressiveness; first the rapidly growing tumours, then those of moderate growth, and finally the slow-growing non-aggressive tumour. The distribution of these emerging cases mirrors the pool of cases that is sojourning during their pre-clinical detectable phase, so that mathematical analysis of the rates of incident cases can be used to calculate the time by which diagnosis has been advanced by screening and its distribution. Shapiro and his colleagues used both parametric and non-parametric equations based on this 'escape' model to estimate lead-time in the HIP study, which is reported to vary between from one to over two years.

A second method used to calculate lead-time in the HIP project was to compare, in women developing breast cancer in study and control populations, the times between date of entry to the trial and that of diagnosis up to the 'catch-up' point when the total number of cases in each population were about equal. Two such calculations were performed, one including cases diagnosed to 71, the other to 77 months. The average time of advancement of diagnosis in the study group was 10·4 months (177).

Models. Since screening started, statisticians have used mathematical models to ascertain the benefits and costs (e.g., risk of radiation cancers) of mammographic and clinical screening. Prior to reports of the HIP study, these were based on comparative data (e.g., between BCDDP and the SEER programme), but there was no way by which they could be validated. The availability of the results of the first randomised controlled trial (HIP study) presented an opportunity to validate mathematical models, which statisticians were not slow to take up. The various models that have been used have been reviewed by Prorok (256). Any attempt to describe or to compare them is beyond my competence;

but the general conclusions, as summarised by Prorok, are (i) that annual screening by mammography and physical examination reduces mortality from breast cancer by from 10 to 40 per cent; (ii) that the radiation risk of mammography is relatively small at low doses, particularly if life expectancy is used as a measure of benefit; (iii) that the screening of women of less than 50 years of age requires further study; (iv) that annual physical examination alone cannot realise a significant percentage of the gain realised by its combination with mammography; (v) that breast self-examination may have significant potential to reduce mortality; and (vi) that the use of two-stage screening strategies should be explored.

These conclusions, based on calculations from models to estimate benefit from the HIP trial were important, but the availability of reports of further controlled randomised trials have redirected efforts into using models to determine the efficiency of screening and to predict the optimum frequency. As has been mentioned earlier in this chapter, models that take account of the distribution of cancers in the pre-clinical detectable phase (sojourn time) have been developed. Thus, from the rates of cancers emerging after a negative screen related to the proportion of cases detected on the prevalent screen, one can calculate the distribution of tumours in their sojourn phase and derive the length and distribution of the lead-time and the sensitivity of the screening test. The methods used to perform these calculations have been fully described by Day and Walters (82, 257–260), who have applied them to compare the efficiency of HIP, the Two-Counties trial, and the population screening project in Malmo. The results indicate that screening in Sweden and in Utrecht has improved characteristics compared to (HIP. Appendix table 23, p. 206).

Stage Distribution. Mortality and sensitivity are only two of the measures that can be applied to assess the efficiency of screening. Another is the distribution of the stage of the disease. There is no doubt that mammographic screening, if effective, will discover the disease at an earlier stage, and it is now well documented that such cancers as are detected by

TABLE 34. *Stage II and more advanced cancers reported in controlled trials for H.I.P. Two-Counties and Edinburgh data pathological 'staging' is given* (177, 211, 213, 219, 225)

Trial	Total Cancers	Stage II and Advanced		
		Number	Percent	Percent Invasive
H.I.P.				
Study	304	133	43·8	
Control	295	160	54·2	
TWO-COUNTIES				
Study	1295	460	35·5	(38·6)
Control	768	453	59·0	(60·8)
MALMO				
Study	579	190	32·8	(31·0)
Control	443	231	52·1	(58·8)
STOCKHOLM				
Study	371	143	38·5	
Control	257	150	58·4	
EDINBURGH				
Study	395	198	50·1	(58·2)
Control	268	183	68·3	(70·1)

screening are more likely to be non-invasive, or if invasive to be of smaller size and to have a lower frequency of involvement of the axillary lymph nodes.

Comparisons of stage distribution are fraught with error, particularly when, as in several reported studies, they are based on retrospective analyses of hospital records, which are notoriously inaccurate. The classification of stages or the methods used may not be defined. It may not be clear whether tumour size has been measured by clinical, mammographic, or pathological measurements, whether a diagnosis of *in situ* disease has been validated by a review panel (and in the HIP study discordance was reported), or whether lobular carcinoma *in situ* (which is not relevant) was excluded.

To rationalise on the use of staging and allow comparisons of the efficiency of screening projects, Tabar and his colleagues proposed that the incidence of *in situ* disease should largely be disregarded. As non-invasive cancers do not surface as invasive disease for many years, their detection cannot contribute immediately to any reduction in mortality. It was believed that the reduction in mortality in the Two-Counties trial was dependent upon the detection of invasive cancers when still small and non-disseminated. Success in their detection was therefore monitored by the cumulative rates of stage II and more advanced cancers. These were assessed on the basis of the 1978 UICC system

33. Comparison of cumulative rates of stage II and more advanced cancers in Swedish and Edinburgh trials (from Table 34).

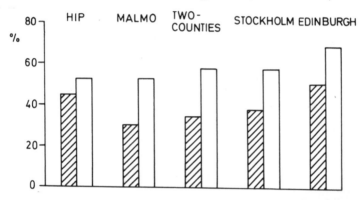

of staging, using pathological criteria to measure tumour size and axillary lymph node status. 'Advanced' tumours were those over 2 cm in size; those that were node-positive, irrespective of size; and those that were locally advanced or disseminated.

Consideration of cumulative rates indicated an initial excess of advanced cases in the study population. At two years this crossed over with that in the controls and then diverged in favour of the study group. The cross-over effect preceded that of mortality by two years. The cumulative rates reported in the Malmo trial have a similar pattern, as do those from Stockholm (when not corrected for 'hidden' cases in the control population), but those from Edinburgh are radically different, suggesting that the efficiency in detecting early disease has been poor compared to Swedish studies (see Figs 24, 26, 28, 30, 33).

While for comparative purposes it is more satisfactory to express the numbers of node positive and advanced cancers as the rates per 100,000 women, they are also reported as the proportion of cancers diagnosed. In Table 34 a comparison of such proportions has been made. Edinburgh would appear to compare badly with Swedish centres. Not that screening failed to have an effect: for as was shown in Appendix table 16 the incidence of stage III and IV (advanced) disease was markedly reduced. But it is the detection of the small invasive cancer at a node-negative stage which is critical for success. An estimate of the proportion of such cases based on pathological data in the *Two-Counties* and *Edinburgh* trials is given in Table 35: again to the disadvantage of the Edinburgh programme.

TABLE 35. *Comparison of proportion of invasive cancers which are under 2 cm in size and node negative on pathological assessment. For Edinburgh data only those tumours in which size and node status are known are included* (213, 219)

		2 cm node negative	
	Invasive Cancers	Number	%
TWO-COUNTIES			
Study	1191	686	57·6
Control	745	273	36·7
EDINBURGH			
Study	333	134	40·2
Control	239	50	20·9

Although the detection of breast cancer at an *in-situ* stage may only prove beneficial after many years, this cannot be disregarded.

The proportion of *in situ* disease reported in *five studies* is given in Table 36. With the exception of the Malmo trial, in which a substantial proportion of the control population had a screening mammogram, this is clearly increased in those offered screening. In some programmes of screening in U.K. the proportion of *in situ* cancers now exceeds 20 per cent.

It has been suggested by Day that the relative deficit of cancers of 'advanced' type can be used to monitor the early

TABLE 36. In situ (non-invasive) cancers in controlled randomised trials and one comparative study as percent of all cancers detected (177, 211, 219, 213, 212)

| | STUDY POPULATION | | | | CONTROLS | |
| | Screen-Detected | | Total Study | | | |
	Total Cancers	% In situ	Total Cancers	% In situ	Total Cancers	% In situ
HIP	132	19·7	304	12·8	295	8·1
Two-Counties	1156	8·4	1295	8·0	768	3·0
Malmo	374	16·4	579	16·1	443	11·3
Edinburgh	243	14·4	395	10·1	268	2·6
TEDBC	—	—	748	11·8	1472	3·3

success of a screening programme. The distribution of these stages of cancer emerging after a negative screen will reflect the number left undetected in their sojourn phase (248). This requires an estimate of their proportional incidence in the screened population following a negative screen to that in the absence of screening, and this can be made available from unscreened controls.

It is proposed to use this method of monitoring as an early indicator of effect in one of the controlled randomised trials that are now being initiated in Britain, that comparing different lengths of intervals between screens, and also to determine the efficiency of current new programmes of population screening.

CONCLUSIONS

It is difficult to draw any firm conclusions from these comparisons. If the Two-Counties trial is regarded as representing the ideal situation for mammographic screening— with high compliance, excellent mammography and dedicated investigation of abnormal findings—one can only explain the inferior results of the U.K. programmes on the basis of poor compliance or poor screening, or both. In Malmo, screening was of a high standard, but the high incidence of mamography of the control population and the low power of the trial are confounding factors. If there is any doubt about the HIP study, it is why the results are so good, particularly when compared to the Two-Counties trial. But it should be noted that the performance of mammography in 13 per cent of the control population in Sweden may have diluted the full effect. The response rate in HIP was not high, and by modern standards the quality of mammography was poor. Only 55 per cent of screen-detected cancers were visualised; and Egan, who reviewed a 10 per cent sample of all mammograms, regarded the quality to be 'inferior'. On the other hand, clinical examination was performed by trained physician and, from personal observation in one centre, was meticulous.

It has been suggested that a substantial selection bias may have affected the results, this from the unusually low incidence of breast cancer in those refusing screening. But, as indicated above, this is not likely to have represented an under-reporting of breast cancer deaths. Further, considerable effort has gone into validating the comparability of study and control populations.

The British results are disappointing. But, at the start of the trials in Britain, we were criticised that the standards of mammography were not comparable to those in Sweden; a position now hopefully reversed. According to Lundgren, unlike their British counterparts, Swedish women are strongly motivated towards health, have confidence in their health-care system, and rarely present to a doctor with other than early cancer of the breast (261). The ratio between breast cancer mortality and incidence in Sweden is reported to have decreased from 60 per cent in 1960 to 36 per cent in 1982–84. The corresponding figure for Britain is 60 per cent. Sweden has no 'class system', which regretfully we are unable to abolish, little poverty, and the attitude of the population to instructions 'from above' is compliant. Population registers are efficient and complete. Lundgren suggests that in Britain, 'poverty ... ignorance, alienation, suspicion—combined with the slightly paranoic civil attitude may well be responsible for a largely ill-founded lack of confidence in medicine ... the high rate of advanced cancer, the strikingly high breast cancer death rate ... and the low compliance in screening ... ', a round condemnation of our system of health (not sickness) care.

It has been reported that only 9 per cent of women in Norway and 11 per cent in the USA have locally advanced disease when breast cancer is first diagnosed. Similar figures are reported in the control population in Malmo (Table 37). In the Edinburgh control population this was 35 per cent, little different from that reported a decade ago (262).

Further, as has been pointed out by Barbara Thomas, the mortality from breast cancer in the Malmo control population was lower than that of our screened groups (263). The message is clear.

TABLE 37. *Contrasting stages in Sweden and other countries. Edinburgh and Malmo are for control populations in screening trials: percentages of invasive cancers* (211, 213, 227, 273)

1960–70		I	II	III	IV
Gavlëberg	1961–74	11	57	24	8
Göteborg	1968–69	12	38	48	2
1975–85					
Havana	1980	12	50	32	4
Dublin	1975–85	16	42	27	14
Edinburgh	1979–86	14	50	31	5
Malmo	1976–86	41	44	7	8

8

DOUBTS ON RECOMMENDATIONS

IN THEIR REPORT THE WORKING GROUP STRESSED THAT their recommendations regarding the age of the target population, the type of basic screening (whether single- or two-view mammography) and the interval between screens were to be regarded as initial, and that with experience modifications might be required. There was uncertainty as to the role of breast self-examination and whether this should be actively promoted. These four factors will now be considered.

AGE

The recommended age of the target population to be screened in the U.K. was 50–64 years. The upper age limit reflected the fall-off in response rates in older women that has been observed in all except the Göteborg study. Response for six rounds of screening in Nijmegen are given in

TABLE 38. *Attendance of invited women at screening clinic in Nijmegen* (237)

| Age (yr) | % Attending 2-Year Screens | | | | | |
	1	2	3	4	5	6
<50	86·9	77·3	72·0	68·9	67·4	66·7
40–64	82·7	69·4	61·2	56·9	52·3	50·1
65+	—	39·5	26·6	20·3	14·4	11·6

SOURCE: International Journal of Cancer, Wiley-Liss Inc., with permission.

Table 38. But it was recommended that women of 65 years and over who wished to have a screening mammogram should have free access to an NHS screening clinic.

The recommendation not to start mammographic screening until the age of 50 years was based on lack of evidence of

129

34. Comparison of results of trials and case-control studies in women of 35–50 years. Note contrast with Figure 32. For data consult Appendix table 24.

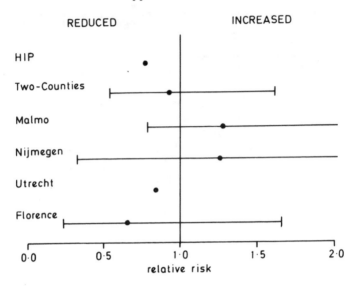

benefit in younger women. In neither the HIP nor the Two-Counties study was there a significant reduction in mortality in this age group; this has been confirmed in the Malmo trial and also by age-specific analyses of the case-control studies (Fig. 34) (Appendix 24, p. 207). It was believed that this was due to two factors: a relative lack of sensitivity of mammography in younger women with more glandular breasts, and too long an interval between screens. In the HIP study, mammography visualised only 33 per cent of cancers in women aged 40–49 compared to 58 per cent in older women; and the calculated lead-time for diagnosis for those 40–44 years was 15·8 compared to 25·2 months for those 50–59 years. In the Two-Counties study, the proportional interval cancer rates within 24 and 48 months of a negative screen were, at 38 and 68 per cent, much greater than in older women (13 and 29 per cent) (Fig. 35 (131)).

A recent analysis of the Nijmegen screening data, using mathematical modelling, suggests that the sensitivity of mammography in this age group is in the order of 85 per

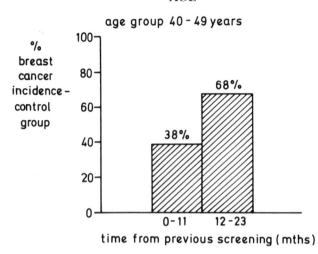

age group 40 - 49 years

% breast cancer incidence – control group

time from previous screening (mths)

Tabar et al. 1987

35. Proportional rates of interval cancers following a negative screen in women of 40–49 years of age in the Two-Counties trial (264).

cent, and that the high rate of interval cases is most likely due to tumours spending less time in the sojourn (pre-clinical detectable) phase (265).

In the HIP trial a reduction in mortality did emerge in women under the age of 50 years at eight years after entry and has persisted for the full 18 years of follow-up (Fig. 36). But, owing to the small numbers of women under 50 years, the statistical analysis had insufficient power to indicate significance either way. Other investigators have con-structed case-fatality tables from date of entry to the study (not date of diagnosis) for all cases of breast cancer in study and control populations diagnosed to a 'catch-up' point of 6 to 7 years. They doubt that there is a threshold at age 50 years for the observed reduction in mortality (218,266). In the most recent study, a significant mortality reduction of 24 per cent (3–41 per cent), emerged nine years after entry in younger women (Fig. 37).

Corroborative evidence has come from BCDDP, in which, even after adjustment for lead-time, women of 40–49 years whose breast cancers were screen-detected had improved survival compared to historical controls. In this age group

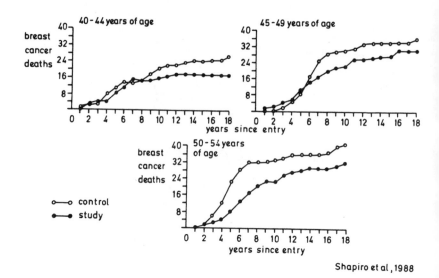

Shapiro et al, 1988

36. Cumulative mortality from breast cancer for cases within 5 years
of entry of different ages (177).
SOURCE: Johns Hopkins University Press, with permission.

85·4 per cent of cancers were detected by mammography
(63).

In the U.S. a baseline screening mammogram is now
recommended for women at 40 years of age, this to be
repeated annually; in Sweden, also, screening starts at that
age. But there are objectors. In an analysis of the potential
health and economic benefits of mammography, as an
addition to clinical examination in women of 40–49 years,
Eddy et al. have concluded that mammography should be
made available only to those who 'understand the limits of
its benefits, . . . its risks, and who are willing to pay its costs';
an opinion that has been violently opposed by Tabar
(267–70).

Existing data cannot resolve this critical question. The
Canadian national trial, which is addressing it, lacks power
and considers only a select group of women. In the 'Two-

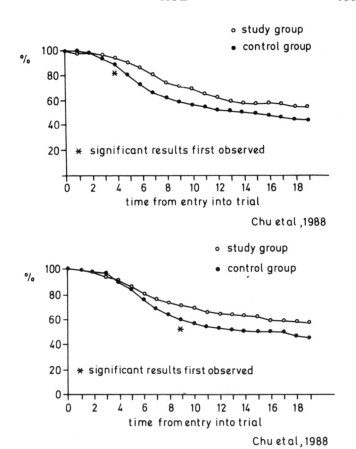

37. Survival rates from date of entry into trial for women aged (a)
40–49 and (b) 50–64 years of age with breast cancer diagnosed within
6 years of entry (266).
SOURCE: J. Nat Cancer Inst, with permission.

Counties' of Sweden, women of 40–49 years are being
randomised for immediate screening or for screening starting at age 50; and a similar trial is reported to be in progress
in Göthenberg. But in view of the low incidence of breast
cancer in this age group, and its relatively low mortality,
larger numbers are required than are available in either
study.

To provide a definite answer to this outstanding problem, a national U.K. study has been set up by the Breast Screening Research Subcommittee (BSRS) of the U.K. Co-ordinating Committee for Cancer Research (UKCCCR), in which a cohort of 195,000 women aged 40–41 years will be allocated randomly to study or control groups in a ratio of 2:1 for 7 years. Women in the study group will attend existing screening clinics for annual screening by clinical examination and mammography until the age of 50 years, at which time both study and control populations will join the national screening service. Mortality from breast cancer is the endpoint of the trial. This is a large and costly study, and one that we are uniquely able to perform. And it is critical that it should be done; for there is no other way by which the role of mammography for screening young women can be determined with certainty (271–2).

SINGLE-VIEW MAMMOGRAPHY

The decision to recommend medio-lateral oblique mammography of each breast as the sole screening procedure in the U.K. was based on Swedish and Dutch experience. Single-oblique-view mammography was the only screening method used in the Two-Counties and Stockholm randomised trials, and in the population screening programme in Nijmegen (273). In Malmo, Göteborg, Utrecht, and Florence, two-view mammography was preferred, which Tabar now supports.

British radiologists have been critical of the recommendation that single-oblique-view mammography alone should be used in the U.K. screening service, at least for the initial (prevalence) screen. In Edinburgh (but not in Guildford), oblique plus cranio-caudal films had been taken at the prevalence screen. A retrospective review of prevalence screen films in Edinburgh indicated that reading two views detected more cancers than oblique alone, but only by 4 per cent. In 100 consecutive cases of cancer detected in screened women, the 'miss rate' on single-oblique compared to two-view mammography was 6 per cent (274).

TABLE 39. *Comparison of detection of cancer on different mammographic views in 491 patients with breast cancer* (275)

Mammographic Projection(s)	Detection in 491 Patients	
	No.	(%)
Medio-lateral oblique alone	440	89·6
Oblique plus cranio-caudal	463	94·3
All three views	467	95·1

From Andersson *et al.*, 260.

There are now a number of reports of retrospective comparisons of the accuracy of single-oblique versus oblique-plus-craniocaudal mammography, and in one also a third medio-lateral view. These indicate that cancer detection rates may be less by up to 5% compared to two-views. But even two-views will miss cancers compared to three views (275–80). In Malmo, the 'miss rate' of cancers on the oblique view alone was 10 per cent; however, 6 per cent of cancers were also missed on two (oblique and craniocaudal) compared to 5 per cent on all three views (Table 39) (275).

TABLE 40. *Results of study of single- versus two-view mammography in 169 patients with cancer and 194 healthy controls* (276)

	Cancer Patients		Normal Women	
	Oblique View Only	Oblique + Cranio-caudal	Oblique View Only	Oblique + Cranio-caudal
Interpreted as abnormal	90%	84%	39%	12%
Recommendation for additional view	23%	4%	32%	5%
Recommendation for biopsy	67%	80%	7%	7%

Three radiologists interpreted each case.

SOURCE: Radiological Society of North America, with permission.

Recall rates must also be considered. In a study reported from North America, three experienced radiologists interpreted a random selection of films in 169 women with cancer and 194 health controls, reading first the single-oblique view and six months later both oblique and craniocaudal (276). Reliance on the single view would have missed only a small number of cancers, but would have increased greatly recall and biopsy rates (Table 40). But this study was in no way representative of screening. Not only were young women of 28 years of age and over included, but the radiologists were asked to make recommendations for

TABLE 41. *Retrospective study of interpretation of single medio-lateral oblique and two-view mammography by the same radiologist in 2500 consecutive women* (277)

	Number (%) Women	
	Oblique View Only	Oblique + Craniocaudal
Interpreted as abnormal	642 (25·7)	179 (7·2)
Generated biopsy	76 (3·0)	83 (3·3)
Generated diagnosis of cancer	25 (1·0)	27 (1·8)

SOURCE: American J. Roentgenology, with permission.

biopsy on the single view alone, which is quite contrary to screening procedure.

The study of Sickles is taken to be more representative of screening requirements and has been widely quoted as supporting two-view screening mammography (277). Single-oblique and subsequently oblique-plus-craniocaudal views of the screening mammograms of 2500 asymptomatic women were separately reported. Reading the oblique view alone generated a suspicion of an abnormality three-and-a-half times more frequently than when two views were available; these most commonly being due to composite (overlapping) breast shadows or calcifications (Table 41). On seven occasions an abnormality seen only on the craniocaudal view generated a biopsy that in two women uncovered an impalpable cancer; a miss rate for the diagnosis of cancer of

8 per cent (0·8 per 1000 women examined). It should be noted that five separate radiologists participated in this study, that women of young age were again included, and that this group have reported the screening of 15 women a day as 'large-scale operation' (278). This is very different from the real-life situation of population screening, where one radiologist is expected to regularly read the films of some 70–80 women from one day's screening. One cannot compare 'screening mammography' as practised in the U.S. with the screening services now being set up in Europe.

None of these studies represent 'real-life' screening, in which a decision for action (i.e., to recall or not for review) has to be made. Experience in the U.K. now suggests that not more than 6 per cent of women will be recalled following a single-view mammographic screen, a situation closer to Swedish figures (<5 per cent) than those suggested by these retrospective studies. But we do not know the truth, which can be determined only by a controlled randomised trial in which women invited to be screened are randomly allocated either for single-oblique or two-view mammography, on each of which a decision must be made. Strict monitoring of recall, cancer detection and interval (missed) cancer rates and cost is necessary.

In the U.K. such a study has been planned under the auspices of the BSRS (271). This will include 70,000 women (270). By using two radiological assessors at each screening centre, it is intended to compare not only the rates of recall and cancer detection in different women having one or the other form of mammography, but also to compare these in the same women, dependent upon which of the two radiologists' recommendation had been acted upon. A pilot study to test feasibility has now started.

Meantime, single-view mammography remains the recommended basic screening method in the U.K. Exceptions may be necessary in outlying rural communities, where recall for additional mammographic views can cause difficulties; although this does not appear to have been so in Gavlëborg. In Sweden the National Board of Health and Welfare recommended single-oblique-view mammography for women over 50 years of age, but that two-view mammography was necessary for screening women of less than 50. But age is another question. And, clearly, the ultimate choice of single versus two-view screening mammography will depend on the results of the U.K. trial.

Two-view mammography costs more than the single-view—in Clarke and Fraser's survey about 20 per cent more—but this does not take into account a reduction in numbers requiring to be recalled (281). Although, from the figures from Swedish centres, this does not appear to be a major issue (Table 51).

The role of double-reading of mammograms is another question which requires to be addressed.

FREQUENCY OF SCREENING

The recommendation that mammographic screening should be repeated at intervals of three years was based on the results of the Two-Counties study, which had shown a significant reduction in mortality from breast cancer in women of 50–64 years screened by single oblique-view mammography each 33 months. Screening at an interval of three years was also in practise in Gavlëborg. But there are no direct comparisons of the effect of different intervals of screening on breast cancer mortality.

As already indicated, a guide to the efficiency of screening is the number of interval cancers that surface following a negative screen, expressed as the proportion of the expected incidence of cancer without screening. Proportional interval cancer rates for women aged 50–69 years in the Two-Counties study climbed rapidly between the second and third year after the initial screen, suggesting that the interval of three years was too long (264). Current recommendations in Sweden favour 24 months (Fig. 38).

Attempts to determine the optimum frequency of screening from mathematical modelling also have been made. But to know for certain which of the possible intervals between screens is most cost-effective, a direct comparison of different intervals is required.

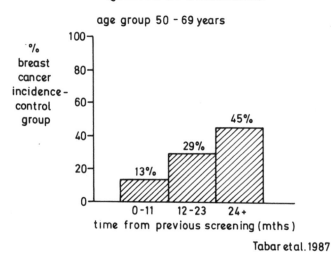

Tabar et al. 1987

38. Proportional rates of interval cancers following a negative screen in women of 50–69 years of age in the Two-Counties trial (264).

This is being conducted in the third controlled randomised trial planned in the U.K. by BSRS (257). It is intended that 130,000 women invited to attend the national service for screening will be randomised for attendance at three-year or one-year intervals in a ratio of 2:1. The end point of the trial is mortality, but an interim analysis will be conducted on the basis of tumour size, node status and grade of malignancy of the cancers detected in study and control groups, which will be used to forecast likely mortality effects. This trial, which will be conducted in five screening centres, has entered its pilot phase.

BREAST SELF-EXAMINATION (BSE)

Regular clinical examination of the breasts by a physician is more commonly practised in the United States than in the U.K. This was normal practice in over 93 per cent of a sample of the 280,000 women who participated in BCDDP. Regular breast examination by doctors or nurses was included in the HIP and TEDBC trials and DOM (Utrecht) programme, but there are no data from which its effect in reducing mortality from breast cancer, either alone or as an addition to mammography, can be assessed. This is being addressed in older women (>50 years) in the Canadian national trial.

In Tampere, Finland, 20,644 women aged 41–60 years were invited for a clinical examination of the breasts. 617 were believed to have an abnormality, for which all but 2 returned for further investigations. Twenty-seven had cancer. Compared to mammographic detection the prevalence rate of 1·3 cancers per 1000 women examined is low. So also is the positive predictive value of a detectable abnormality, only one in twenty-three proving to be cancer (282). The detection rates for cancer at clinical and clinical plus mammographic screens in the Edinburgh programme also indicate the lower sensitivity of clinical examination (Fig. 39).

Despite the opinions of some (283), it would appear that when screening mammography is of high quality, the addition of a clinical examination has little to offer in

39. Cancer detection rates in the Edinburgh trial comparing clinical plus mammography and clinical only screens (213).

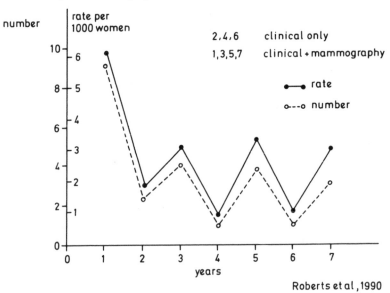

Roberts et al, 1990

terms of the detection of additional cancers. In the HIP trial, in which clinical examination and mammography were both performed annually, 45 per cent of cancers detected through screening would have been missed had clinical examination not been performed. Ten years later in BCDDP, in which the pattern of screening was similar, the contribution of clinical examination in detecting additional cancers was small. Only 257 to 3437 (7 per cent) of screen-detected cancers were detected by clinical examination alone (63). In Edinburgh and Guildford also, clinical examination did not add greatly to the diagnostic yield from mammography. In the prevalence screen in Edinburgh the two modalities (mammography and clinical examination) were independently assessed; without clinical examination, only 4 per cent of cancers would have been missed (214): in Guildford the corresponding figure was 9 per cent. (263) And this was at a time when mammography in Edinburgh was thought to be relatively insensitive.

The small contribution which clinical examination makes to the detection of cancer in addition to modern mammography must not be construed as indicating that the majority of mammographically detected cancers are impalpable. Regretfully, the opposite is the case. In the prevalence screen in Edinburgh 74 per cent of cancers detected by screening were clinically palpable. It is for this reason that a clinical examination should be included early in the review procedure for assessing mammographic abnormalities, and why examination of the breasts should be an essential part of the medical examination of any woman who consults her doctor for any reason. This is far from being routine in Britain.

It has been recognised for many years in hospital practice that most cases of breast cancer come to light because the woman herself discovers a lump in her breast. And it is obvious that a woman who examines her own breasts regularly is more likely to become conversant with their texture and structure than an occasional medical examiner. All with experience of breast disease have been consulted by women who have detected a tiny 'rice-grain' or 'match-head'

TABLE 42. *Overview of six studies in which practice of breast self-examination was related to the size and state of the axillary nodes of breast cancer* (288)

| | Tumour Size <2 cm | | Axillary Nodes Not Involved | |
	Total No. Women	% <2 cm	Total No. Women	% Negative Nodes
Practised BSE	2137	43·6	2852	60·9
Did not practise BSE	2260	33·6	2713	50·3
Odds ratio	0·56	(0·38–0·81)	0·66	(0·59–0·74)
Percent	—		0·03	

nodule lying superficially in the breast that subsequent investigations have revealed to be a cancer. Haagensen went as far as to suggest that ' . . . from the point of view of the greatest possible gain in early diagnosis, teaching a woman how to examine their own breasts is more important than teaching the technique of breast examination to physicians' (284).

While there would not appear to be any argument against breast self-examination (BSE) as good practise, its promotion on a population basis as a method of reducing mortality from breast cancer is much less certain. For its value must be equated against the risk of anxiety caused by repeatedly 'looking for cancer' or of having unnecessary investigations, the potential morbidity of a surgical biopsy, or the dangers of false re-assurance. The pros and cons of BSE have been extensively reviewed (285–7).

In an attempt to assess the value of BSE, a series of studies have been conducted in which the stage of cancers detected by women practising BSE has been used as an index of benefit. A meta-analysis of 12 such studies, including 8118 women, has been reported in which the variable assessed was the state of the axillary nodes, i.e., whether disease-free or involved (288). This was determined either indirectly by clinical examination or directly by histopathology of excised nodes. In those women who had practised BSE before their breast cancer was diagnosed, the likelihood of having involved nodes was significantly reduced. Tumour size followed the same pattern, being smaller in those who regularly practised BSE (Table 42).

A British study, not included in the meta-analysis, was reported by Mant and colleagues from Oxford, in which the relationship between the teaching and practise of BSE and the stage of breast cancer on diagnosis was examined in 616 women aged 15–59 years (289). They also reported that those who were taught and practised BSE had smaller tumours and a reduced incidence of axillary node involvement (Table 43).

A problem with all such studies is that the stage of the cancer has been determined retrospectively from hospital records, which are notoriously inaccurate. They are also confounded by the variability of the methods used to determine stage and their inherent errors. This is well exemplified in the Oxford report by lack of information on pathological lymph-node status. It is hoped that more accurate information can come from the prospective comparative study now being conducted as part of TEDBC and the controlled randomised trial of BSE being carried out in 200,000 factory workers in Leningrad (290).

TABLE 43. *Clinical size and axillary node status (where known from histological report) in 616 women related to practise of breast self-examination* (289)

	Clinical Size of Tumour		Histological Confirmation or Node Status	
	Number of Women	Size <2 cm (%)	Number of Women	Nodes Not Involved
Not done	294	33·2	214	36·9
Done but not taught	96	34·4	68	44·1
Done and taught <monthly	82	43·6	54	46·3
Monthly or more often	144	45·3	93	50·5

From Mant *et al.*, 271.

TABLE 44. *Tumour size and histological node status in 751 cancers emerging in women offered intruction in breast self-examination compared to a consecutive series of 751 historical controls* (293)

	Number	(%)	Characteristics of Cancer Number	(%)
In situ and <2 cm	351	46·7	281	37·4
Node negative 2	319	42·5	250	33·3
Grade I	109	14·5	70	9·3

Differences reached significant levels when stratified by Nottingham prognostic index, their prognosis is more favourable (from Locker *et al.*).

In the intervention districts in TEDBC (Huddersfield and Nottingham) not offering active clinical and mammographic screening over 70,000 women aged 45–64 (22,484 in Huddersfield, 49,573 in Nottingham) were invited to attend for formal instruction in BSE. For those who detected abnormalities, self-referral clinicals were set up where clinical examination and mammography were performed. In Nottingham the study has been extended to women of 40–64 in a second district, so that between 1979 and 1986 a cohort of 89,010 women have been enrolled in the study group in that city (291–2).

Response to a personal invitation to attend was moderate: 30 per cent in Huddersfield and 42 per cent in Nottingham. The stage distribution of cancers detected in those women who attended in Huddersfield was little different from those who did not. But in Nottingham, compared to historical controls, there was a reduction in the stage of 751 cases of breast cancer diagnosed in the study population compared to historical controls. However, this has not yet been reflected in a mortality advantage compared to TEDBC comparison districts (Table 44; Fig. 40).

From Nottingham a case-control study has recently been reported in which 201 women dying from breast cancer between the time of receiving their invitation and December 1987 have been age-matched with three healthy controls who also had been sent an invitation for BSE education

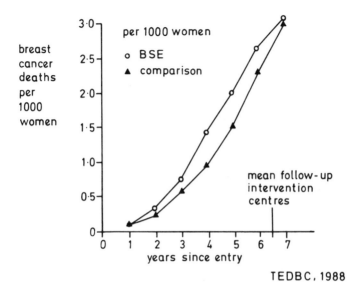

breast cancer deaths per 1000 women

per 1000 women

o BSE
▲ comparison

mean follow-up
intervention
centres

years since entry

TEDBC, 1988

40. Cumulative mortality rates in TEDBC: for BSE and comparison
districts (212).

(293). Women diagnosed as having breast cancer within 3
months of their invitation to be screened were subsequently
excluded leaving 43 premenopausal and 137 postmenopausal cases with 540 controls, in whom a history of having
attended or not attended for education could be compared.

In postmenopausal (but not premenopausal) women the
relative risk of dying was significantly reduced by attending
for education (0·66 (0·45–0·97)).

No difference in survival of study versus historical controls was noted, but within the study group those attending
for BSE education had significantly improved survival. Possibly another example only of the strength of bias due to the
self-selection of highly motivated and health aware women.

An examination of the effect of BSE and routine physician examination on breast cancer mortality was reported by
Greenwald and colleagues. They interviewed 293 women
with breast cancer to determine the method of detection of
their tumour, the stage of which had been recorded. The
distribution of stage in those whose cancers were detected

by BSE implied an expected reduction in mortality of around 20 per cent (294).

The practical question that requires to be answered is whether the role of BSE in population screening requires to be formally examined, either as a sole method of 'screening' in young women or as an adjunct to the national screening programme. The large population study in Finland (295) lacks a control population; and it would appear that only TEDBC and the controlled randomised trial in Leningrad will provide an answer. But whatever the outcome, it must be appreciated that the positive predictive value for a diagnosis of cancer of self-referral on account of finding an abnormality is low. And BSE can never meet the primary objective of screening, which is to detect breast cancer during its sojourn (pre-clinical-detectable) phase.

Acceptance to an invitation to attend a BSE class is not as good as that to a screening clinic, partly on account of dislike of group compared to individual activities, but also from belief that active screening is more 'medical' and more likely to be effective (296–7).

9

QUESTIONS OF MORBIDITY
AND COST

RISKS AND BENEFITS

ONE CRITIC HAS SUGGESTED THAT WOMEN ARE BEING hookwinked in being offered benefit that cannot be delivered. For those whose breast cancers are detected on screening, there is no guarantee that treatment will cure or that survival will be prolonged.

As stressed by Miller, in his discussion of the ethics, risks, and benefits of screening, one cannot imply that every screenee will derive benefit; some are bound to be disadvantaged (298). There is potential anxiety, and also risks of false re-assurance in those screened. But this may happen irrespective of population screening, particularly in those countries where routine medical checks, which include mammography, are accepted as the norm. Attendance may not be without risk. One of Miller's screenees, travelling to a screening clinic from an outlying district in Canada, was killed in a plane crash!

One would expect, as a result of the earlier detection of cancer through screening, that treatment would be less arduous and morbid. But this is not necessarily so. Many surgeons still prefer to recommend mastectomy for *in situ* disease, and there is a real danger that borderline lesions may be unnecessarily treated radically due to the over-diagnosis of pre-malignant or malignant change. It is also said that treatment which does not prolong life, by advancing the time of diagnosis, increases the duration of morbidity.

This is a situation where the risks for some may outweigh the benefits for others, a difficult equation to solve. Yet it has been solved in other situations, for example, organ transplantation from living donors.

Benefits must also be considered. Most important is an improved life-span, which if the disease is treated early, should be symptom-free. Mortality from breast cancer in Utrecht, where screening started in 1973, has shown a marked reduction compared to other Dutch cities without a screening service (299,300). So also has that in Nijmegen fallen compared to Arnheim, which before screening started, had identical mortality rates (300). The mortality from breast cancer in Sweden has steadily fallen over the past decade (301) (Fig. 41).

Less radical treatment is another possible benefit, and, although some surgeons still prefer to use radical treatment for early disease, this is not the general pattern. In Scotland, mastectomy is now performed only in a minority of patients for those with tumours less than 4 cm in size (302).

In Gavlëborg County, Sweden, where up to 1974 the incidence of locally advanced and disseminated breast cancer (stages III and IV) was similar to that now recorded in

41. Comparison of breast cancer mortality in the city of Utrecht (where screening was introduced in 1974) with other urban areas in Netherlands. Women born 1911–1925 (299).

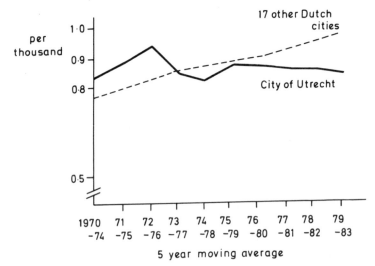

Day & Chamberlain, 1988

the control population in Edinburgh, there has been a
steady decline in the number of such cases. Seventy-four per
cent of newly diagnosed breast cancers are now of stage I,
i.e., less than 2 cm in size and without-involved axillary
lymph-nodes. The policy of treatment has changed to one of
local excision of a segment of the breast alone without post-
operative radiation of systemic therapy. Outlays on screening are now retrieved by reduced treatment costs. Relapse
rates are not high: 11 per cent of 160 patients at four years
follow-up. It is hoped that these women will also be spared
the hazards of advanced disease with its diminished quality
of life (261).

In Edinburgh, a comparison of the treatment of breast
cancer in screen-detected and control women has indicated
that in the former conservation of the breast is more
practicable. But, as will be discussed, a particular problem
arises in the management of *in situ* cancer (see below) (Table
45).

TABLE 45. *Surgical treatment of operable (Stages I and II)*
invasive cancer at Longmore Breast Unit, Edinburgh (213)

| | Treated by Conservation | |
	Screen-Detected 287 Cases	Controls 129 Cases
1979–81	0	3
1982	35	2
1983	46	6
1984	31	3
1985	61	4
1986–87	77	14

Almost all cases detected by screening and 57% of cases in the control
population were referred to that unit for treatment. This was independent of the source of referral. Since 1982, breast conservation therapy
has been considered for all tumours up to 4 cm in size.

And to many women knowledge of a negative 'screen' is
reassuring.

If benefits are to outweigh risks, risks must be minimised.
The quality of screening must be high. This includes every
step in the screening process—from the original listing of

women in the target population to the follow-up of the patient with cancer after treatment. The need for close monitoring of all aspects of screening was stressed by the Working Group, which saw considerable advantage in asking central authorities to advise health departments on the introduction of breast cancer screening programmes, to monitor effectiveness and efficiency and to keep progress under review. This has been done, and a series of guidelines for all aspects of screening have been drawn up by expert working parties and are being implemented (195,303–7). Further, an extensive programme of education has been implemented including the regular issue, with the support of the Cancer Research Campaign, of *Network*, a newsletter produced by Muir Gray and his editorial team that is circulated to all those concerned with screening. Monitoring and evaluation systems based on mathematical models have also been proposed by Day and his colleagues (260).

A description of details of propositions for the assurance of quality is beyond the scope of this monograph; but it is reassuring that they reflect the endeavour of the health departments to get it right. For screening of poor quality is worse than no screening.

Quality depends on people, and it is also reassuring that throughout U.K. radiologists, pathologists, surgeons and community medicine specialists are together seizing the opportunity not only to provide a model service, but also to use it as a valuable source of new knowledge.

PSYCHOLOGICAL EFFECTS

The psychosexual morbidity that can follow a diagnosis of breast cancer has already been referred to (page 40). There is concern that breast cancer screening by itself may have undesirable psychological or psychiatric effects, which may disadvantage those who participate. But, until now, this has been largely a matter of opinion. Facts from two recent British studies suggest that it is an unwarranted fear.

To assess psychiatric morbidity of women attending the Edinburgh Breast Screening Clinic, Dean and her colleagues invited a random sample of 151 women to complete a 30-item General Health Questionnaire (GHQ) while waiting to be screened and again six months after screening (308). The GHQ is an instrument that is widely used to test for psychiatric disability, particularly anxiety and depression (309). Women also were asked to allow a trained researcher to interview them in their home six months after being screened. She enquired about their attitudes to screening, to breast cancer and to BSE, and assessed mental state with a psychiatric assessment schedule. A successful interview was achieved in 132 women. Controls, matched for age, marital status, social class and employment, factors which are known to affect psychiatric morbidity and could cause bias, were randomly selected from the normal population. They also were invited for interview: 117 matched pairs were available for analysis.

An additional sample of 158 women attending the screening clinic during a one-week period were also invited to complete the GHQ before being screened and by post six months after attendance. Data were complete for 139.

Of the 117 pairs interviewed, the prevalence of a psychiatric disorder among the screened population did not differ from that in their matched partners. Nor did the type of 'case', whether depressive or anxious, vary between the two groups (Table 46).

TABLE 46. *Estimated prevalence of psychiatric disorder among interviewed women* (308)

| | Number (%) of Women | |
RDC Diagnosis Nature of Disorder	Screening Sample (117 women)	Community Sample (117 women)
Major depressive	7	9
Minor depressive	6	6
Generalised anxiety	4	5
Panic	1	0
TOTAL	18	20

Comparison screening and community samples.

TABLE 47. *General Health Questionnaire 'case rate' in 269 women in interview and postal samples before and 6 months after screening* (308)

	Number of Women	
	Before Screening	*6 Months After*
'Cases' before not after screening	20	—
'Cases' after not before screening	—	21
'Cases' on both occasions	26	26
TOTAL	46	47

Mean symptom scores were 1·766 and 2·048, respectively; difference not significant.

The information obtained from the interview was used to determine a 'cut-off point' for a psychiatric disorder on the GHQ of these same women. There were 28 cases before and 28 six months after screening. This same cut-off point was then applied to the GHQs of the second, 'postal', sample; 18 were cases before and 19 six months after screening. Although different women were classified as 'cases' before or after screening, no significant differences were found (Table 47).

TABLE 48. *General Health Questionnaire scores of 5 or more in women attending screening clinic, at initial visit and 3 months later* (310)

	% Prevalence of GHQ Score of 5+	
	At Time of Review	*3 Months Later*
Screened: no abnormality detected	24·0	19·2
Recalled for review: no cancer	30·1	18·8
Symptomatic: no cancer	35·7	31·0
New diagnosis breast cancer	35·1	45·9
Previous breast cancer	21·4	21·4

The only significant difference between groups on initial attendance at the relevant clinic was that between routine screening and those symptomatic but without cancer. At 3 months, significant differences were observed for symptomatic benign and cancer patients.

Women in whom an abnormality was detected on their screening mammogram, and as a result had to return to the clinic, were not included in the Edinburgh study. They were the subject of that carried out in Guildford. For this, five consecutive attenders for screening each week and five consecutive attenders at the review clinic (these being women recalled for further assessment) were invited, on attendance, to complete a 28-item GHQ designed to test for anxiety and depression of recent onset. Three months later the same women were again asked to complete the questionnaire. Women referred to a hospital out-patient clinic with breast symptoms were similarly assessed (310).

In total, 733 of 774 invited women completed both questionnaires. They fell into five groups:

1. Screened and no abnormality detected

2. Recalled for review but considered, after further investigation, to be normal

3. Symptomatic women in whom the diagnosis was of benign disease

4. Women, either symptomatic or on review from screening, who were newly diagnosed to have breast cancer

5. Women with a previous history of breast cancer.

TABLE 49. *Distribution of scores in subgroups before and 3 months after screening* (310)

	Group 1 (no. 295)	Group 2 (no. 271)	Group 3 (no. 134)	Group 4 (no. 38)	Group 5 (no. 14)
Somatic symptoms					
before	38	40	44	45	36
3 months after	34	26	43	62	29
Anxiety					
before	35	44	50	42	43
3 months after	26	29	38	41	36
Social dysfunction					
before	35	33	37	47	36
3 months after	30	29	37	68	21
Depression					
before	14	14	16	11	7
3 months after	10	10	16	14	7

Group 1 are in the middle of the range expected for community-based samples.

The prevalence of psychiatric morbidity in these five groups is given in Table 48, and the breakdown into anxiety, depression, social dysfunction, and somatic symptoms in Table 49.

The scores for psychiatric morbidity were in the middle of the range expected from other community-based studies of women in this age group. There was no evidence of excess morbidity in women attending for screening; confirming the Edinburgh results. Women who attended the review clinic on account of a screen-detected abnormality did have significantly greater anxiety, but not more so than that experienced by symptomatic women attending the hospital out-patient clinic. Nor did it last; the score returned to 'normal' levels at three months.

In only one group did significant and lasting anxiety cause psychiatric morbidity—those with a diagnosis of breast cancer.

At interview women were asked how best anxiety might be minimised. Shortening of periods of waiting and good communication were regarded as paramount.

These two studies provide strong evidence that participation in a screening programme does not lead to any sustained increase in psychiatric morbidity. Fear that the anxiety provoked by screening outweighs its benefits are groundless. Not that women are not anxious. In the Edinburgh study 30 per cent admitted to anxiety on receiving the invitation and 20 per cent on being examined, particularly by mammography. But this is not of morbid proportions; 86 per cent found the experience reassuring. And even being recalled for further tests provoked no greater anxiety than attending a doctor's surgery (311–2).

The value of nurse counsellors in a symptomatic clinic has already been referred to. So also have they a critical supportive role in screening.

TABLE 50. *Work scheme for screening in Stockholm trial with actual numbers of women involved* (225)

	Number of Women (%)	
	1st Screen	2nd Screen
Number of participants	32,555 (100)	30,765 (100)
Recalled for 3-view mammography	1,655 (5·1)	989 (3·2)
Recalled for clinical exam and other investigations	482 (1·5)	246 (0·8)
Biopsy performed	207 (0·6)	122 (0·4)
Histology cancer	128 (0·4)	95 (0·3)
Histology benign	79 (0·2)	27 (0·09)

Similar proportions are described in Gavlëborg, Two-Counties trial, Malmo and Göteborg.

SOURCE: Breast Cancer Research & Treatment. Klomar Academic Publishers, with permission.

BASIC SCREENING AND RECALL

In the U.K. women are now being screened in static and mobile screening units, each examining 12,000 women a year. The poor predictive value of a basic screening mammogram has been a cause for concern. Even at most, only two or three out of each ten women with a detectable abnormality on their basic single-view screen will prove to have cancer. In the BCDDP, this was the case in one out of each ten women with an abnormality on screening with two-view mammography and clinical examination.

Before condemning screening on account of the potential anxiety which a false-positive test may cause, it must be realised that a woman who visits her doctor with a lump in her breast and who is referred to a hospital out-patient department is equally anxious. And even a smaller proportion (1 in 10) prove to be cancer. According to the survey of Edinburgh and Aberdeen women, this fact was known to only one-third of women. The psychiatric morbidities caused by attending a screening review clinic and a hospital out-patient department are identical; fears of psychological stress from screening have been overstated.

But, it is essential to the success of a screening service that the number of women who are brought back for assessment is kept as low as possible. This depends upon the quality of the radiography and the experience and confidence of the radiologist. In Stockholm, the percentage of women who are recalled after a single view for additional mammography is 5% and for full examination just over 1% (225) (Table 50, Table 51).

The quality of screening mammography is critical to the success of the whole programme. A proportion of films may not be of suitable standard for interpretation. In our feasibility study with a mobile screening unit, 3 per cent of 6008 women were recalled owing to unsatisfactory films. Most were due to dense breasts, a problem now reduced by the use of grid-films. Only in 77 women was a poor film alone the reason for recall, and then faulty packing of the film was mainly responsible (313). Poor radiography accounted only for eight failures. The College of Radiographers has insisted that radiographers responsible for screening mammography should have attended an approved course and be accredited; and that performance indicators should be applied to ensure that quality is maintained.

The quality of interpretation of the initial screening mammogram is also critical. This initial interpretation is not diagnostic; the radiologist only decides whether a set of films are normal, abnormal, or not interpretable. Training courses have been set up in five approved centres, and the Royal College of Radiology has taken an active interest in both initial and continued programmes of education for screening radiologists. The proportion of 'false-negative' tests due to faulty interpretation can be determined by reviewing the original screening mammograms of interval cases, as has been done in Malmo and in Canada. The rate of 'true misses' in Canada was less than two per 1000 sets of films (186).

Realisation for the need of quality prompted the Radiation Advisory Committee to invite a group of experts to recommend standards for the performance of mammography, to provide guidelines for testing available systems, and to advise how best quality might be monitored. The

Pritchard report, which has been widely circulated, provides comprehensive advice on all aspects of screening mammography, including the evaluation of equipment, the performance of the screening process, and the identification of deficiencies (195). Of major importance is their recommendation that in each region a Quality Assurance Manager should be appointed and that a reference centre should act as a focus for the 'development, monitoring and review of a programme of quality assurance'. Managers would maintain links with the five training centres and the central evaluation unit. The guidelines for quality in the Pritchard report are exacting, and imply a degree of monitoring and supervision not usually encountered in the NHS. But, high quality can be achieved only if their proposals for continued assessment of all aspects of the mammographic screen are accepted as necessary constraints on the freedom of those concerned.

Modern high-quality mammography is the only test available for the detection of breast cancer at an early stage. Provided the requirements for quality are met, it is difficult to understand those who would not wish to utilise the benefits it can bring, particularly when questions of real concern, such as the benefits and costs of single- versus two-view type mammography and the optimal interval for screening, are also being addressed.

ASSESSMENT AND BIOPSY RATES

An important principle of screening is that facilities for the investigation and treatment of screen-detected abnormalities are adequate. The Working Group was conscious that if the number of surgical biopsies were to be kept to a minimum, the assessment of screen-detected abnormalities had to be exact. A surgical biopsy of the breast may be regarded as a minor procedure by the surgeon; but even minor surgery is a major event for the patient. It can cause physical morbidity and by distorting the breast may compromise the interpretation of subsequent mammograms. A biopsy, particularly for a non-palpable lesion is also expensive; in the Edinburgh analysis, the cost of a localisation biopsy which involves a general anaesthetic and hospital stay was £250 (1983 prices) (281).

The assessment of an abnormality seen on a single-view mammogram may require additional mammograms including magnification views, clinical examination, ultrasonography, fine-needle aspiration (FNA) and FNA cytology. For the non-palpable lesion this includes stereotactic radiological guidance. The performance of these tests requires the skills of different specialists—clinical, radiological, cytological. The Working Group recommended the establishment of multidisciplinary 'assessment teams', each of which would serve the needs of up to 2–3 basic screening units. This view was endorsed by committees advising the Health Department, and such formal assessment is being implemented.

In Sweden, the first step in the assessment of patients with mammographic abnormality is 'complete mammography', which is an extension of the basic screening process. The woman is seen by a clinician only if the radiologist is convinced that the abnormality, suspected on the single-oblique view screening mammogram is still present. The Working Group believed that a similar pattern would evolve in the U.K., and that a number of women would be recalled only for an additional cranio-caudal view, fuller assessment being reserved for those in whom an abnormality was confirmed (or those with symptoms). But it has become apparent that, in women requiring additional views, the radiologist is likely to wish magnification films and often an ultrasonogram: and that a clinical examination is desirable.

Our decision to perform a clinical examination early in the assessment procedure was based on experience that three-quarters of mammographically detected abnormalities were palpable. Further investigation of a palpable lump by FNA cytology, as in a symptomatic woman referred to a breast clinic, allows an unequivocal diagnosis in 95 per cent of patients, and avoids the need for sophisticated imaging.

These investigations belong more to assessment than to screening and increasingly are being carried out at a first-stage (lo-tech) review clinic. This is best held outside the hospital in the screening clinic, where women can be counselled as necessary. This pattern has been adopted in Edinburgh, where the central clinic services two mobile units and is equipped with a sophisticated mammographic unit. Women with an abnormality detected on their initial screen or who have symptoms are invited to return (or if initially screened in a mobile unit to attend) the central screening clinic, where their additional x-rays are taken and a clinic doctor or radiologist examines their breasts and they can be seen by a nurse-counsellor. There is no need for a surgeon to be involved at this stage. But as a surgeon must have an opportunity to examine a suspected cancer before it is needled (which distorts clinical features), only cystic lesions confirmed by ultrasound are aspirated at first-stage assessment.

Should the radiologist suspect a cancer, the woman proceeds to the second-stage (hi-tec) assessment, which in Edinburgh is carried out in a dedicated breast unit. This involves a review of the mammographic and clinical findings with a surgeon, and the performance of FNA-cytology, which in the non-palpable lesion requires stereotactic guidance. The surgeon, radiologist and cytologist then can decide in consultation whether a biopsy is indicated. This system has many advantages. At the first-stage assessment at the screening clinic, the majority of women recalled for review can immediately be assured all is well, and so avoid the psychiatric morbidity of attending a hospital clinic; the skills of surgeon and cytologists are more economically used, for they need consult only those who require their services; a firm diagnosis can be made in many patients, in whom surgery becomes a question of management rather than diagnosis; and the patient can be appropriately counselled. Cytological aspirates are prepared under safe conditions for the handling of human tissues. The 'hi-tec team' is also available to provide a service for the symptomatic hospital clinic.

The value of a formal assessment procedure was shown by a study of 437 localisation biopsies for non-palpable lesions carried out in Edinburgh in 304 women referred from the screening clinic (with its formal multi-disciplinary assessment procedure) and 130 from the hospital breast clinic (where the decision for biopsy was made by the surgeon on

TABLE 51. *Comparison of findings in patients referred for the screening clinic (where assessment was formalised) and from hospital out-patient clinic (where no formal assessment was used)* (314)

| | Source of Referral | |
	Screening Clinic	Symptomatic Out-Patient Clinic
Number	304	130
Age	$55 \cdot 2 \pm 7 \cdot 1$	$49 \cdot 6 \pm 9 \cdot 4$
Malignant histology	108 (35·5%)	17 (13·1%)
Benign:malignant	1·8 to 1	6·6 to 1

the report of the mammogram) (314). Biopsy rates and the ratio of benign to malignant histology confirm the higher efficiency of the formal team approach. This study was carried out before guided FNA-cytology was available. From Italy it is reported that the introduction of stereotactic FNA decreased the ratio of benign to malignant biopsies from 1·7 to 1 to 0·5 to 1 (315).

Stereotactic FNA cytology in the non-palpable lesion has many advantages. Should a diagnosis of cancer be confirmed, a biopsy is no longer appropriate. The further management of the patient, including the operation, is for cancer. Before stereotactic FNA cytology was introduced a diagnostic operation incompletely removed half of all non-palpable cancers, necessitating the unpleasantness and risk of a second operation (18).

Cytology is now also being used to confirm that an abnormality believed radiologically to be benign is such, allowing it to be observed rather than removed. The safety of this procedure has been demonstrated in a report from Stockholm, in which 2005 women with non-palpable mammographic abnormalities without either mammographic or cytological suspicion of malignancy were observed for a period of 2–6 years. In only one had breast cancer been missed.

TABLE 52. *Rates of biopsies (per 1000 women) and benign:malignant ratios reported in screening trials* (213, 227, 229, 219, 225, 207)

Age (years)	Prevalence Screen		Incidence Screen	
	rate	b:m ratio	rate	b:m ratio
TWO-COUNTIES				
50–69	14·0	1·0	4·6	0·3
STOCKHOLM				
40–64	6·0	0·5	4·0	0·3
GÖTEBORG				
40–49	6·3	1·0	4·1	1·2
50–59	16·4	0·6	5·9	1·1
NIJMEGEN				
35–49	7·8	2·3	5·2	1·9
50–64	11·0	1·0	6·4	0·4
EDINBURGH				
45–64	16·6	2·7	6·1	1·8
GUILDFORD				
45–64	15·6	1·8	3·7	0·5

From Italy it is reported that the introduction of stereotaxic FNA decreased the ratio of benign to malignant biopsies from 1·7 to 1 to 0·5 to 1 (315).

The success of assessment in discriminating between benign and malignant lesions can be monitored by the rate

TABLE 53. *Comparison biopsy rates (per 1000 women) and benign:malignant ratios in USA and Nijmegen over similar periods of screening* (177, 63, 237)

Age (yr)	Screens	Biopsies over programme	
		rate	b:m ratio
HIP			
40–64	4 annual	32·1	3·9
BCDDP			
35–74	5 annual	99·6	5·7
NIJMEGEN			
35–49	2 biennial	12·3	1·7
50–64		16·2	0·8

of biopsies and the ratio of benign to malignant lesions on histological examination. Sweden and Holland provide the standard, but British rates are reasonable. In the U.S., where every mammographic abnormality is excised, the reported ratios are disturbing (Tables 52,53). The results of six rounds of screening in Nijmegen indicate that positive predictive values of referral for the assessment of a mammographic abnormality and for biopsies increase with each

TABLE 54. *Predictive value if referral generated by a mammographic biopsy for diagnosis of cancer in Nijmegen programme of screening (237)*

24-month screens	Percent positive for cancer			
	of mammographic abnormalities referred for investigation		of biopsies	
	< 50 yr	50–64 yr	< 50 yr	50–64 yr
1	20·5	38·0	29·6	51·0
2	21·3	49·3	34·0	69·4
3	27·1	45·5	34·2	62·5
4	22·2	51·0	31·6	71·4
5	43·2	64·8	59·3	87·5
6	64·3	36·5	85·7	96·7

SOURCE: International Journal of Cancer. Wiley-Liss, with permission.

TABLE 55. *Relationship age to benign:malignant ratio of biopsies generated by screening in BCDDP (241)*

Age (yr)	Benign/Malignant Ratio
35–39	16·4
40–44	9·5
45–49	6·5
50–54	5·2
55–59	3·8
60–64	3·4
65–69	3·2
70–74	2·7

From Baker, 241.
SOURCE: American Cancer Society, with permission.

screening round (Table 54). According to Hendriks, predictive values for referral of 30 per cent in the first and 70 per cent in subsequent rounds should be attainable in a successful programme; a figure contrasting with that of 8 per cent for mammographic screening in the first round of the Canadian trial (316, 317). Excess biopsies are commoner in the young (Table 55).

Different methods of assessing mammographic abnormalities are used in different screening districts. These are discussed in the Breast Screening publication on *Organising Assessment*, which has been widely circulated (305). But irrespective of the system, assessment teams must be expert and experienced. Therefore, they must be limited in number.

The performance of the biopsy and its interpretation also requires a team approach. This team is likely to be the same as the assessment team. The performance and interpretation of biopsies by surgeons and pathologists inexperienced in the techniques are to be discouraged. This is particularly so for the non-palpable lesion, when radiologist, surgeon, and pathologist must work closely together. The insertion of a localising device by a radiologist remote from the operating suite is not ideal practise. Nor is a lack of close liaison between surgeon and pathologist. Conditions for the immediate preparation and dispatch of the specimen must be met. The pathologist cannot be expected to make a quick diagnosis. In the preparation of tissues he requires to use radiological and subgross techniques; the microscopic interpretation of borderline lesions requires experience and wisdom (19).

Review sessions, at which the pathologist discusses his findings with radiological and surgical members of the screening team, are critical to the quality of this complex exercise, and are held regularly in well-organised programmes.

The interpretation of *in situ* cancers and atypical hyperplastic lesions requires particular care. A system of review, with a panel of experts, is nationally available to ensure uniformity for the borderline lesion.

The Royal Colleges of Pathologists and of Surgeons have issued guidelines for the requirements of screening services.

Reviews of the role of pathologists and surgeons have recently been published (303–4,307). The removal and interpretation of screen-detected abnormalities is not a responsibility to be undertaken occasionally, and it is regretful that some clinicians do not accept this.

TREATMENT

Concern is expressed that screen-detected cancers may be over-treated. But in a well-organised programme, the opposite is the case. In Gavlëborg, local excision of a segment of the breast alone is practised for small (<2 cm) invasive tumours. A controlled randomised trial is under way in Sweden in which stage I tumours are being treated either by 'sector resection' alone or with radiotherapy. The preliminary results are promising; but longer follow-up is required to confirm the safety of the more conservative approach. Over-diagnosis of borderline lesions is another concern; but in the U.K. this is guarded against by pathological review (318).

The problem of treating *in situ* disease has already been referred to. Its incidence has increased dramatically since the introduction of mammographic screening, so that it now accounts for 15 per cent of all screen-detected cancers. For lobular carcinoma *in situ* (LCIS), there is no logic in other than adopting a conservative approach. It is a histopathological entity, a marker of unstable breast epithelium rather than of malignancy. The risk of invasive cancer is small and long delayed. Bilateral mastectomy is only exceptionally performed; a trial of long-term tamoxifen therapy is under way in Europe.

Ductal carcinoma *in situ* (DCIS) is frankly malignant and if left untreated will develop into invasive cancer in at least 30 per cent of involved breasts within three to ten years. There is also the risk that foci of micro-invasion may be present, associated in a small percentage (2 per cent) with axillary lymph-node metastases. Multi-focal deposits of tumour are common, and reported to be present in 30 per cent of mastectomy specimens (319). It is on account of these risks that some surgeons still prefer mastectomy as the treatment of choice, knowing that it achieves cure. But most now suggest this to be unnecessarily radical (302–3).

The risk of relying on local excision to treat DCIS has recently been assessed in a report of 115 mastectomy specimens removed after an area of DCIS has been excised. Provided local excision was regarded as adequate and the margins of the specimen were clear of tumour, residual invasive disease in the mastectomy specimen was found only when the extent of DCIS exceeded 45 mm. In 60 patients with disease of 25 mm or less in diameter, only one had residual foci of invasive cancer—and this was following an incomplete excision (64).

The size of DCIS detected by mammography is much smaller than that which previously became clinically apparent by a mass or nipple discharge. Not that mammographically detected DCIS is free from recurrence. In a series of 80 cases treated by local excision alone, this proved to be 10 per cent at 48 (1–136) months; but only half were invasive (63).

A detailed radiological-pathological study has recently been reported from Holland on 82 mastectomy specimens removed for the treatment of DCIS (47 screen-detected). There were 50 cases of so-called comedo DCIS and 32 of cribriform or micropapillary type. Notable was that in the latter the size of the tumour exceeded that suspected from the mammographic appearances and commonly extended over more than one quadrant, such spread being contiguous rather than as a result of multifocal disease.

The type of calcification on the mammogram—linear and branching 'casts' of ducts or coarse granules—in comedo DCIS was distinct from the clusters of fine granular calcifications found in cribriform and micropapillary disease, forming a useful guide to the surgeon as to the need for an extensive resection (320).

In Europe local excision is now the preferred treatment for DCIS, provided the margins of the excised tissue are not involved (321). But there is concern about the incidence of local recurrence and uncertainty as to the role of radiation therapy (322–6). Some information is available from a subset of the NSABP trial in the U.S. and from a retrospective European study, which suggests that radiotherapy may be protective, but the numbers are small (327–8). Randomised trials in progress in Europe (EORTC) and the U.S. are addressing this question by comparing local excision with local excision and radiotherapy, but, because of the favourable outcome of *in situ* cancer (329), large numbers are required (19). In the U.K., the Breast Cancer Trials Co-ordinating Subcommittee (BCTCS) of UKCCR has initiated a study in screen-detected DCIS. This trial is testing not only the effect, following local excision, of post-operative radiation, but also of long-term tamoxifen therapy in a 2×2 factorial design, which will answer both questions in one cohort of patients (330).

Some have proposed that those cancers which emerge after a negative screen (interval cancers) have a particularly bad prognosis and therefore require more aggressive treatment. But in a comparison of 94 interval cancers and 179 cancers diagnosed independently of screening in the control population during the same time period, reported from Sweden, no difference in outlook was obvious (331). In the HIP trial case fatality rates of interval cases were also similar to those of the controls. (Fig. 42).

SELECTIVE SCREENING

Factors of Risk

The cost-effectiveness of screening for breast cancer could be greatly enhanced were it to be confined to those at risk from the disease. There is an extensive literature on factors affecting risk (312–15). These have been defined mainly by retrospective studies in which their presence in women with breast cancer is compared with that of controls. Controls are either hospital patients without breast cancer or healthy women in neighbouring communities (332–6).

Sex and Reproduction. Breast cancer is a disease of females. Functioning ovaries are necessary for its initiation, both in experimental animals and in women. Surgical removal of the

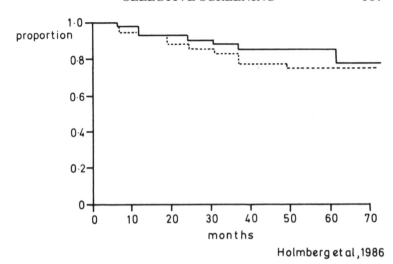

Holmberg et al, 1986

42. Proportion of 94 interval and 178 control cancers surviving in the
Two-Counties trial (331).

ovaries, if performed before the age of 40 years, reduces the
incidence of breast cancer by half (337).

The duration of a woman's active reproductive life is
related to her risk of developing breast cancer. Early menarche, (before the age of 15 years) and late menopause,
(after 50 years of age) are associated with a modest but
signifiant increase of breast cancer risk in later life. Some
consider that it is the time of the start of regular ovulatory
menstrual cycles and the total number of functional cycles
that a woman experiences which are relevant.

The human ovary secretes oestrogens and progesterone
during the menstrual cycle. Oestrogen was once believed to
be the only promoting agent, but there is increasing evidence that progesterone is also implicated. The administration of exogeneous oestrogens alone—for example, as
hormone-replacement therapy after the menopause or during a pregnancy (once used to prevent miscarriage)—only
increases risk slightly (338–9). The effect of oestrogen (and
progesterone) may be age-related. There is increasing evidence that oestrogen-containing contraceptive pills, when

taken early in life, are associated with an increased incidence of breast cancer, at least in young women (340).

A large case-control study carried out in 11 geographical areas in Britain has now indicated that for young women who develop breast cancer before the age of 36 years, there is a highly significant trend in risk with duration of pill usage (341). The authors tentatively suggest that 20 per cent of breast cancers in this age group may be pill-related. Fortunately, breast cancer at so young an age is not common.

Married compared to single women enjoy protection against breast cancer. So also do those who bear children, particularly in early life. A unique international study carried out by McMahon and colleagues in seven geographical areas showed that it was the age at which a woman had her first pregnancy that was the critical factor (342). A woman whose first child was born before the age of 20 years has one-third to one-half of the risk of developing breast cancer compared to one having her first child when over 35 (343). There is a cross-over effect: nulliparous women have a risk intermediate to these two extremes (Fig. 55).

The protective effect of a pregnancy only occurs with full-term deliveries, even if still-born. There is evidence that abortions during the first three months of pregnancy may aggravate risk, but this has not been supported in a recent Swedish study (344).

Race and Environment. Breast cancer is a disease of western women and is strongly age-related. There are wide variations in incidence and mortality between countries (Fig. 9) (345). Sex-related and reproductive factors influence risk within any one country, but they do not account fully for international variations.

These differences are not genetically determined. Migrants from low-incidence to high-incidence countries take on the incidence of their new host; but only after a generation: exposure to the new environment must be at an early age (346) (Fig. 56). Of the possible environmental factors concerned, diet takes precedence (347). Obesity is associated with an increased incidence of breast cancer in postmenopausal women; and a relationship between the intake of dietary fat and breast cancer incidence and mortality and prognosis has been described (348–9) (Fig. 57). And there is new evidence implicating high-density lipoproteins with breast cancer risk (351). So also with alcohol (350).

But these factors may only be markers of increasing affluence, and are not necessarily cause-related. Fat cannot be separated from calories or body weight, which influences also the date of menarche. In those countries with low fat intake, children are small and therefore menstruate late. But, as indicated on page 184, there are new data implicating oestrogens as a related factor.

The aetiology of breast cancer in pre-menopausal and post-menopausal women may differ. That in older women may be of environmental origin (352); a belief supported by the increasing incidence of breast cancer in post-menopausal women in Japan, coincidental with its westernisation (Fig. 58).

As has already been indicated radiation during childhood may also be an environmental factor of importance. From a recent follow-up report of children in Israel who were treated by scalp irradiation, it is apparent that a relatively small dose of radiation (16 mGy 1·6 rad) to the breast during its development (age 5–9) increases the risk of cancer in later life (183).

Genetic Factors. There is strong evidence that genetic factors may be associated with breast cancer. The disease is more common in those with an affected first-degree relative (mother or sister). But, as the environment during childhood is the same, this is not necessarily a genetic effect. Not so for those with affected paternal relatives or for those who belong to those rare families in which the disease, frequently bilateral, appears in dominant fashion and affects 50 per cent of young female members.

The potential for investigating these families by modern molecular genetic techniques is great, and such studies are under way in several centres in Britain, including Edinburgh (353).

Hormonal Profiles. It was hoped that the availability of assays for cirulating hormones, particularly oestrogens, would unravel the cause of these various relationships, whether within or between populations. Unfortunately, this has not yet proven to be the case (354).

Many problems affect such studies. Sampling is one; blood sampling is invasive, urine collections are difficult to monitor. Salivary sampling is non-invasive and has recently been used in an international comparative study, but methodology for hormonal assays are restricted (355). Circulating hormone levels may vary from second to second, and are influenced by medication and stress. Further, the relationship between circulating hormonal levels and those within the breast is quite obscure. Breast fluid is rich in precursor steroids of adrenocortical origin, which can be synthesised to oestrogen by breast fat and by the tumour. Local concentrations may bear little relationship to those in the circulating plasma.

The results of these studies tend to confuse rather than clarify issues of risk; although, on balance, they do support the importance of oestrogens and other steroid hormones as permissive agents. Without oestrogen (and probably progesterone) one does not get breast cancer, and excess is probably bad (332).

Benign Disease. A history of benign breast disease, particularly when requiring a biopsy, is more frequent in women with breast cancer than normal controls. Epithelial proliferation is believed to be the main risk factor; this indicating early instability.

In 1976, Wolfe reported that the parenchymal pattern of the breast on xeromammography, was related to subsequent risk of breast cancer (356). Breasts with prominent ducts and dense 'dysplasia' were more at risk. His findings were not universally accepted, partly on account of the difficulty in detecting small cancers in mammograms with these characteristics. Several studies have shown a relationship between mammographic patterns and risk factors; for example, family history and age at first pregnancy. And it may be that they relate to cancer risk; but not to the extent initially reported by Wolfe (357–9).

More important risk factors are tabulated (Table 56)

TABLE 56. *Factors influencing risk of developing breast cancer* (360)

Factors	High v Low Risk	Relative Risk
SEX AND REPRODUCTION		
Sex	Female v male	Absolute (almost)
Menarche	Early v late age	2–4
Menopause	Late v early age	<2
Ovarian function	Artificial menopause v normal	Age-dependent
	Nulliparous v parous	<2
Pregnancy	Early v late age (first)	2–4
HORMONE EXPOSURE		
Oral contraceptives	Use v non-use	Age-dependent
Postmenopausal oestrogen	Use v non-use	<2
HORMONE PROFILES		
Circulating oestradiol	High v low	Uncertain
RACE AND ENVIRONMENT		
Race	Westernised v developing	>4
Socioeconomic status	High v low	2–4
Body habitus	Obese v lean	<2
Diet	High v low fat calories	Uncertain
Radiation exposure	Childhood v none	2–4
FAMILY HISTORY		
First-degree relative	Breast cancer v no breast cancer	2–4
Premenopausal bilateral breast cancer	History v no history	Dominant
MEDICAL HISTORY		
Age	Old v young	>4
Previous benign disease, particularly biopsy	History v no history	2–4
Mammographic pattern	Prominent ducts v no prominent ducts	2–4
	Dense v not dense	2–4

(360). Two points of importance are (i) that relative risk relates only to that compared to the control population in the study concerned and not to the population in general; (ii) that those factors described as 'risk factors' are not causative; many are but markers of another agent yet to be defined.

Application to Screening. Risk factors have been used to determine whether selective screening of a high-risk group is practical. For this purpose, only those factors elicited on simple enquiry are relevant. Although mammographic patterns and even estimates of urinary steroids have been included in some studies. A study in Guernsey, in which specimens of urine were collected from 5000 healthy women to relate to risk of developing breast cancer, was at its time (1961) unique (361). But, attention has been focused mainly on those factors related to reproduction (age at menarche, menopause, and first pregnancy), family history, and a history of benign breast disease, which can readily be defined by enquiry.

Before risk factors can be applied, it must be confirmed that they are 'active' discriminants of breast cancer in the population to be screened. In the HIP study, all 20,000 women attending for their first screen were surveyed (340–1). In other screening projects, case-control studies have been performed to compare the prevalence of risk factors in cases of cancer and matched healthy controls. Relative risk is calculated by linear or multivariate analysis, which allows the identification of factors which best can discriminate between cases (breast cancer) and controls (362–7).

Having defined risk factors of relevance, their prevalence, individually and in combination, is tested in patients with cancer and healthy women, either by simple addition of the most significant factors or by logistic regression. This further analysis is best done on a separate population from which the discriminant has been calculated, but in most studies subsets of the original populations have been used.

A study carried out by Alexander and her colleagues in Edinburgh is representative (368). From the screening clinic, 186 cases of breast cancer detected by screening or presenting within 12 months of a negative screen were identified, for each of which four controls matched for age and time of screening were randomly selected. These were women who had attended for screening within 12 months of the case but who had not developed breast cancer. Fifteen separate factors known to be associated with risk were examined by multivariate analysis, of which four proved significant: age at menarche, family history, previous benign breast disease and (barely) age at first pregnancy. To these was later added menopausal (versus other menstrual) status. The prevalence of the four most readily determined (family history, benign breast disease, menopausal status and first full-term pregnancy) in a subset of 98 women whose cancer was detected at their first screen was then compared with that in the invited and screened healthy population from which women in the study had been selected. The best discriminant, using all four factors was present in 56 per cent of those with cancer and 48 per cent of the healthy population.

The results of other studies give little grounds for optimism (Table 57). A screening programme designed to miss 20 per cent of the detectable breast cancers is not likely to find favour, unless it can be confined to a small proportion (less than 20 per cent) of the population.

TABLE 57. *The application of risk factor analyses to selective screening* (282,361–8)

| | | Discriminant for Cancer (%) | |
	Number of Factors in Analysis	Women with Cancer	Healthy Population
Guernsey	5	82	55
New York	5	33	54
Finland	20 and 4	84	65
Italy	15 and 4	74–97	51
Holland	6	63	37
Scotland	4	48	56
Canada	12	85	40

For a suitable test, one should be able to define 80% of cancer cases in 20% of the population. Italian and Canadian studies included symptoms as a risk factor (from 340–347).

The results of a recent Canadian study associated with the national screening programme, in which logistic regression was used to examine the prevalence of 12 risk factors in women with breast cancer and healthy women, are reported to be more optimistic. When symptoms were included, this analysis allowed the detection of 85 per cases in 40–50 per cent of the population (367). But, as Tabar has pointed out, studies that utilise women who have attended for screening are subject to selection bias (369). Further, the inclusion of women with symptoms is misleading, as all symptomatic women attending for screening must be recalled for review.

Risk factor analyses have also been used to determine whether the type or frequency of screening can be modified in those in different categories of risk. In particular, these have been aimed at determining whether the addition of mammography to clinical examination can be omitted. But this is not relevant to current European programmes in which mammography alone is the screening method.

Risk factors have not been found to differentiate between those with screen-detected and interval cancers. There is some evidence to support the hypothesis that during the menopause the growth rate of breast cancers may be more rapid and that screening should be more frequent at that time (370–71). An interesting, but unconfirmed report suggested that women might be selected on account of their psychological make-up (372). But, in general, the determination of the need for screening by risk factor analysis is 'not on' (373).

A different approach has been reported recently in which an attempt has been made to categorise risk on an individual basis. This was from a large case-control study including 2852 white women whose breast cancers were detected in BCDDP and 3136 controls. As in other studies, the main factors to emerge were age, year of menarche, age at first live birth, number of previous breast biopsies, and a history of breast cancer in first-degree relatives (374). Relative risks for each of these factors alone and in combination were calculated and used to construct a table from which an individual woman can determine her probable risk of developing breast cancer at 10, 20, and 30 years. It would then be up to her to decide what action she would wish to take. As pointed out in an accompanying editorial, oral contraceptives and oestrogen and alcohol use, which are avoidable hazards, should be included in a future analysis, which willl require larger numbers if valid guidance on individual risk is to be given (375). And it is important to remember that 75 per cent of women who develop breast cancer may not have any of these recognisable risk factors; and therefore cannot assess their likelihood of developing the disease by these parameters (363).

COST

The economics of screening are beyond the scope of this monograph. At the time the Working Group reported, there were few studies of the cost of screening asymptomatic women for breast cancer; and these related to the costs of screening mammography rather than those of population mammographic screening. Only one was from Britain (376). However, a study was ongoing in Edinburgh by Clarke and Fraser (281) and a second had started in Guildford, from both of which preliminary figures were available. The Working Group included an economist, now Director of the Scottish Health Services Economic Unit in Aberdeen, who conducted an economic appraisal based on Edinburgh costs and mortality reduction on nine years of follow-up in the Two-Counties trial in Sweden, supplemented for long-term mortality projections by data from HIP. Her analysis was based on life-years gained, which were also adjusted for quality (QALYS).

In calculating the costs of the screening in Edinburgh, Clarke and Fraser did not only consider the basic screen (which in the U.K. costs, to the NHS, about £15), but also the additional costs of initial assessment. Such costs as those incurred by women in travelling to the clinic and losing time off work were included. So also were gains from production during the additional life-years experienced by those whose cancers were detected by screening. The additional costs of biopsy and treatment compared to those presenting symptomatically in the absence of screening and potential savings as a result of reduced treatment costs were not included. Discounting at 5 per cent to compensate for costs and benefits occurring in different time periods was applied.

Assuming an acceptance rate of 70 per cent, the cost of establishing a national service for screening by single-view mammography at an interval of three years approximated £3000 per life-year gained, which, when adjusted for qual-

TABLE 58. *Comparison of costs per quality-adjusted life years (QALY) gained from various health-care procedures* (3)

Procedure	Cost 1983–84
Pacemaker implantation for Atrioventricular heart block	700
Hip replacement	750
Coronary artery bypass graft (CABG) for main vessel disease	1,040
Kidney transplantation	3,000
BREAST CANCER SCREENING	3,500
Heart transplantation	5,000
CABG for moderate angina with OLC vessel disease	12,000
Hospital haemodialysis	14,000

From ref 3.

ity, was £3500. This spanned the costs to the NHS of kidney and liver transplantation, both of which now are included as a necessary part of the delivery of national health care (Table 58). Screening for breast cancer was considerably less expensive than hospital haemodialysis.

Since that time an interim final report has been submitted by Fraser and Clarke that supports their original figures. When one considers that screening by single-view mammography with attendance, if necessary, at a review clinic costs less than £15, one cannot deny that the British system of health care can deliver good value for money!

In the Netherlands, screening for breast cancer has also started on a national level. Basic screening units, both static and mobile, serve each region. Administration is regional; but evaluation of the screening programme is a national responsibility. A very detailed report of costs of a number of alternative programmes has been produced. This includes estimates of all costs and savings connected with assessment, treatment, and treatment for advanced disease. The alternative recommended as the 'best buy' is screening, by single oblique-view mammography, between the ages of 50 and 70 at an interval of two years. Costs in terms of life-years gained cannot be compared with those estimated in the U.K., as there is no parity-conversion system for health service costs, but it was concluded that, compared to other health costs, screening for breast cancer was cost-effective (377). Further it has been estimated that one third of the cost of a national programme will be earned back by savings in other health sectors (378). A national programme of screening is under way in Sweden (378–9). Some preliminary figures on cost have been reported but, again, these are not comparable.

It must be emphasised that the estimated costs of screening must include all the costs and savings incurred by a comprehensive screening service and not only the provision of screening mammography. The objective of population screening for breast cancer is to make this full-screening process available to all women in the target population, so that the definition and invitation of the women is the starting expenditure, while the follow-up of the patient with cancer is the last. Some are concerned that there may be a large additional workload on the hospital service. In a study of two regions in Sweden, in one of which only population screening was in force, screening of 90 per cent of two-thirds of women over 40 resulted in a twofold increase in in-patient operations for breast cancer; this in women over 50 years of age. Notable was the great increase in women over 70 years (Fig. 43). But there has been no increase in the number of operations for benign breast disease, confirming the excellence of the assessment procedure (380–1).

The importance of compliance cannot be over-estimated. In the Dutch assessment of costs and efficiency of screening, increasing attendance rates is the most efficient way to increase life-years gained at lowest cost.

Some have suggested that the money required to institute mammographic screening in the U.K. would better have

43. Annual number of operations in Kopparberg and Uppsala counties in Sweden (a) for benign disease (b) for cancer. Only Kopparberg had a screening programme in operation (380).

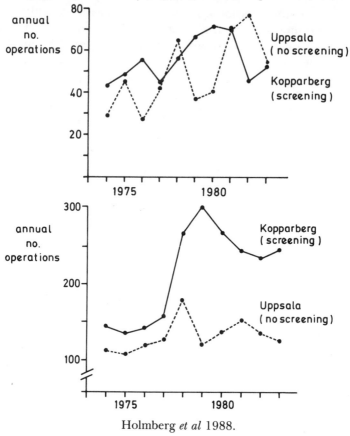

Holmberg *et al* 1988.

been spent on other health-care needs, or even for the support of scientific research. But this argument is spurious.

There could be no guarantee that the money found by government to support screening would have been available for other health-care or scientific needs. Screening for breast cancer is not cheap, but for those women whose cancer is detected at a pre-clinical stage it must be good value. It is regretful that response rates do not reflect greater confidence by the public in this addition to their health-care system.

10

WHERE NOW?

TREATMENT

THE PAST FEW DECADES HAVE SEEN ENORMOUS ADVANCES
in the treatment of some forms of cancer. Lymphomas,
leukaemia, ovarian and testicular cancer are now curable
diseases, while, through the availability of cervical cytology,
mortality from cancer of the cervix has decreased (382).
None of these advances are cheap. Accurate staging by
modern methods of imaging, aggressive chemotherapy and
bone marrow transplantation have added to health service
costs; but no one denies that they are worthwhile.

But for the other more common solid tumours, affecting
the lungs, gastro-intestinal tract and female breast, mortality
remains largely unchanged.

Breast cancer is moderately sensitive to available chemotherapeutic drugs. The current trend of treating locally
advanced disease primarily by systemic therapy has uncovered the potential of multiple-drug regimens to rapidly
shrink large tumours (383). The synthesis, by recombinant
technology, of factors that normally stimulate the bone
marrow has provided a method of combatting the depletion
of white blood cells, which made dose-intensive regimens of
chemotherapy hazardous (384–5). And autologous bone
marrow transplantation is also available to reconstitute the
depleted marrow.

To date such intensive chemotherapy has been used only
to treat locally advanced and disseminated disease. But it is
now being considered for earlier stages, even for disease
regarded as amenable to primary surgical treatment.
Whether the micrometastatic deposits of tumour which are
the cause of breast cancer mortality will be eliminated is yet
a matter for conjecture. And, on account of the slow-

growing nature of the disease, this may take many years to prove; which is why it is essential that such treatment is given only within the context of meticulously controlled trials.

A method to monitor the growth of these small tumour deposits could help rationalise therapy; and the application of immunohistochemical techniques to detect malignant cells in aspirates of bone marrow is being pursued (386). Detection by imaging using positron-emission tomography (PET scanning) or selective labelling of the tumour using monoclonal antibodies is also under active investigation (387–8).

Targetted chemotherapy, by encapsulation in liposomes or liposomal membranes, by attachment to a chemical substrate (ligand) that binds to a specific cell receptor, or attachment to an antibody to a specific antigenic protein cell constituent, is opening the way to selective therapy. This may be used not only for the carriage and delivery of cell toxins, but to carry radioisotopes into the cell, which then can deliver high-dose radiation selectively to the tumour (389–93).

The 'recruitment' of quiescent tumour cells into an active phase, by oestrogen stimulation, when they are responsive to chemotherapy is a method now being put to practical use in breast cancer treatment (394–6).

But breast cancer is not only sensitive to chemotherapy. About 60 per cent of tumours share with cancers of the prostate and endometrium a reliance on sex hormones, deprivation of which leads to suppression of growth. The antioestrogen tamoxifen and other endocrine-suppressing agents have long been used for the control of advanced disease; and there are now many trials supporting a beneficial role for tamoxifen in early disease (397). Unlike chemotherapy, tamoxifen is relatively non-toxic and free from side effects, and compliance for taking the drug is good. In a report of a recent U.S. trial, only 4 per cent of women discontinued its use over a period of five years (398).

The fundamental problem of anti-oestrogen therapy is that only a proportion of breast cancers will be influenced beneficially. To give tamoxifen to all patients with primary invasive breast cancer may be therapeutically simple; but it is wasteful and may deny a non-responsive patient the potential benefit of chemotherapy. It was hoped that assays for oestrogen-receptor protein in the primary tumour would have given guidance to which patients would benefit, but this is uncertain. Women with tumours containing high concentrations of receptor would appear to be more likely to have prolongation of disease-free survival; but this may still occur in those with low or even absent receptor (397). Nor does oestrogen receptor activity relate to the response to chemotherapy (399).

The first step in the orthodox treatment of invasive breast cancer of operable stage is to remove the primary tumour, following which the patient may receive 'adjuvant' systemic therapy. As the only measurable disease is no longer present, there is no means by which the response to systemic treatment can be assessed—a situation not generally accepted in modern therapeutics. The wish to select *appropriate* systemic therapy for women with large (over 4 cm) tumours which, although still operable, have a poor outlook prompted us to reverse this orthodox procedure. Initial treatment was by anti-oestrogens; to which the response was assessed before further treatment was considered. Those not responding to this simple hormonal treatment were given chemotherapy for three months; only then was local treatment by mastectomy carried out (400).

In this study, the concentration of oestrogen receptor protein in the primary tumour proved to be a good discriminant of response to anti-oestrogens. Tumours with low levels did not benefit, so that anti-oestrogens are now given only to those with receptor-rich tumours (401). Those with receptor-poor tumours and those which, although receptor-rich, had tumours that did not respond to hormonal treatment received aggressive chemotherapy. The majority have responded.

This reversal of orthodox treatment, by which the local treatment has become the 'adjuvant' to systemic treatment, is logical. Currently its value is being compared to 'orthodox' treatment by mastectomy followed by tamoxifen in a controlled randomised trial.

But this approach does not lessen the importance of

defining those tumour factors including gene expression that may determine outlook and give guidance for appropriate therapy (402–3). Molecular science is being applied to the investigation of the nature of resistance of breast cancer cells to therapeutic agents, which could in time become a reversible phenomenon (404–6).

The identification of those factors which influence the growth of the tumour and its ability to extend is opening the way to the development of new therapeutic agents which inhibit normal responses. Some of these are already being tested in the clinic (407–8). And new understanding of the mechanism of the immune reaction against foreign cells has stimulated novel methods of attack, using such agents as interleukin-2 and immunologically competent killer cells (409).

PREVENTION

The ideal solution to the problem of breast cancer is to determine its cause. For then, true prevention could be within reach. Unless, as with lung cancer, the means of prevention involves the discarding of a pleasurable, and to some addictive, habit.

As indicated above, the geographic variations in the incidence of the disease and the behaviour of migrants suggest an environmental cause; and there is evidence that human breast secretions may contain mutagenic substances (410). But the application of suction to the nipple withdraws fluid which will have been stagnating in the largest ducts and which may be quite unrepresentative of lobular secretion.

We are now living through an enormous explosion in knowledge of the genetic constitution of breast cancer cells. At present, eight separate mutational anomalies have been detected; and a loss of genetic constituents has been observed in five separate chromosomes, some of which have been identified in Edinburgh (404,411–4). Of greatest interest are the deletions of fragments of DNA that occur close to those sequences that are known to be promoters of growth. The latter comprise the family of oncogenes, which normally are believed to be kept in check by neighbouring genes so that they lie dormant as 'proto-oncogenes'.

Studies of the initiation of tumour development in mice provide strong evidence that these changes may contribute to the initiation and progression of human breast cancer. So also may they indicate metastasising potential and prognosis (415). Thus the amplification of a specific gene may indicate a 'bad tumour'. But there are pitfalls in such simplistic use of complex technology.

Specific use of definable changes in the constitution of genetic material is being put, in Edinburgh and elsewhere, to the exploration of those families in which breast cancer behaves as an autosomal dominant disease. Such breast cancers are characterised by an early age of onset, bilaterality, 'vertical' transmission from mother to daughter. They also are reported to have impaired survival compared to sporadic forms. The genetic study of these families is in progress. This involves 'linkage analysis', by which a marker gene close to that assumed to be associated with the disease can be identified and used to trace related inherited characteristics within the family. If the gene responsible for inherited breast cancer can be identified, it may become possible to 'tag' those members of the family likely to develop the disease (331).

Role of Oestrogens

Because of its known role in the genesis of human breast cancer, attention has focussed on the actions of oestrogen on normal and malignant breast cells. The model used to elucidate its effects at a molecular level is the *in vitro* culture of both hormone-dependent and -independent human breast cancer cell lines. Cell cultures are uninfluenced by other oestrogen-mediated effects in the intact host; and also allow the identification of such factors as may be 'secreted' into the culture medium following oestrogen stimulation. By implanting cultured cells into immune-deprived mice, the hormone sensitivity of the resulting tumour *in vivo* can also be tested (416–9).

As a result of such studies, it is now well established that the action of oestrogen is mediated through the expression of growth factors which act in autocrine (its own cell) and paracrine (neighbouring cells) fashion. The genes responsible for some of these effects have been identified, and hormone dependence can be altered by the insertion into a cell of a foreign gene which stimulates cellular proliferation in the absence of oestrogen (419). Understanding of the nature of the hormone dependence of human breast cancer cannot long be delayed.

Plans for Prevention

It has been suggested that deprivation of oestrogen may be one means of preventing breast cancer, and discussions have been taking place to determine whether this is a justifiable approach. Two methods of intervention are being considered: antioestrogen therapy and reduction in dietary fat.

Anti-Oestrogen Therapy. In 1986 Cuzick and his colleagues, on reviewing the evidence implicating oestrogen as a causal agent in human breast cancer, suggested that continuous tamoxifen administration should be explored in those at risk from the disease (420). In rats this anti-oestrogen had been shown to prevent carcinogen-induced breast cancer (421). It was proposed that women with three of five risk factors related to age at first pregnancy, family history, previous benign disease, mammographic type and serum sex-hormone-binding globulin (which had been shown to be low in those at risk) might form a volunteer group who would be prepared to be allocated randomly to receive tamoxifen.

Discussions concentrated on the potential risks of long-term anti-oestrogen therapy: bone demineralisation, changes in serum lipoproteins, thrombosis, coronary heart disease. Tamoxifen also has some oestrogen-agonist effects which could increase the risk of cancer of the endometrium and liver, the latter having been reported in experimental animals (422–3). The report of an increased incidence of endometrial cancer in women given tamoxifen as adjuvant therapy in Stockholm was worrying; but this has not been confirmed in the long-term follow-up of the Scottish trial, in which tamoxifen had been given for five years (424–5). Nor is there any evidence that tamoxifen is tumorigenic to the endometrium in experimental animals (426). These various aspects of tamoxifen therapy were recently addressed in a workshop in Wisconsin where a study of the effect of tamoxifen in normal women is in progress (427).

A feasibility study was initiated by Powles and his colleagues in London in 1986. Between 1986 and 1988, 200 women of 35–65 years of age with at least one first-degree relative with breast cancer gave consent to be randomised to receive tamoxifen 20 mg or an inactive placebo tablet daily for three years (428–9). Women were carefully screened for a breast abnormality before entry. Monitoring was by serum oestradiol, sex-hormone-binding globulin, the clotting factors fibrogen and antithrombin-III and fasting lipoprotein profiles. Bone mass was measured by single-photon absorptiometry of the forearm.

The only acute toxicity observed was a significant increase in the incidence of mild hot flushes in those receiving tamoxifen, but 85 per cent of women in both groups continued to take their tablets over 12 months. No long-term adverse effects have so far been recorded. Rather the reverse: lowering of the ratio of fibrinogen to antithrombin-III and of the low-density lipoprotein fraction of cholesterol is favourable for the avoidance of thrombotic and cardiac disease. This finding may account for the lowered incidence of non-cancer deaths in the Scottish and NATO tamoxifen trials (144,430).

Large adjuvant tamoxifen trials also offer an opportunity to assess the complications of long-term tamoxifen therapy, at any rate in women with breast cancer. They have also allowed monitoring of second tumours in the contra-lateral breast, and so provide evidence for a protective effect. Breast cancer is prone to bilaterality, the incidence of a second 'primary' tumour in the opposite breast being, in a recent British study, 0·8 per cent per annum (431). It has been reported that the incidence of second tumours in those given adjuvant tamoxifen is halved, but this evidence must be taken with some caution (432). Not only has no difference emerged in the Scottish trial, in which follow-up was meticulous, but the definition of a contralateral primary tumour in the reported studies is unclear (Table 59). A contralateral breast tumour may be metastatic and not a second primary; a possibility guarded against in the Scottish trial by accepting as primary tumours only those which were without evidence of recurrent disease elsewhere within a period of 12 months (144,433).

Novel anti-oestrogens which, unlike tamoxifen, have no oestrogenic action are under development (434).

Ovarian Ablation. Reversible and temporary ablation of ovarian function by gonadotrophin-releasing hormone (GnRH) agonists has been proposed as an alternative method of reducing hormonal stimulation of the breast by Pike and his colleagues (435). Noting that oral contraceptives have a protective effect on cancer of the ovary and endometrium but increase breast cancer risk, they have suggested that while unopposed oestrogen is a risk factor for endometrial cancer (as is clear from the effect of exogenous oestrogen administration), it is not so for cancer of the breast. They suggest that the evidence that oestrogen alone increases breast cancer risk is sparse and that it is the combination of oestrogen and progesterone that is important. Support for this hypothesis comes from studies of epithelial cell turnover in the resting human breast, such as those reported from Edinburgh, which indicate that the greatest proliferative activity occurs during the follicular phase of the menstrual cycle when both oestrogen and progesterone are being secreted (436). On this basis, delaying the onset of regular ovulatory cycles ought to protect against the disease in the same way as does surgical oophorectomy early in life.

A reversible medical oophorectomy can be achieved by desensitising the pituitary to the normal pulsatile stimulation of gonadotrophin-releasing hormone (GnRH) by the administration of pharmacological doses of synthetic agonist analogues. Pike proposes that this method of delaying ovulatory cycles should be considered the lack of oestrogen being compensated for by oestrogen-replacement therapy for 21 of each 28 days. He does not believe that, by itself, this would increase breast cancer risk and suggests that this

TABLE 59. *Incidence of contralateral breast cancer in controlled randomised trials of adjuvant therapy for primary breast cancer in which tamoxifen has been given in one arm alone (424,425,430–433)*

	Dose Tamoxifen mg/day	Duration (years)	Follow-up (years)	Tamoxifen		Controls	
				Pts	Cancers	Pts	Cancers
Cancer Research Campaign	20	2	2	—	3	—	10
Christie Hospital	20	1	5–10				
premenopausal				199	2	174	1
postmenopausal				282	6	306	4
Stockholm	40	2 or 5	0·5–10·5	931	18	915	34
Scotland	20	5	4–10	539	7	531	7
NSABP	20	5	1–6	1318	13	1326	29

Controls not receiving any form of systemic therapy.

combination would provide effective contraception, without
the dangers of the pill. It would reduce the incidence of
cancer of the breast by half, and that of the ovaries by two-
thirds. The increased risk of endometrial cancer might be
prevented by the addition of progesterone at such planned
intervals as would not enhance the risk of breast cancer. This
is an attractive proposition, and one which in young women
is more logical than the administration of tamoxifen.

Diet. An alternative approach to reducing oestrogen secretion is by dietary intervention. This possibility has gained
support from a recent study reported by the Women's
Health Trial Study Group in the U.S. In 73 post-menopausal
women, aged 45–69 years, not taking exogenous oestrogen,
serum hormones were measured before and after reduction
of their fat intake from 40 per cent of total kilocalories to 20
per cent over a period of 10–22 weeks. Plasma concentrations of total and of weakly bound oestradiol were reduced
by 17 per cent. Data obtained from a case-control study,
which we had carried out in Edinburgh in association with
the Tenovus Institute in Cardiff, was used to estimate the
reduction of risk which a 17 per cent reduction in circulating oestradiol would achieve. In this study oestradiol and
other steroid hormone levels had been estimated at 15-
minute intervals over a 6-to 8-hour period. This was four- to
fivefold; an amount which the authors consider sufficient to
explain international differences of the disease (437–8).
Dietary regulation of oestrogen levels may well yet be
feasible.

Risk Factors Again

If interventional studies are to be carried out, it will be
necessary to define those women to be included on account
of an increased risk from the disease. It has already been
pointed out that combinations of those risk factors, which
can readily be obtained on enquiry, do not allow good
discrimination between those at risk and those not. New
systems of computer modelling may help, but what is
required is a new marker of risk that can easily be applied to

normal women. The transformation of normal breast epithelium through hyperplasia to malignancy is a series of events which will be better understood in time. And, perhaps like cervical cancer, a cytological specimen taken by suction applied to the nipple or by fine-needle aspiration will provide an answer to the degree of risk that a woman is carrying; although, even then the only certain form of intervention required to counter it is unlikely to be acceptable to many.

MAMMOGRAPHY AND SCREENING

Where do these considerations leave the future of screening by mammography. Hopefully not at the top of the list; for mammography is not a good screening test (439). It is not simple and quick to administer, easy to interpret, or cheap. It is reasonably reliable, but its validity depends upon the skill of the observer. Acceptability is in doubt. But it does not cause risk, either of serious psychological problems or of radiation-induced effects.

But mammography is all we are likely to have for some time to come. For even if more sensitive methods of imaging are developed, they are not likely to be applicable for population screening. Efforts to improve sensitivity by better equipment and more sensitive film-screen combinations are bound to continue; and this has particular importance for those under 50 years of age. Research into methods to facilitate interpretation, for example, by digitalisation of the film image or of the image recording system, is also being pursued (440). So also are improved methods of assessment, which allow a firm diagnosis to be reached quickly. But these cannot resolve a primary problem, which is the definition of those women who require to be regularly screened and those in whom perhaps one or two screens during their lifetime will suffice.

Admittedly it is a relatively small number of women who have benefitted from current programmes—a fact seized upon by those who are opposed. But it is only those who have breast cancer who can benefit: and for them there is no other measure of equal proven value.

But if population screening is to work well, women must attend. The low response rates already reported from some centres must be a cause for concern (441). Errors of address accounted for 5·25 per cent of non-attenders; no doubt disinterest and lack of awareness for the rest. The Chief Medical Officer has drawn attention to the intent that the system 'be organised as part of primary care in which the woman's general practitioner, with nursing support, had an essential role in inviting the women to come forward and counselling them at every stage as necessary' (442). The general practitioner has a large responsibility to fulfill; for the British public still adheres to the traditional 'whatever you say, doctor' approach, and will look to their doctor, and other health professionals, to give guidance. Which they can do only if they are certain not only that screening is beneficial, but that the quality of the service is beyond reproach. And this requires the commitment and enthusiasm of all those people of many differing skills who are responsible for each stage of the screening process.

A recent survey of 1029 general practitioners in USA revealed a change of attitude over the past 5 years. In 1984 only 41 per cent advised women to follow the guidelines of the American Cancer Society for mammographic screening: by 1989 72 per cent did so. A similar change of attitude in this country is a necessary prerequisite of successful screening (443).

But it also requires that women in the U.K. become increasingly aware of the importance of facing up to breast cancer as a disease, becoming knowledgeable about its management, and appreciating that it is in their hands that action must lie. In the U.S. very positive steps are being taken to bring the attention of Congress to the increasing public outrage over the thousands of lives lost through this disease (444). Included is a request for a mandate for coverage for screening mammograms, under a new bill, which now bears the name of Rose Kushner, a proponent of all breast cancer issues until her recent death from breast cancer. It is from women such as her that leadership is required to ensure that here also there is constant pressure on the need to determine how breast cancer can be conquered.

Evidence has been presented to indicate that screening mammography can prolong life to a greater extent than any other change in the management of breast cancer. To dispense with it, without having something better to put in its place, would be a brave decision.

TABLE 60. *Controlled randomised trials under way in U.K. national breast cancer screening service*

Question	Study Population	Control Population
How screen?	2-view oblique + craniocaudal mammography	Single-oblique mammography
How often?	Repeat screens at 1 year	Repeat screens at 3 years
At what age?	40–41 yr, annual screening until 47, then national programme	40–41 yr, no screening until age 50, then national programme
How treat *in situ* cancer?	Local excision ± tamoxifen	Local excision ± radiation ± tamoxifen

EPILOGUE

In his Haddow Memorial Lecture, the Chief Medical Officer, Sir Donald Acheson, reviewing progress in implementing breast screening within the NHS, concluded: 'We have made a good start on a great adventure' (441).

A recent report in the *British Medical Journal* indicates that this is so. In England and Wales, 30 of 77 screening centres covering 190 Health Authorities, some with mobile units, had already accumulated sufficient data for analysis. Of 164,000 women invited to be screened, 67·5 per cent had responded, ranging from 38 to 83 per cent. Recalled for assessment were 8238 (7·4 per cent); 1410 (1·3 per cent) had a surgical biopsy with a yield of 733 cancers: a malignant:benign ratio of 1:1. The rate of cancer detection was 6·6 per 1000 (413).

These figures indicate that breast cancer screening within the NHS can work; for which much credit must be given to those responsible for its implementation. And to those who have done so much to see that information and training go hand in hand with monitoring and evaluation.

But we have also made a good start to a great experiment, this by the support of the Health Departments, the Medical Research Council, the Cancer Research Campaign and the Imperial Cancer Research Fund, which has allowed a unique series of controlled trials to be embedded within the national screening service (Table 60). These will resolve some very important issues. The comprehensiveness of this joint service and research programme is unparalleled in any other country. And we all have a national responsibility to see that its objectives are achieved.

It is my hope that this Queen Elizabeth, the Queen Mother, monograph may help to realise this responsibility by bringing to the notice of doubters the need to use this and every other means at our disposal continuously to fight this dread disease.

APPENDIX TABLES

APPENDIX 1. *Some characteristics of samples of study and control populations entering during 1964 (177)*

Study	Percent	Control
Age (yr):		
40–50	47·9	48·1
50–60	40·9	40·6
60–64	11·2	11·3
Jewish	32·8	32·9
College education	30·9	32·9
Ever married	91·3	90·7
Ever pregnant	79·7	77·0
At or past menopause	70·9	74·1
Previous breast lump	9·5	11·8

SOURCE: Johns Hopkins University Press, with permission
[also for Tables 2, 3, 4, 5, 6].

APPENDIX 2. *Rates of detection of breast cancer (per 1000 person-years) during five years from entry to the trial (177)*

	Number of Cases	Rate
STUDY POPULATION		
Screened	225	2·26
Detected on screening	132	—
Prevalence screen	55	2·72
Incidence screen	77	1·49
Interval cancers	93	0·92
Refused screening	79	1·61
TOTAL	304	2·05
CONTROL POPULATION	295	1·95

For prevalence screen, rate is per 1000 persons.

APPENDIX 3. *The method of detection of 132 histologically confirmed breast cancers diagnosed as a result of screening* (177)

Method of Detection	Number of Women	Percent
Mammography only	44	33·3
Clinical examination only	59	44·7
Both modalities	29	22·0

APPENDIX 4. *Proportions of* in situ *and proven (histological) axillary node-negative cancers in study and control populations* (177)

		Percent	
	Number of Cases	In situ Cancer	Negative Nodes
STUDY POPULATION			
Detected on screening	132	19·7	70·5
Not detected on screening	172	7·6	45·9
TOTAL	304	12·8	56·6
CONTROL POPULATION	305	8·1	46·1

APPENDIX 5. *'Stage' of cancers diagnosed within five years of entry in study and control populations* (177)

Stage	Study Population 304 Cases	Controls 295 Cases
'Operable' tumour, no node involvement	56·3	45·8
'Operable' tumour, nodes involved	29·6	35·6
Skin or chest wall involvement	5·9	11·5
Distant metastases	4·3	2·4

Axillary nodes staged by histology (unknown in 3·9 and 4·7%, respectively).
Staging by unique classification.

APPENDIX 6. *All-cause mortality (excluding breast cancer) in study and control population during the first 10 years after entry per 10,000 person-years* (177)

	Population	
	Study	Control
Malignant disease	20·7	20·3
(respiratory)	(2·4)	(2·2)
Circulatory disease	29·8	31·2
(ischemic heart disease)	(19·6)	(20·3)
Respiratory and digestive disease	6·1	5·6
All others	9·6	8·8
Unknown	2·3	3·0
TOTAL	68·6	68·9

APPENDIX 7. *Rates of detection of invasive cancer per 1000 person-years in Two-counties trial* (207)

	Number of Cases	Rate
STUDY POPULATION		
Screened		
Detected on screening	797	—
Prevalence screen	387	5·56
Incidence screen	410	—
Interval cancers	261	—
Refused screening	133	—
Total	1191	2·19
CONTROL POPULATION	745	1·91

For prevalence screen rate per 1000 persons.

APPENDIX 8. *Stage of 1295 breast cancers diagnosed in the study population and 768 in controls* (219)

Stage	% of All (Invasive) Cancers Study	Control
In situ cancer	8·4	3·0
Tumour <2 cm, no node involvement (Stage I)	53·0 (57·6)	35·6 (36·6)
Tumour >2 cm, or nodes involved or clinically advanced (Stages II–IV)	35·5 (38·6)	59·0 (60·8)
Nodes involved and/or disseminated disease (Stages II and IV)	24·6 (26·8)	37·2 (38·2)

TNM (1978) classification with pathological size and axillary node status. Lobular carcinoma–*in situ* was discounted. Percentages are of all cancers with those of invasive cancer in parentheses.

SOURCE: International Union Against Cancer, with permission.

APPENDIX 9. *Analysis of mortality from causes other than and including breast cancer adjusted for county and age* (207)

Mortality From	Relative Risk of Death (95% confidence limits)	(%)
All cancers except breast cancer	1·00 (0·96–1.04)	0·9
All cancers including breast cancer	0·99 (0·95–1·03)	0·5
Other cancers amongst breast cancer cases	1·06 (0·75–1·49)	0·7

Differences on analysis of unadjusted mortality were similar.

APPENDIX 10. *Numbers of cases detected in Malmo trial* (211)

STUDY POPULATION	
Screened	581
Detected on screening	374
prevalence screen	—
incidence screen	—
Interval cancers	100
Refused screening	107
CONTROL POPULATION	497

APPENDIX 11. *Stage of 579 breast cancers diagnosed in the study population and 443 in controls* (211)

Stage	% of All (and Invasive) Cancers	
	Study	Control
In situ cancer	16·0	11·3
Tumour <2 cm, no node involvement (Stage I)	51·1 (60·9)	36·6 (41·2)
Tumour >2 cm, or nodes involved or clinically advanced (Stages II–IV)	32·8 (39·1)	58·8 (52·1)

TNM (1978) classification (presumably by pathological size and node status but not stated). Lobular carcinoma–*in situ* (LCIS) may have been included. Percentages are of all cancers with those of invasive cancer in parentheses.

APPENDIX 12. *Causes of death in study and control populations during seven years from start of trial. Overall mortality was not significantly different between the two groups* (211)

	% of Population Dead	
	Study (21,088)	Control (21,295)
Malignant tumours	3·35	3·49
Cardiovascular disease	3·42	3·18
Respiratory and gastrointestinal disease	0·68	0·73
Suicide/injuries unknown	0·47	0·57
Others	0·50	0·57
Total	8·42	8·54

APPENDIX 13. *Number of cases detected in Stockholm trial (corrected for size of populations)* (225)

Study Population	Number of Cases
Screened	
Detected by screening	217
prevalence screen	124
incidence screen	93
Interval cancers	102
Refused screening	43
Total	371
CONTROL POPULATION	257

APPENDIX 14. *Cancers diagnosed in screening centres during the first 5–7 years of study* (212)

	Edinburgh		Guildford		Total	
	Number	Rate	Number	Rate	Number	Rate
Prevalence screen	78	5·5	78	4·8	156	5·2
Incidence screens (clinical only)	51	1·4	44	1·2	95·	1·3
Incidence screens (clinical+mammography)	95	3·0	141	3·6	236	3·3
Interval cancers	47	—	68	—	115	—
Non-attenders	89	1·7*	57	1·7*	146	1·7*
TOTAL	360	—	388	—	748	2·57

Rates are per 1000 women and per 1000 women-years (*). Cumulative diagnosis rate for comparison centres is 1·70*.

APPENDIX 15. *Numbers of cancers detected in the Edinburgh trial* (213)

Study Population	Number of Cases	Rate
Screened		
Detected on screening	797	—
prevalence screen	387	5·56
incidence screen	410	—
Interval cancers (total)	261	—
Refused screening	123	—
Total	1191	2·18
CONTROL POPULATION	745	1·91

APPENDIX 16. *Clinical staging by UICC classification (1978) of 395 breast cancers diagnosed in the study and 268 in the control populations* (213)

Stage	% of All Cancers Detected	
	Study	Control
In situ cancer (Stage 0)	10·1	2·6
<2 cm, no palpable nodes (Stage I)	31·9 (35·5)	13·1 (13·4)
>2 cm or palpable nodes (Stage II)	41·8 (46·5)	47·8 (49·0)
>5 cm, involving skin or chest wall, fixed nodes (Stage III)	12·7	29.9
Distance metastases (Stage IV)	3·3	4·9
Not known	0·3 (0·3)	1·9 (1·9)

Figures in parentheses are percent of invasive cancers (355 and 261 in study and control populations).

APPENDIX 17. *Size and node status of cases of Stage I and II cancer in study population determined histopathologically (279 with size and 265 with lymph-node status known) compared to control (152 and 129) (213)*

	≤10 mm	Node Negative
STUDY		
Detected by screening	27·2	74·7
Interval (all)	9·3	60·0
Non-attenders	7·3	48·6
Total	21·5	69·1
CONTROL	13·8	60·5

Expressed as % of size and node status known in each category.

APPENDIX 18. *Clinical staging by UICC classification of cancers in trial according to participation.*
Percent of invasive cancers is in parentheses (213)

	No.	In Situ	% of All Cancers Detected			
			I	II	III and IV	NK
STUDY POPULATION						
Detected by screening	243	14·4	42·0 (49·0)	40·3 (47·1)	3·3 (3·9)	—
All interval cases	60	5·0	25·0 (26·3)	53·3 (56·1)	15·0 (15·8)	2·0 (1·8)
Non-attenders	92	2·2	9·8 (10·0)	38·0 (38·9)	50·0 (51·1)	—
Total	395	10·1	31·9 (35·5)	41·8 (46·5)	15·9 (17·7)	0·3 (0·3)
CONTROL POPULATION	268	2·6	13·1 (13·4)	47·8 (49·0)	34·7 (35·6)	1·9 (1·9)

APPENDIX 19. *All-cause mortality in study and control populations by primary registered causes of death during seven years of follow-up from date of entry per 10,000 women–years*

	Population	
	Study	Control
Cardiovascular disease	29·2	42·1
Lung cancer	9·1	10·4
Gastrointestinal cancer	8·8	9·4
Geniro-urinary and lymphatic cancer	6·1	6·7
Breast cancer	4·3	5·1
Other causes and unknown	33·2	27·1
All causes	80·7	100·8

The differences in all-cause and cardiovascular mortality are significant, even when adjusted for age and socio-economic status of general practice (P. B. Donnan, personal communication).

APPENDIX 20. *The method of detection of histologically confirmed breast cancers diagnosed as a result of screening in BCDDP* (63)

Method of Detection	Number of Women	(%)
Mammography only	1375	40·0
Clinical examination only	257	7·5
Both modalities	1805	52·5

SOURCE: American Cancer Society, with permission.
[also Appendix Tables 21 and 22].

APPENDIX 21. *Characteristics of 3548 breast cancers detected by screening in BCDDP* (63)

	Number	Number known	(%)
Of all			
in situ cancer	614	3548	17·3
Of invasive size known			
<1 cm	279	2809	9·9
Of invasive stage known			
Stage I	880		33·2
II	1083	2653	40·8
III	690		26·0
Of invasive nodes known			
node-negative	1750	2281	76·8

APPENDIX 22. *Cumulative relative survival rates for invasive breast cancer in cases detected by screening and white females in the SEER programme* (63)

	No. of Cases	Survival Rate (%)		No. of Cases	Survival Rate (%)	
		5 yr	8 yr		5 yr	8 yr
Node Negative						
<2 cm	880	94	90	5479	96	92
2–5 cm	511	89	80	3831	88	82
5+ cm	182	86	80	2622	77	70
Node Positive						
<2 cm	171	84	74	1802	83	70
2–4·9 cm	219	72	66	8522	72	58
5+ cm	76	64	56	3146	57	43

Available comparisons included from Seideman *et al.* (64).

SOURCE: American Cancer Society, with permission.

APPENDIX 23. *Examples of application of model to evaluate efficiency of screening programmes* (258)

Programme	Age	Prevalence Screen		Proportional Rate Interval Cancers		Sojourn Time (yr)	Sensitivity (%)
		Rate	Proportional	0–12 mo.	12–24 mo.		
HIP	40–64	2·93	1·30	31·7	57·2	1·7	82
Two-Counties	40–49	2·15	1·95	37·8	67·6	3·8	54
	50–59	4·63	3·09	11·6	29·9	4·2	89
	60–69	9·08	4·59	14·3	28·1	—	—
Utrecht	50–59	6·20	2·95	17·0	57·8	2·8	99
	60–64	9·51	3·80	13·9	59·3		

Source: International Union Against Cancer, with permission.

APPENDIX 24. *Available information on age differential in relation to mortality from breast cancer in trials*

	Relative Risk of Death		
	Age 40–<55 Years Range		Age 40–>55 Years Range
HIP	40–49	23·5% reduction	50–59 31·1% reduction
Two-Counties	40–49	0·92 (0·52–1·60)	50–59 0·60 (0·40–0·90)
Malmo	45–54	1·29 (0·74–2·25)	55–70 0·79 (0·51–1·24)
Edinburgh	45–50	3·18 v 3·25	50–64 0·80 (0·54–1·17)
Nijmegen	35–49	1·23 (0·31–4·81)	50–64 0·26 (0·10–0·67)
Utrecht	50–54	0·82 (—)	55–64 0·31 (—)
Florence	40–49	0·63 (0·24–1·64)	50–70 0·51 (0·29–0·89)

Number of rounds variable (Florence data after 1 and 2 rounds). Relative risk of death between study (or screened) and controls (or non-screened).

REFERENCES

1. BLAXTER, M., 'The causes of disease: women talking'. *Social Sci. Med.*, 1983; 17:59–69.

2. Parliamentary Debates *Hansard* 6 series Vol 3 1986–7, p. 272. Report of House of Commons, 25 February 1987.

3. *Breast Cancer Screening*. Report to the Health Ministers of England, Wales, Scotland and Northern Ireland by a Working Group chaired by Sir Patrick Forrest. Her Majesty's Stationery Office. 1987.

4. Commission on Chronic Illness. *Chronic illness in the United States.* Cambridge, Mass., 1957, 1, 45 (cited by 5).

5. WHITBY, F. G., 'Screening for disease: definitions and criteria', *Lancet*, 1974; 2:819–21.

6. WILSON, J. M. G., JUNGNER, G., *Principle and Practice of Screening for Disease.* World Health Organisation Public Health Paper, 1968.

7. SHAPIRO, S., VENET, W., STRAX, P. *et al.* 'Ten-to-fourteen-year effect of screening on breast cancer mortality', *J. Natl. Cancer Inst.*, 1982; 69:349–55.

8. TABAR, L., FAGERBERG, C. J. G., GAD, A., BALDETORP, L., HOLMBERG, L. H. *et al.*, 'Reduction in mortality from breast cancer after mass screening with mammography: Randomised trial from the Breast Cancer Screening Working Group of the Swedish National Board of Health and Welfare', *Lancet*, 1985; 1:829–32.

9. VERBEEK, A. L. M., HENDRICKS, J. H. C. L., HOLLAND, R., MRAVUNAC, M., STURMANS, F. *et al.*, 'Reduction of breast cancer mortality through mass screening with modern mammography: first results of the Nijmegen project, 1975–1981', *Lancet*, 1984; 1:1222–4.

10. COLLETTE, H. J. A., DAY, N. E., ROMBACH, J. J., DeWAARD, F., 'Evaluation of screening for breast cancer in a non-randomised study (the DOM project) by means of a case-control study', *Lancet*, 1984; 1:1224–6.

11. BOLMGREHN, J., JACOBSON, B., NORDENSTROM, B., 'Stereotaxic instrument for needle biopsy of the mamma', *A.J.R.*, 1977; 129:121–5.

12. LOFGREN, M., ANDRESSON, I., BONDESON, L., LINDHOLM, K., 'X-ray guided fine-needle aspiration for the cytologic diagnosis of non-palpable breast lesions', *Cancer*, 1988; 61:1032–7.

13. AZAVEDO, E., SVANE, G., ANER, G., 'Stereotactic fine-needle biopsy in 2594 mammographically detected non-palpable lesions', *Lancet*, 1989; 1:1033–5.

14. FRANK, H. A., HALL, F. M., STEER, M. L., 'Pre-operative localisation of non-palpable breast lesions demonstrated by mammography', *Eng. J. Med.*, 1976; 296:259–60.

15. SIMON, N., LESNICK, G. J., LERER, W. N., BACHMAN, A. L., 'Roentographic localisation of small lesions of the breast by the spot method', *Surg. Gynec. Obstet.*, 1972; 134:572.

16. FORREST, A. P. M., 'The surgeon's role in breast screening', *World J. Surg.*, 1989; 13:19–24.

17. CHETTY, U., KIRKPATRICK, A. E., ANDERSON, T. J., LAMB, M. M. *et al.*, 'Localisation and excision of occult breast lesions', *Br. J. Surg.*, 1983; 70:607–10.

18. AITKEN, R. J., MACDONALD, H. L., KIRKPATRICK, A. E., ANDERSON, T. J., CHETTY, U., FORREST, A. P. M., 'The outcome of surgery for non-palpable mammographic abnormalities', *Br. J. Surg.*, 1990 (in press).

19. ANDERSON, T. J., 'Breast cancer screening: principles and practicalities for histopathologists,' *Recent Advances in Histopathology*, 1989; 14:43–61.

20. BAILAR, J. C., 'Mammography: a contrary view', *Ann. Intern. Med.*, 1976; 84:77–84.

21. SKRABANEK, P., 'False premises and false promises of breast cancer screening', *Lancet*, 1985; 2: 316–20.

22. SKRABANEK, P., 'The physician's responsibility to the patient', *Lancet*, 1988; 1:1155–6.

23. SKRABANEK, P., 'Breast cancer screening: a UK showdown', *Br. J. Hosp. Med.*, 1988; 40:419.

24. SKRABANEK, P., 'Pros and cons of breast cancer screening', *Irish Med. J.*, 1989; 82:41.

25. SKRABANEK, P., 'Shadows over screening mammography', *Clin. Radiol.*, 1989; 40:4–5.

26. SKRABANEK, P., 'The debate over mass mammography in Britain: the case against', *Br. Med. J.*, 1989; 297:971–2.

27. WRIGHT, C. J., 'Breast cancer screening: a different look at the evidence', *Surgery*, 1986; 100:594–7.

28. WRIGHT, C. J., 'Should the hunt for non-palpable breast lesions be called off', *Canad. J. Surg.*, 1986; 29:299–300.

29. ROBERTS, M. M., 'Breast screening: time for a rethink', *Br. Med. J.*, 1989; 299:1153–5.

30. ISACSSON, S. O., LARSSON, L. G., JANZON, L., 'Debatt om mammografi', *Lakartidningen*, 1985; 82:2672–3.

31. FORREST, A. P. M., HAWKINS, R. A., MILLER, W. R., 'Breast', in: Jamieson and Kay's *Textbook of Surgical Physiology*, LEDINGHAM, I. B. (ed.). Edinburgh and London, Churchill-Livingston, 1989, pp. 85–94.

32. AZZOPARDI, J. G., *Problems in Breast Pathology*. London, J. B. Saunders, 1979.

33. PAGE, D. L., ANDERSON, T. J., *Diagnostic Histopathology of the Breast*. Edinburgh, Churchill-Livingston, 1988.

34. PETRAKIS, N. L., EMSTER, V. L., SACKS, S. T., 'Epidemiology of breast fluid secretion association with breast cancer risk factors and cerumen type', *J. Natl. Cancer Inst.*, 1981; 67:277–84.

210

REFERENCES

35. MILLER, W. R., HUMENIK, V., FORREST, A. P. M., 'Factors affecting dehydroepiandrosterone sulphate levels in human breast secretion', *Breast Cancer Res. Treat.*, 1981; 1:267–72.

36. YAP, P. L., MILLER, W. R., HUMENIK, J., PRYDE, E. A. D., MIRTLE, C. L., McCLELLAND, D. B. L., 'Milk protein concentrations in the mammary secretions of nonlactating women', *J. Reprod. Immunol.*, 1981; 3:49–58.

37. PETRAKIS, N. L., 'Oestrogens and other cytological and biochemical components in nipple aspirates of breast fluid: relationship of 15 risk factors for disease', *Proc. Roy. Soc. Edinb.*, 1989; 95B:169–81.

38. WELLINGS, S. R., JENSEN, H. M., MARCUM, R. G., 'An atlas of subgross pathology of human breast with special reference to possible pre-cancerous lesions', *J. Natl. Cancer Inst.*, 1975; 55:231–73.

39. Editorial. Metastatic fundamentals, *Lancet*, 1989; 1:1052–4.

40. LIOTTA, L. A., 'Gene products which play a role in cancer invasion and metastases', *Breast Cancer Res. Treat.*, 1988; 11:113–24.

41. FIDLER, I. J., RADINSKY, R. 'Genetic control of cancer metastases', *J. Natl. Cancer Inst.*, 1990; 82:166–8.

42. BRINKLEY, D., HAYBRITTLE, J. L., 'A 15-year follow-up study of patients treated for carcinoma of the breast', *Br. J. Radiol.*, 1968; 41:215–21.

43. DAWSON, E. K., 'Carcinoma in the mammory lobule and its origin', *Edinb. Med. J.*, 1933; 40:57–82.

44. GALLAGHER, H. S., MARTIN, J. E., 'Early phases in the development of breast cancer', *Cancer*, 1969; 24:1170–8.

45. CAHILL, C. J., GIBBS, N. M., BOULTER, P. S., 'Invasive breast cancer—the tip of an iceberg', *Ann. Royal Coll. Surg. Eng.*, 1963; 65:356–9.

46. SANDISON, A. T., 'An autopsy study of the adult human breast', *Natl. Cancer Inst.*, Monograph 1962, No. 8.

47. FRANTZ, V. K., PICKREN, J. W., MELCHER, G. W., AUCHINCLOSS, H., 'Incidence of chronic cystic disease in so-called normal breasts. A study based on 225 post-mortem examinations', *Cancer*, 1951; 4:762–3.

48. NEILSON, M., THOMSEN, J. L., PRINDAHL, S., DYREBORG, U., ANDERSON, J. A., 'Breast cancer and atypica among young and middle-aged women: a study of 110 medico legal autopsies', *Br. J. Cancer*, 1987; 56:814–9.

49. POLLEI, S. R., METTLER, F. A., BARTOW, S. A., MORADIAN, G., MOSKOWITZ, M., 'Occult breast cancer: prevalence and radiographic detectability', *Radiology*, 1987; 163:459–62.

50. DUPONT, W. D., PAGE, D. L., 'Risk factors for breast cancer in women with proliferative breast disease', *N. Engl. J. Med.*, 1985; 312:146–51.

51. PAGE, D. L., VANDER SWAGG, R., ROGERS, L. W., WILLIAMS, L. T., WALKER, W. E., 'Relation between component parts of fibrocystic disease complex and breast cancer', *J. Natl. Cancer Inst.*, 1978; 61:1055–63.

52. STILES, H., 'Contributions to the surgical anatomy of the breast', *Med. J. Edinb.*, 1891–2, 37:1099–12; 37:1892–3, 38:26–43.

53. QUALHEIM, R. E., GALL, E. A., 'Breast carcinoma with multiple sites of origin', *Cancer*, 1957; 10:460–8.

54. STEWART, H. J., 'Unpublished observations', in FORREST A.P.M. Fifteenth Lister Memorial Lecture: 'Rationalisation in the management of breast cancer', *Can. J. Surg.*, 1971; 14:244–52.

55. ANDERSON, T. J., LAMB, J., ROBERTS, M. M., FORREST, A. P. M., 'Multi Foetal cancers in a breast screening programme'. Third European Organisation for Research and Treatment of Cancer—Breast Cancer Working Conference, Amsterdam, 1983.

56. URBAN, J. A., PAPACHRISTOV, D., TAYLOR, J., 'Bilateral breast cancer: biopsy of the opposite breast', *Cancer*, 1977; 40:1968–73.

57. EREMIN, O., Editorial: 'Second primary breast cancer', *Br. Med. J.*, 1988; 296:1755–6.

58. FENIG, J., ARLEN, M., LIVINGSTON, S. F., LEVOWITZ, B. S., 'The potential for carcinoma existing synchronously on a microscopic level within the second breast', *Surg. Gynec. Obstet.*, 1975; 141:394–6.

59. OHUCHI, N., PAGE, D. L., MERINO, M. J., VIGLIONE, M. J., KUFE, D. W., SCHLOM, J., 'Expression of tumour-associated antigen (DF3) in atypical hyperplasia and in situ carcinomas of the human breast', *J. Natl. Cancer Inst.*, 1987; 79:109–17.

60. THAM, K. T., PAGE, D. L., 'Agnor and Ki-67 in breast lesions', *Am. J. Clin. Path.*, 1988; 92:518–20.

61. SWAIN, S. M., LIPPMAN, M. E., 'Intraepithelial carcinoma of the breast: LCIS and DCIS. In: *Diagnosis and Management of Breast Cancer*, LIPPMAN, M. E., LICHTER, A. S., DANFORTH, D. N. (eds). Philadelphia, W. B. Saunders, 1988, pp. 296–325.

62. SCHNITT, S. J., SILEN, W., SADOWSKY, N. L., CONNOLLY, J. L., HARRIS, J. R., 'Ductal carcinoma-in-situ (intraductal carcinoma of the breast)', *N. Engl. J. Med.*, 1988; 318:898–903.

63. SEIDMAN, H., GELB, S. K., SILVERBERG, E. *et al.*, 'Survival experience in the Breast Cancer Detection Demonstration Project'. CA 1987; 37:258–90.

64. LAGIOS, M. D., MARGOLIN, F. R., WESTDAHL, M. D., MARYE, R., 'Mammograpically detected duct carcinoma in situ', *Cancer*, 1989; 63:618–24.

65. GALLAGHER, H. S., MARTIN, J. E., 'An orientation to the concept of minimal breast cancer', *Cancer*, 1971; 28:1505–7.

66. GALLAGHER, H. S., 'Minimal breast cancer: results of treatment and the long-term follow-up'. In: *Breast Carcinoma: Current Diagnosis and Treatment*, FEIG, S. A., McLELLAND, R. (eds). New York, Masson Publishing USA Inc., 1983, pp. 291–4.

67. 'Report of the Working Group to Review the National Cancer Institute-American Cancer Society Breast Cancer Detection Demonstration Projects', *J. Natl. Cancer Inst.*, 1979; 62:639–709.

68. CARTER, C. L., ALLEN, C., HENSON, D. E., 'Relation of tumor site, lymph node status and survival in 24,740 breast cancer cases', *Cancer*, 1989; 63:181–7.

69. BRINKLEY, B., HAYBITTLE, J. L., 'The curability of cancer', *Lancet*, 1975; 2:95.

70. TABAR, L., DUFFY, S. W., KRUSEMO, U. B., 'Detection method, tumour size and node metastases in breast cancers diagnosed during a trial of breast screening', *Eur. J. Cancer Clin. Oncol.*, 1987; 23:959–62.

71. TUBIANA, M., KOSCIELNY, S., 'The natural history of breast cancer. Implications for patient management'. IV Internatl. Conf. on Senology Opening Lecture, 1986.

72. KOSCIELNY, S., TUBIANA, M., LE, M. G., VALLERON, A. J., 'Breast cancer: relationship between the size of the primary tumour and the probability of metastatic dissemination', *Br. J. Cancer*, 1984; 49:709–15.

73. DIXON, J. M., PAGE, D. L., ANDERSON, T. J., LEE, D., ELTON, R. A. *et al.*, 'Long-term survivors after breast carcinoma', *Br. J. Surg.*, 1985; 72:445–8.

74. BLOOM, H. J. B., RICHARDSON, W. W., 'Histological grading prognosis in breast cancer: study of 409 cases of which 359 have been followed up for 15 years', *Br. J. Cancer*, 1957; 11:35–77.

75. McGUIRE, W. L., CLARK, G. M., FISHER, E. R., HENDERSON, I. C., 'Predicting recurrence and survival in breast cancer', *Breast Cancer Res. Treat.*, 1987; 9:27–38.

76. SPYRATOS, F., MAUDELONDE, T., BROUILLET, J-P., BRUNET, M., DE-FRENNE, A., ANDRIEU, C., HACENE, K., DESPLACES, A., ROUESSE, J., ROCHE-FORT, H., 'Catheps-in-D: an independent prognostic factor for metastasis of breast cancer', *Lancet*, 1989; 2:1116–8.

77. TOIKKANEN, S., JOENSUU, H., KLEMI, P., 'The prognostic significance of nuclear DNA content in invasive breast cancer', *Br. J. Cancer*, 1989; 60:693–700.

78. GULLICK, W. J. 'Expression of c-erb B2 proto-oncogene protein in human breast cancer', *Recent Results Cancer Research*, 1989; 113:51–56.

79. LOCKER, A. P., DOWLE, C. S., ELLIS, I. O. *et al*, 'c-myc oncogeme product expression and prognosis in operable breast cancer', *Brit. J. Cancer*, 1989; 60:669–72.

80. OSBORNE, C. D. 'DNA flow cytometry in early breast cancer: a step in the right direction', *J. Nat. Cancer Instit.*, 1989; 81: 1344–5.

81. HARRIS, A. L., NEALE, D. E., 'Epidermal growth factor and its receptor in human breast cancer'. In: *Oestrogen and Human Breast Cancer*, BECK, J. S. (ed.). *Proc. Roy. Soc.*, Ed B, 1989; 94:60–90.

82. WALTER, S. D., DAY, N. E., 'Estimation of the duration of a preclinical disease state using screening data', *Am. J. Epidemiol.*, 1983; 118:865–86.

83. *Facts on Cancer*. Annual Report of the Cancer Research Campaign, 1988.

84. *Washington Post*, Jan. 21, 1990.

85. DE BONO, A. M., PILLERS, M. K., 'Carcinoma of the breast in East Anglia 1960–75: a changing pattern of presentation', *J. Eupidemiol Comm. Med*, 1978; 32:178–82.

86. WHITE, E., DALING. 'Rising incidence of breast cancer among young women in Washington State', *J. Nat. Cancer Instit.*, 1987; 79: 239–43.

87. ADAMS, M. J. T., SPICER, C. C. 'Recent mortality from breast cancer', *Lancet*, 1965; 11:732–34.

88. OLSSON, H., MOLLER, T. R., RAMSTAM, J. 'Early oral contraceptive use and breast cancer amongst pre-menopausal women: final report from a study in Sweden', *J. Nat. Cancer Instit.*, 1989; 81:1218–23.

89. SILVERBERG, E., BORING, C. C., SQUIRES, T. S. *Cancer Statistics*. CA 1990; 40:9–26.

90. CLEMMENSON, J., 'On the aetiology of some human cancers', *J. Natl. Cancer Inst.*, 1951; 12:1–21.

91. HAYBITTLE, J. L., 'The evidence for cure in female breast cancer'. In: *Commentaries on Research in Breast Disease*, BULBROOK, R. D., TAYLOR, D. J. (eds). New York, Alan Liss, 1983; 3:181–94.

92. KIRCHER, T., NELSON, J., BURDO, H., 'The autopsy as a measure of accuracy of the death certificate', *N. Engl. J. Med.*, 1985; 313:1263–9.

93. WALDRON, H. A., VICKERSTAFF, L., 'Necropsy rates in United Birmingham Hospitals', *Br. Med. J.*, 1975; 2:326–8.

94. CAMERON, H. M., McGOOGAN, E., 'A prospective study of 1152 hospital autopsies. I. Inaccuracies in death registration', *J. Path.*, 1981; 133:273–83.

95. HEASMAN, M. A., LIPWORTH, L., 'Accuracy of certification of cause of Death', London, 1–1. M.S.O., 1986.

96. BRINKLEY, D., HAYBITTLE, J. L., ALDERSON, M. R., 'Death certification in cancer of the breast', *Br. Med. J.*, 1984; 289:465–7.

97. EASSON, E. C., RUSSELL, M. H., *The curability of cancer in various sites*. London, Pitman, 1968.

98. BRINKLEY, D., HAYBITTLE, J. L., 'Long-term survival of women with breast cancer', *Lancet*, 1984; 1:1118.

99. ADAIR, F., BERG, J., JOUBERT, L., ROBBINS, G. F., 'Long-term follow-up of breast cancer patients: the thirty-year report', *Cancer*, 1974; 33:1145–50.

100. MUELLER, C., AMES, F., ANDERSON, G. D., 'Breast cancer in 3558 women; age as a significant determinant in the role of dying and causes of death', *Surgery*, 1978; 83:123–32.

101. LANGLANDS, A. O., POCOCK, S. J., KERR, J. R., GORE, S. M., 'Long-term survival of patients with breast cancer; a study of the curability of the disease', *Br. Med. J.*, 1979; 2:1247–51.

102. LE, M. G., HILL, C., REZVANI, A., SARRAZIN, D., CONTESSO, G., LACOUR, J., 'Long-term survival of women with breast cancer', *Lancet*, 1984; 2:922.

103. RUTQVIST, L. E., WALLGREN, A., 'Long-term survival of 458 young breast cancer patients', *Cancer*, 1985; 55:658–65.

104. ANDERSON, T. J., LAMB, F., ALEXANDER, F. *et al.*, 'Comparative pathology of prevalent and incident cancers detected by breast screening', *Lancet*, 1986; 1:519–22.

214 REFERENCES

105. ANDERSSON, I., ANDREN, L., HILDELL, J., LINELL, F., LJUNGQVIST, U., PETTERSSON, H., 'Breast cancer screening with mammography', *Radiology*, 1979; 132:273–6.

106. HARMER, M. H. (Ed.) *TNM classification of malignant tumours.* 3rd edition. International Union against Cancer, Geneva 1978.

107. HERMANEK, P., SOBIN, L. H. (Ed.) *TNM classification of malignant tumours.* 4th edition. International Union against Cancer, Berlin, 1987.

108. SOBIN, L. H., HERMANEK, P., HUTTER, R. V. P., 'TNM classification of maligant tumours. A comparison between the new (1987) and old editions', *Cancer*, 1988; 61:2310–14.

109. BROWN, J., 'Rab and his friends'. In: Collected Papers. 1890.

110. FORREST, A. P. M., 'Lister Oration: breast cancer—121 years on', *J. Royal Coll. Surg. Edinb.*, 1989; 34:239–48.

111. HALSTED, W. S., 'The results of radical operations for the cure of carcinoma of the breast', *Ann. Surg.*, 1907; 46:1–19.

112. MEYER, W., 'Carcinoma of the breast—10 years experience with my method of radical operation', *J. Am. Med. Assoc.*, 1907; 65:297–313.

113. HANDLEY, S. W., *Cancer of the Breast and its Operative Treatment.* London, John Murray, 1906.

114. VIRCHOW, R., *Cellular Pathology.* (Trans. by F. Charet) Philadelphia, Lippincott, 1863.

115. CUZICK, J., STEWART, H. J. S., PETO, R., 'Overview of randomised trials of post-operative adjuvant radiotherapy in breast cancer', *Cancer Treat. Rep.*, 1987; 71:15–29.

116. CUZICK, J., STEWART, H. J. S., PETO, R., 'Overview of randomised trials comparing radical mastectomy without radiotherapy against simple mastectomy with radiotherapy in breast cancer', *Cancer Treat. Rep.*, 1987; 71:7–14.

117. HAYBITTLE, J. L., BRINKLEY, D., HOUGHTON, J., A'HERN, R. P., BAUM, M., 'Postoperative radiotherapy and late mortality: evidence from the Cancer Research Campaign trial for early breast cancer', *Br. Med. J.*, 1989; 298:1611–4.

118. PATEY, D. H., DYSON, W. H., 'The prognosis of carcinoma of the breast in relation to the type of operation performed', *Br. J. Cancer*, 1948; 2:7.

119. MCWHIRTER, R., 'Simple mastectomy and radiotherapy in the treatment of breast cancer', *Br. J. Radiol.*, 1955; 28:128–39.

120. FORREST, A. P. M., KUNKLER, P. B., 'Breast cancer: management of the early case', *Hosp. Med.*, 1968; (Jan):398–407.

121 KEYNES, G., 'Radium treatment of carcinoma of the breast', *Lancet*, 1928; 2:108–11.

122. KEYNES, G., 'Carcinoma of the breast: the unorthodox view', *Proc. Cardiff Med. Soc.*, 1953; 4:40–9.

123. KEYNES, G., 'Conservative treatment of cancer of the breast', *Br. Med. J.*, 1937; 2:643–7.

124. VERONESI, U., SACCOZZI, R., DEL VECCHIO, M. *et al.*, 'Comparing radical mastectomy with quadrantectomy axillary dissection and radiotherapy in patients with small cancers of the breast', *N. Engl. J. Med.*, 1981; 305:6–11.

125. FISHER, B., BAUER, M., MAGROLESE, R. *et al.*, 'Five-year results of a randomized clinical trial comparing total mastectomy and segmental mastectomy with or without radiation in the treatment of breast cancer', *N. Engl. J. Med.*, 1985; 312:665–73.

126. HAYWARD, J. L., 'The Guy's Hospital trials in breast conservation'. In: *Conservative Management of Breast Cancer*, HARRIS, J. R., HELLMAN, S., SILEN, W. (eds). Philadelphia, Lippincott, 1983, pp. 77–90.

127. MORRIS, T., STEVEN-GREER, H., WHITE, P., 'Psychological and social adjustment to mastectomy (a two-year follow-up study)', *Cancer*, 1977; 40:2381–7.

128. MAGUIRE, G. P., LEE, E. G., BEVINGTON, D. J., 'Psychiatric problems in the year after mastectomy', *Br. Med. J.*, 1978; 1:963–5.

129. DEAN, C., CHETTY, U., FORREST, A. P. M., 'Effects of immediate breast reconstruction on psychological morbidity after mastectomy', *Lancet*, 1983; 1:459–62.

130. FALLOWFIELD, L. J., BAUM, M., MAGUIRE, G. P., 'Effects of breast conservation on psychological morbidity associated with diagnosis and treatment of early breast cancer', *Br. Med. J.*, 1986; 293:1331–4.

131. BEATSON, G. T., 'On the treatment of inoperable cases of the mamma', *Lancet*, 1986; 2:104–7, 162–9.

132. POTT, P., 'Ovarian hernia'. In: *Chirurgical Works*. London, 1775, pp. 791–2.

133. HUGGINS, C., BERGENSTAL, D. M., 'Inhibition of human mammary prostatic cancer by adrenalectomy', *Cancer Res.*, 1952; 12:134–41.

134. LUFT, R., OLIVECRONA, H., SJORGEN, B. J., 'Hypophysektomie pa manniska', *Nordisk Med.*, 1952; 47:351–4.

135. FORREST, A. P. M., PEEBLES-BROWN, D. A., 'Pituitary radon implant for breast cancer', *Lancet*, 1955; 1:1054–5.

136. FORREST, A. P. M., BLAIR, D. W., VALENTINE, J. M., 'Screw-implantation of the pituitary with yttrium–90', *Lancet*, 1958; 2:192–3.

137. FORREST, A. P. M., 'Endocrine management of breast cancer'. In: *Oestrogen and Human Breast Cancer*, BECK, J. S. (ed.). *Proc. Royal Soc. Ed. B.*, 1989; 94:1–10.

138. LOESER, A. A., 'Hormone therapy in mastitis and breast cancer', *Br. Med. J.*, 1938; 2:319.

139. ULRICH, P., 'Testosterone (hormone male) et son role possible dans le traitment de certains cancers du sein', *Acta un Int. Contra. Canc.*, 1939; 4:377–80.

140. HADDOW, A., WATKINSON, J. M., PATERSON, E., 'Influence of synthetic oestrogens for advanced malignant disease', *Br. J. Med.*, 1944; 2:393–8.

141. HARPER, M. J., WALPOLE, A. L., 'Contrasting endocrine activities of cis- and trans-isomers in a series of substituted triphenyl ethylenes', *Nature*, (London) 1966; 212:87.

142. PATERSON, R., RUSSELL, M. H., 'Clinical trials in malignant disease: value of irradiation of the ovaries', *J. Fac. Radiol.*, 1959; 10:130–3.

143. EARLY BREAST CANCER TRIALIST'S COLLABORTIVE GROUP, 'Effects of adjuvant tamoxifen and of cytotoxic therapy on mortality in early breast cancer. An overview of 61 randomized trials among 28,896 women', *N. Engl. J. Med.*, 1988; 319:1681–91.

144. BREAST CANCER TRIALS COMMITTEE, SCOTTISH CANCER TRIALS OF-FICE (MRC), 'Adjuvant tamoxifen in the management of operable breast cancer: the Scottish trial', *Lancet*, 1987; 2:171–5.

145. SALOMON, A., 'Beitrage zur pathologie und klinik der mammarcar-cinome', *Arch. Klin. Chir.*, 1913; 101:573–68.

146. LEBORGNE, R., 'Diagnosis of tumors of the breast by simple roentgenography. Calcifications in carcinomas', *Am. J. Roent. Rad. Ther.*, 1951; 65:1–11.

147. EGAN, R. L., *Breast Imaging: Diagnosis and Morphology of Breast Disease*. Philadelphia, W. B. Saunders, 1988.

148. WARREN, S. L., 'Roentgenologic study of breast', *Am. J. Roent. Rad. Ther.*, 1930; 24:113–4.

149. EGAN, R. L., 'Experience with mammography in a tumour institution. Evaluation of 1000 studies', *Radiology*, 1960; 75:894–900.

150. EGAN, R. L., 'Mammography, an aid to diagnosis of breast carcinoma', *J. Am. Med. Assoc.*, 1962; 182:839–43.

151. GROS, C. M., 'Les cancers occultes du sein et la de la mamelle tumorale', *J. Radiol. Electrol.*, 1952; 33:602–5.

152. GROS, C. M., *Les Maladies du Sein*. Paris, Masson, 1963.

153. INGLEBY, H., GERSHON-COHEN, J., *Comparative Anatomy, Pathology and Roentgenology of the Breast*. Philadelphia, Univ. of Pennsylvania Press, 1960.

154. GERSHON-COHEN, J., STRICKLER, A., 'Roentgenological examination of the normal breast: its evaluation in demonstrating early neoplastic change', *Am. J. Roent.*, 1938; 40:189–201.

155. GROS, C. M., 'Methodologie: symposium sur le sein', *J. Radiol. Electr.*, 1967; 48:638–55.

156. LOGAN, W. W., MUNTZ, E. P., *Reduced Dose Mammography*. New York, Masson, 1979.

157. BRUNNER, S., LANGFELDT, B. (eds), 'Breast Cancer: Present Perspective of Early Diagnosis', *Recent Results in Cancer Research*, Vol. 105. Berlin, Springer-Verlag, 1984.

158. STANTON, L., DAY, J. L., VILLAFANA, T., MILLER, C. H., LIGHTFOOT, D. A., 'Screen-film mammographic technique for breast cancer screening', *Radiology*, 1987; 163:471–9.

159. HAUS, A. G., Recent trends on screen-film mammography: technical factors and radiation dose. *Recent Results in Cancer Research*. Heidelberg, Springer-Verlag, 1987, Vol. 105, pp. 37–51.

160. DANCE, D. R., DAVIS, R., 'Physics of mammography'. In: *Diagnosis of Breast*, PARSONS, C. A. (ed). Baltimore, Univ. Park Press, 1983.

161. LANYI, M., *Diagnosis and Differential Diagnosis of Breast Calcifications*. Berlin, Springer-Verlag, 1987.

162. KIRKPATRICK, A. E., LAW, J., 'The usefulness of a moving grid in mammography', *Br. J. Radiol.*, 1989; 58:257–8.

163. SICKLES, E. A., 'The role of magnification technique in modern mammography'. *Recent Results in Cancer Research*. Heidelberg, Springer-Verlag, 1987, Vol. 105, pp. 19–24.

164. LUNDGREN, B., 'The oblique view mammography', *Br. J. Radiol.*, 1976; 50:626–8.

165. LUNDGREN, B., JACOBSEN, S., 'Single view mammography: a simple and efficient approach to breast cancer screening', *Cancer*, 1976; 38:1124–9.

166. LUNDGREN, B., 'Population screening for breast cancer by single-view mammography in a geographic region in Sweden', *J. Natl. Cancer Inst.*, 1979; 62:1373–9.

167. YOUNG, G. B., 'Improving contrast in mammography', *Br. J. Radiol.*, 1966; 39:230–2.

168. YOUNG, G. B., 'Mammography in carcinoma of the breast', *J. Royal Coll. Surg. Edinb.*, 1968; 13:12–33.

169. SAMUEL, E., 'Diagnostic radiology in diagnosis of carcinoma of the breast', *Br. J. Surg.*, 1964; 51:221–4.

170. APSIMON, H. T., STEWART, H. J., WILLIAMS, W. J., 'Recording the gross outlines of breast tumours. A pathological assessment of the accuracy of radiographs of breast cancers', *Br. J. Cancer*, 1968; 22:40–6.

171. GEORGE, W. D., GLEAVE, E. N., ENGLAND, P. C. *et al.*, 'Screening for breast cancer', *Br. Med. J.*, 1976; 2:858–60.

172. STARK, A. M., 'Screening for breast cancer', *Lancet*, 1970; 2:407–9.

173. FURNIVAL, I. G., STEWART, H. J., WEDDELL, J. M., DOVEY, P., GRAVELLE, I. H., EVANS, K., FORREST, A. P. M., 'Accuracy of screening methods for the diagnosis of breast disease', *Br. Med. J.*, 1970; 4:461–3.

174. DAVEY, J. B., McKINNA, J. A., GREENING, W. P., 'Is screening for cancer worthwhile. Results from a well woman clinic for cancer detection', *Br. Med. J.*, 1970; 3:696–9.

175. CHAMBERLAIN, J., CLIFFORD, R. E., NATHAN, B. E., PRICE, J. L., BURN, I., 'Error rates in screening for breast cancer by clinical examination and mammography', *Clin. Oncol.*, 1979; 5:135.

176. DAVEY, J. PENTNEY, H., TUCKER, A., WRIGHT, H. B., BAILEY, A., 'Screening for breast cancer. A report of 11654 examinations', *Clin. Oncol.*, 1976; 2:317–22.

177. SHAPIRO, S., VENET, W., STRAX, P., VENET, L., *Periodic screening for Breast Cancer. The Health Insurance Plan Project and its Sequelae 1963–1986*. Baltimore and London, The Johns Hopkins Univ. Press, 1988.

178. *Report of EECESO Advisory Group. Periodic Mammographies and the Risk of Radio-Induced Cancers*, 1990.

179. BARENIDSEN, G. W., 'Effects of radiation on the reproductive capacity and proliferation of cells in relation to carcinogenesis'. In: *Radiation Carcinogenesis*, UPTON, A. C., ALBERT, R. E., BURNS, F. J., SHORE, R. E. (eds). Amsterdam, Elsevier Science Publ., 1986, pp. 85–105.

180. BRESLOW, L., HENDERSON, B., MASSEY, F., PIKE, M., WINKELSTEIN, W., 'Mammography in screening for breast cancer group reports', *J. Natl. Cancer Inst.*, 1977; 59:481–95.

181. BOICE, J. D., LAND, C. E., SHORE, R. E., NORMAN, J. E., ROKUNAGA, M., 'Risk of breast cancer following low-dose radiation exposures', *Radiology*, 1979; 131:589–97.

182. KAMADA, N., SHIGETA, C., KURAMOTO, A. *et al.*, 'Acute and late effects of A-bomb radiation: studies in a group of young girls with a defined condition at the time of bombing'. *J. Radiation Res.*, 1989; 30:218–225.

183. MODAN, B., CHETRIT, A., ALFARIDARG, E., 'Increased risk of breast cancer after low-dose irradiation', *Lancet*, 1989; 1:629–30.

184. GOHAGAN, J. K., DARBY, W. P., SPITZNAGEL, E. L., MONSEES, B. S., TOME, A. E., 'Radiogenic breast cancer effects of mammographic screening', *J. Natl. Cancer Inst.*, 1986; 77:71–6.

185. FEIG, S. A. 'Dose and quality control of mammographic screening', In *Practical Modalities for an Efficient Screening for Breast Cancer in the European Community*, G. ZIANT, International congress series 865, *Exercpta Medica*, 1989; 60.

186. BAINES, C. J., CHRISTEN, A., SIMARD, A., WALL, C., DEAN, D. *et al.*, 'The national breast screening study: pre-recruitment sources of awareness in participants', *Can. J. Pub. Hlth.*, 1989; 63:221–5.

187. WOLFE, J. N., 'Xerography of the breast', *Radiology*, 1968; 91:231–40.

188. SICKLES, E. A., 'Mammographic features of 300 consecutive nonpalpable cancers', *Am. J. Roentgen.*, 1986; 146:661–3.

189. CIATTO, S., CATALIOTTI, L., DISTANTE, V., 'Nonpalpable lesions detected with mammography: review of 512 consecutive cases', *Radiology*, 1987; 165:99–102.

190. MUIR, B. B., LAMB, J., ANDERSON, T. J., KIRKPATRICK, A. E., 'Microcalcification and its relationship to cancer of the breast: experience in a screening clinic', *Clin. Radiol.*, 1983; 34:193–200.

191. MILLIS, R. R., DAVIS, R., STACEY, A. J., 'The detection and significance of calcifications in the breast: a radiological and pathological study', *Br. J. Radiol.*, 1976; 49:12–26.

192. PRICE, J. L., GIBBS, N. M., 'The relationship between microcalcification and in situ carcinoma of the breast', *Clin. Radiol.*, 1978; 29:447–52.

193. COLE, P., MORRISON, A. S., 'Basic issues in population screening for cancer', *J. Natl. Cancer Inst.*, 1980; 64:1263–72.

194. CHAMBERLAIN, J. 'Secondary prevention: screening for breast cancer', *Effective Health Care*, 1985; 2:180–7.

195. *The Pritchard Report. Guidelines on the establishment of a quality assurance system for the radiological aspects of mammography used for breast screening.* Radiation Advisor Committee: Subcommittee on Quality Assurance (The Pritchard Comm.), 1988.

196. ROMBACH, J. J., COLLETTE, B. J. A., DeWAARD, F., SLOTBOOM, B. J., 'The analysis of the diagnostic performance in breast cancer screening by relative operating characteristics', *Cancer*, 1986; 58:169–77.

197. BATES, S. 'The use and potential of serum markers, new and old, *Drugs*, 1989, 38:9–18.

198. COOPER, J. A., SARACCI, R., COLE, P. 'Describing the validity of a screening test' *Brit. J. Cancer*, 1979; 39:87–89.

199. DAY, N. E., 'Estimating the sensitivity of a screening test', *J. Epid. Comm. Med.*, 1985; 39:364–6.

200. SICKLES, E. A., 'Computed tomography scanning, transillumination and magnetic resonance imaging of the breast'. *Recent Results: Cancer Research.* Berlin, Springer-Verlag, 1987, pp. 31–7.

201. MONSEES, B., DESTOUET, J. M., TOTTY, W. G., 'Light scanning versus mammography in breast detection', *Radiology*, 1987; 163:463–5.

202. MONSEES, B., DESTOUET, J. M., GERSELL, D., 'Light scan evaluation of nonpalpable breast lesions', *Radiology*, 1987; 163:467–70.

203. 'Canadian Task Force on the Periodic Health Examination. The periodic health examination', *Can. Med. Assoc. J.*, 1986; 134:721–9.

204. SASCO, A. J., DAY, N. E., WALTER, S. D. 'Case-control studies for the evaluation of screening', *J. Chr. Disease*, 1986, 39:399–405.

205. FARLEY, T. A., FLANNERY, J. T. Late-stage diagnosis of breast cancer in women of lower socio-economic status: public health implications. *Amer. J. Public Hlth.*, 1988, 1989, 79:1508–1512.

206. FREEMAN, H. P., WASFIE, T. J. Cancer of the breast in poor black women. *Cancer*, 1989, 63:2562–2569.

207. TABAR, L., FAGERBERG, G., DUFFY, S. W., DAY, N. E., 'The Swedish two-county trial of mammographic screening for breast cancer: recent results and calculation of benefit', *J. Epidemiol. Comm. Hlth.*, 1989; 43:107–14.

208. VERBEEK, A. L. A., HENDRICKS, J. H. L. C., HOLLAND, R., 'Mammographic screening and breast cancer mortality: age-specific effects in the Nijmegen project 1975–82', *Lancet*, 1985; 1:865–6.

209. PALLI, D., ROSSELLI DEL TURCO, M., BUIATTI, E., CARLI, S., CIATTO, S. *et al.*, 'A case-control study of the efficacy of a non-randomised breast cancer screening program in Florence (Italy)', *Int. J. Cancer*, 1986; 38:501–4.

210. PALLI, D., TURCO, M. R., BUIATTI, E., CIATTO, S., CROCETTI, E., PACI, E., 'Time interval since last test in a breast cancer screening programme. A case-control study in Italy. *J. epidomiol. comm. Hlth.*, 1989; 43:241–248.

211. ANDERSSON, I., ASPERGEN, K., JANZON, L., LANDBERG, T., LINDHOLM, K. *et al.*, 'Mammographic screening and mortality from breast cancer: the Malmo mammographic screening trial', *Br. Med. J.*, 1988; 297:943–8.

212. 'U.K. Trial of Early Detection of Breast Cancer Group. First results on mortality reduction in the U.K. trial of early detection on breast cancer', *Lancet*, 1988; 2:411–5.

213. ROBERTS, M. M., ALEXANDER, F. E., ANDERSON, T. J., CHETTY, U., DONNAN, P. T., FORREST, A. P. M., HEPBURN, W., HUGGINS, A., KIRKPATRICK, A. E., LAMB, J., MUIR, B. B., PRESCOTT, R. J., 'The Edinburgh trial of screening for breast cancer', *Lancet*, 1990 (in press).

214. SHAPIRO, S., STRAX, P., VENET, L., 'Periodic breast cancer screening in reducing mortality from breast cancer', *J. Am. Med. Assoc.*, 1971; 215:1777–80.

215. CLARK, R. C., COPELAND, M. M., EGAN, R. L., GALLAGHER, H. B., GELLER, H., LINDSAY, J. P., ROBBINS, L. C., WHITE, E. C., 'Reproducibility of the technique of mammography (Egan) for cancer of the breast', *Am. J. Surg.*, 1965; 109:127–33.

216. SHAPIRO, S., VENET, W., STRAX, P., VENET, L., 'Current results of the breast cancer screening: the Health Insurance Plan (HIP) of Greater New York Study'. In: *Screening for Breast Cancer*, DAY, N. E., MILLER, A. B. (eds.) Toronto, Hans-Huber, 1988, pp. 3–15.

217. ARON, J. L., PROROK, P. C., 'An analysis of the mortality effect in a breast cancer screening study', *Int. J. Epidemiol.*, 1986; 15:36–43.

218. HABBEMA, J. D. F., van OORTMARSSEN, G. J., van PUTTEN, D. J., LUBBE, J. T., van der MAAS, J., 'Age-specific reduction in breast cancer mortality by screening. Analysis of the results of the Health Insurance Plan of Greater New York study', *J. Natl. Cancer Inst.*, 1986; 77:317–20.

219. FAGERBERG, L., TABAR, L., 'The results of periodic one-view mammography screening in a randomised controlled trial in Sweden. Part I. Background, organisation, screening program, tumour findings'. In: *Screening for Breast Cancer*, DAY, N. E., MILLER, A. B. (eds). Toronto, Hans-Huber, 1988, pp. 33–8.

220. TABAR, L., FAGERBERG, C. J. G., DAY, N. E., 'The results of periodic one-view mammography screening in a randomised controlled trial in Sweden. Part II. Evaluation of the results'. In: *Screening for Breast Cancer*, DAY, N. E., MILLER, A. B. (eds.) Toronto, Hans-Huber, 1988, pp. 39–44.

221. GRONTOFT, O., 'Histopathological investigation of breast cancer lesions detected by mammography with special reference to staging and grading of invasive ductal carcinoma'. In: *Screening for Breast Cancer*, DAY, N. E., MILLER, A. B. (eds). Toronto, Hans-Huber, 1988, pp. 75–7.

222. GRONTOFT, O., 'Staging and grading of invasive ductal carcinoma in a randomised population screened by mammography: the first and second screens', In: *Screening for Breast Cancer*, DAY, N. E., MILLER, A. B. (eds). Toronto, Hans-Huber, 1988, pp. 79–82.

223. ANDERSSON, I., SIGFUSSON, B. F., 'Screening for breast cancer in Malmo: a randomised trial'. In: *Early Detection of Breast Cancer*, BRUNNER, S., LANGFELDT, B., ANDERSON, P. E. (eds). Berlin, Springer-Verlag, 1984, pp. 114–115.

224. FRISELL, J., GLAS, U., HELLSTROM, L., SOMELL, A., 'Randomised trial for breast cancer in Stockholm', *Breast Cancer Res. Treat.*, 1986; 8:45–54.

225. FRISELL, J., EKLUND, G., HELLSTROM, L., GLAS, U., SOMELL, A., 'The Stockholm breast cancer screening trial—5-year results and state at discovery', *Breast Cancer Res. Treat.*, 1989; 13:79–87.

226. VON ROSEN, A., FRISELL, J., GLAS, U., HELLSTROM, L., NILSON, R., SKOOG, L., AUER, G., 'Non-palpable invasive breast cancer from the Stockholm screening project', *Acta Oncol.*, 1989; 28:23–7.

227. BJURSTAM, N., CABLIN, E., ERIKSSON, O., HEFSTROM, F. O., RUDEM-STAM, C. M., SARE-SODERBERGH, J., Breast cancer screening project. Göteborg, Sweden, 4th EORTC Working Conference, London, 1987.

228. U.K. TRIAL OF EARLY DETECTION OF BREAST CANCER GROUP, 'Trial of early detection of breast cancer: description of method', *Br. J. Cancer*, 1981; 44:618–27.

229. THOMAS, B. A., PRICE, J. L., 'The Guildford breast screening project: six-year assessment'. In: *Recent Results in Cancer Research*, Vol. 105. Heidelberg, Springer-Verlag, 1987, pp. 68–72.

230. THOMAS, B. A., 'The Guildford breast screening project', *Clin. Oncol.*, 1983; 9:121–9.

231. 'Screening for Breast Cancer. Report from Edinburgh Breast Screening Clinic', *Br. Med. J.*, 1978; 2:175–8.

232. ROBERTS, M. M., ALEXANDER, F., ANDERSON, T. J., FORREST, A. P. M., HEPBURN, W. *et al.*, 'The Edinburgh randomised trial of screening for breast cancer: description of method', *Br. J. Cancer*, 1984; 50:1–6.

233. MILLER, A. B., HOWE, G. R., WALL, C., 'The national study of breast cancer screening. Protocol for a Canadian randomised controlled trial of screening for breast cancer in women', *Clin. Invest. Med.*, 1981; 4:227–58.

234. MILLER, A. B., 'The Canadian national trial'. In: *Screening for Breast Cancer*, DAY, N. E., MILLER, A. B. (eds). Toronto, Hans-Huber, 1988, pp. 51–8.

235. BAINES, C. J., MILLER, A. B., WALL, C. *et al.*, 'Sensitivity and specificity of first screen mammography in the Canadian Breast Screening Study: a preliminary report from five centres', *Radiology*, 1986; 160:295–8.

236. BAINES, C. J., MCFARLANE, D. V., MILLER, A. B., 'Sensitivity and specificity of first screen mammography in 15 NBSS centres', *J. Can. Assoc. Radiol.*, 1988; 39:273–6.

237. PEETERS, P. H. M., VERBEEK, A. L. M., HENDRICKS, J. H. C. L., VAN BON, M. J. H., 'Screening for breast cancer in Nijmegen: report of six screening rounds 1975–86', *Int. J. Cancer*, 1989; 43:226–30.

238. DEWAARD, F., COLLETTE, H. J. A., ROMBACH, J. J., BAANDERS-VAN HALWIJN, E. A., HONING, C., 'The DOM project for the early detection of breast cancer, Utrecht, the Netherlands', *J. Chronic Dis.*, 1984; 37:1–44.

239. COLLETTE, H. J. A., ROMBACH, J. J., DEWAARD, F., COLLETTE, C., 'An update of the DOM project for the early detection of breast cancer'. In: *Screening for Breast Cancer*, DAY, N. E., MILLER, A. B. (eds). Toronto, Hans-Huber, 1988, pp. 17–27.

240. LUNDGREN, B., 'Efficacy of single-view mammography: rate of interval cancer cases', *J. Natl. Cancer Inst.*, 1979; 62:799–803.

241. BAKER, L. H., 'Breast cancer detection demonstration project: five-year preliminary report', CA 1982; 32:194–225.

242. MORRISON, A. S., BRISSON, J., KHALID, N., 'Breast cancer incidence and mortality in the breast cancer detection demonstration project', *J. Natl. Cancer Inst.*, 1988; 80:1540–7.

243. MOSS, S., DRAPER, S. J., HARDCASTLE, M., CHAMBERLAIN, J., 'Calculation of sample size in trials of screening for early diagnosis of disease', *Int. J. Epidemiol.*, 1987; 16:104–10.

244. TABAR, L., DUFFY, S., 'Malmo mammographic screening trial', *Br. Med. J.*, 1989; 298:48–9.

245. ALEXANDER, F., ROBERTS, M. M., LUTZ, W., HEPBURN, W., 'Randomisation by cluster and the problem of social class bias', *J. Epidemiol. Comm. Hlth.*, 1989; 43:29–36.

246. BLACK, D., MAVIS, J. N., SMITH, C., TOWNSEND, P., *Inequalities and Health. Report of a research working group.* London DHSS, 1980.

247. ALEXANDER, F. E., O'BRIEN, F., HEPBURN, W., MILLER, M., 'Association between mortality among women and socio-economic factors in general practices in Edinburgh: an application of small area statistics', *Br. Med. J.*, 1987; 292:754–6.

248. *Cancer Statistics Review 1973–1986.* Natl. Cancer Int., U.S. Dept. Health and Human Services, 1989.

249. FRENCH, K., PORTER, A. M. D., ROBINSON, S. E., McCALLUM, F. M., HOWIE, J. G. R., ROBERTS, M. M., 'Attendance at a breast screening clinic: a problem of administration or attitudes', *Br. Med. J.*, 1982; 285:617–20.

250. MACLEAN, U., SINFIELD, D., 'Women who decline screening: report to Health Services Research Committee', *J. Epidemiol. Comm. Med.*, 1984; 38:278–83.

251. ROBERTS, M. M., FRENCH, K., DUFFY, J., 'Breast cancer and breast self-examination: what do Scottish women know', *Soc. Sci. Med.*, 1984; 18:791–7.

252. ROBERTS, M. M., FRENCH, K., ROBINSON, S. E., *The Edinburgh Breast Education Project.* 39–48.

253. ROBINSON, S. E., ROBERTS, M. M., 'A women's health shop: a unique experience', *Br. Med. J.*, 1985; 291:255–6.

254. ROBERTS, M. M., ROBINSON, S. E., FRENCH, K., PROUDFOOT, A., TALBOT, H., ELTON, R. A., 'Edinburgh breast education campaign on breast cancer and breast self-examination: was it worthwhile', *J. Epidemiol. Comm. Hlth.*, 1986; 40:338–43.

255. CHAMBERLAIN, J., 'Breast screening: a response to Dr M. M. Roberts'. *Br. Med. J.*, 1989; 299:1336–7.

256. PROROK, P. C., 'Mathematical models of breast cancer screening', In: *Screening for Breast Cancer*, DAY, N. E., MILLER, A. B. (eds). Toronto, Hans-Huber, 1988, pp. 95–104.

257. DAY, N. E., WALTER, S. D., 'Simplified models of screening for chronic disease: estimation procedure from mass screening programmes', *Biometrics*, 1940; 40:1–14.

258. DAY, N. E., WALTER, S. D., TABAR, L., FAGERBERG, C. J. G., 'The sensitivity and lead time of breast cancer screening: a comparison of the results of different studies'. In: *Screening for Breast Cancer*, DAY, N. E., MILLER, A. B. (eds). Toronto, Hans-Huber, 1988, pp. 105–110.

259. DAY, N. E., 'Quantitative approach to the evaluation of screening programmes', *World J. Surg.*, 1989; 13:3–8.

260. DAY, N. E., WILLIAMS, D. R., KHAW, K. T., 'Breast cancer screening programmes: the development of a monitoring and evaluation system', *Br. J. Cancer*, 1989; 59:954–8.

261. LUNDGREN, B., 'Breast screening in Britain and Sweden', *Br. Med. J.*, 1988; 297:1266.

262. LANGLANDS, A. O., KERR, G. R., SHAW, S., 'The management of locally advanced breast cancer x-ray therapy', *Clin. Oncol.*, 1976; 2:365–71.

263. THOMAS, B. A., 'The place of clinical examination in breast cancer screening'. In: *Practical Modalities of an Efficient Screening for Breast Cancer in the European Community*. G. ZIANT (ed.). International Congress Series 865. *Excerpta Medica 1989*, 11–24.

264. TABAR, L., FABERBERG, G., DAY, N. E., HOLMBERG, L. 'What is the optimal interval between mammographic screening: an analysis based on the latest results of the Swedish two-county breast cancer screening trial', *Br. J. Cancer*, 1987; 55:547–51.

265. VERBEEK, A. L. M., STRAATMAN, H., HENDRICKS, J. H. L. C., 'Sensitivity of mammography in Nijmegen women under age 50: some trials with the Eddy model'. In: *Screening for Breast Cancer*, DAY, N. E., MILLER, A. B. (eds). Toronto, Hans-Huber, 1988, pp. 29–32.

266. CHU, C., SMART, C. R., TARONE, R. E., 'Analysis of breast cancer mortality and stage distribution for the health insurance plan clinical trial', *J. Nat. Canc. Inst.*, 1988; 80:1125–32.

267. GORDILLO, C., 'Breast cancer screening guidelines agreed on by AMA, other medically-related organisations', *J. Amer. Med. Assoc.*, 1989; 262:1155.

268. KING, S., 'Not everyone agrees with new mammographic screening guidelines designed to end confusion', *J. Amer. Med. Assoc.*, 1989; 262:1154–5.

269. EDDY, M., 'The value of mammography screening in women under 50 years', *J. Am. Med. Assoc.*, 1988; 259:1512–19.

270. TABAR, L., DEAN, P. B., 'The value of mammographic screening in women under 50 years', *Invest. Radiol.*, 1989; 24:420–4.

271. THE NEW FORREST COMMITTEE, *Network: NHS Breast Screening Project*, GRAY, M. (ed.). Cancer Research Campaign, 1988, No. 2, p.8.

272. *Network: NHS Breast Screening Project*, GRAY, M. (ed.). Cancer Research Campaign, 1988, No. 3, p.1.

273. LUNDGREN, B., 'Screening for breast cancer: a view from the front line', *Biomed. Pharmacother.*, 1988; 42:443–6.

274. MUIR, B. M., KIRKPATRICK, A. E., ROBERTS, M. M., DUFFY, S. W., 'Oblique-view mammography adequacy for screening', *Radiology*, 1984; 151:39–44.

275. ANDERSSON, I., HILDELL, I., MUHLOW, A., PETTERSON, H., 'Number of projections in mammography: influence in detection of breast disease', *Am. J. Roentgen.*, 1978; 130:349–51.

276. BASSETT, L. W., BUNNELL, D. H., JAHANSHAHI, R., GOLD, R. H., ARNDT, R. D., LINSMAN, J., 'Breast cancer detection: one versus two views', *Radiology*, 1987; 165:95–7.

277. SICKLES, E. A., WEBER, W. N., GALVIN, H. B., OMINSKY, S. H., SOLLITTO, R. A., 'Base-line screening mammography: one vs two view per breast', *Am. J. Roentgen.*, 1986; 147:1149–53.

278. SICKLES, E. A., WEBER, W. N., GALVIN, H. B., OMINSKY, S. H., SOLLITTO, R. A., 'Mammographic screening: how to operate successfully at low cost', *Radiology*, 1986; 160:95–97.

279. ANTINEN, L., PAMILO, M., ROIHA, M., SOIVA, M., SURAMO, I., 'Baseline screening mammography with one versus two views', *Europ. J. Radiol.*, 1989; 9:241–3.

280. LOCKER, A. P., MANHIRE, A. R., CASELDINE, J., BLAMEY, R. W., 'A comparison of the detection of breast carcinoma by mammography using one or two views', *Brit. J. Radiol.*, 1988; 61:440.

281. CLARKE, P. R., FRASER, N. M., *Economic Analysis of Screening for Breast Cancer*. Interim Report to Scottish Home and Health Department, 1989.

282. SOINI, I., HAKAMA, M., 'Failure of selective screening for breast cancer by combining risk factors', *Int. J. Cancer*, 1978; 22:275–81.

283. HANSELL, D. M., COOKE, J. C., PARSONS, C. A., 'The accuracy of mammography alone and in combination with clinical examination and cytology in the detection of breast cancer', *Clin. Radiol.*, 1988; 39:150–3.

284. HAAGENSEN, C. D., 'A monograph for the physician', *New York American Cancer Society*, 1950.

285. BAINES, C. J., 'Breast self-examination: the known and the unknown'. In: *Screening for Breast Cancer*, DAY, N. E., MILLER, A. B. (eds). Toronto, Hans-Huber, 1988, pp. 85–91.

286. O'MALLEY, M. S., FLETCHER, S. W., 'Screening for breast cancer with breast self-examination: a critical review', *J. Am. Med. Assoc.*, 1987; 257:2197–2203.

287. FRANK, J. W., MA, V., 'Breast self-examination in young women: more harm than good', *Lancet*, 1985; 2:654–7.

288. HILL, D., WHITE, V., JOLLEY, D., MAPPERSON, K., 'Self-examination of the breast: is it beneficial. Meta-analysis of studies investigating breast self-examination and extent of disease in patients with breast cancer', *Br. Med. J.*, 1988; 297:271–5.

289. MANT, D., VESSEY, M. P., NEIL, A., McPHERSON, K., JONES, L., 'Breast self-examination and cancer stage', *Br. J. Cancer*, 1987; 55:207–11.

REFERENCES 225

290. TSECHKEVSKI, M., SEMIGLASNOV, V., SAGAIDASK, V., MOISEYENKO, V., MIKHAILOV, E., *Role of Breast Self-examiniation in Reduction of Mortality from Breast Cancer*, Protocol of the study. World Health Organisation, 1986.

291. PHILIP, J., HARRIS, W. G., FLAHERTY, C., JOSLIN, C. A. F., RUTAGE, J. H., WIJESINGHE, D. P., 'Breast self-examination: clinical results from a population-based prospective study', *Br. J. Cancer*, 1984; 50:7–12.

292. DOWLE, C. S., MITCHELL, A., ELSTON, C. W., ROEBUCK, E. J., HINTON, C. P., HOLLIDAY, H., BLAMEY, R. W., 'Preliminary results of the Nottingham breast self-examination programme', *Br. J. Surg.*, 1987; 74:217–9.

293. LOCKER, A. P., CASELDINE, J., MITCHELL, A. K., BLAMEY, R. W., ROEBUCK, E. J., ELSTON, C. W. 'Results from a seven-year programme of breast self-examination in 89,010 women', *Br. J. Cancer*, 1989; 60: 401–405.

294. GREENWALD, P., NASCA, P. C., LAWRENCE, C. E., HORTON, J., MCGARRAH, R. P., GABRIELE, T., CARLTON, K., 'Estimated effect of breast self-examination and routine physician examinations on breast-cancer mortality', *N. Engl. J. Med.*, 1984; 299:271–3.

295. GASTRIN, G., 'Breast cancer control: early detection programme'. ALMQVIST AND WISKELL, STOCKHOLM, 1986.

296. CALMAN, M., 'Explaining women's participation in programmes for the early detection of breast cancer', *Conn. Med.*, 1984; 6:204–210.

297. CALMAN, M., 'Women and medicalisation: an empirical examination of a woman's dependence on medical technology in the early detection of breast cancer', *Soc. Sci. Med.*, 1984; 18:561–9.

298. MILLER, A. B., 'The ethics, risks and benefits of screening', *Biomed. Pharmacother.*, 1988; 41:439–42.

299. DAY, N. E., CHAMBERLAIN, J., 'Screening for breast cancer: workshop report. *Europ. J. clin. oncol.*, 1988; 24:55–9.

300. HENDRIKS, J. H. C. L., 'Discussion in *Practical Modalities of an Efficient Screening for Breast Cancer in the European Community*', ZIANT, G. (ed.). Amsterdam. *Excerpta Med.*, 1989: p. 64.

301. ADAMI, H. O., MALBER, B., RUTQUIST, L. E., PERSSON, I., RIES, L., 'Temporal trends in breast cancer survival in Sweden: significant improvement in 20 years', *J. Natl. Cancer Inst.*, 1986; 76:653–9.

302. ROBINSON, S., STEWART, H. J., FORREST, A. P. M., 'Management of operable primary breast cancer in Scotland'. (Submitted for publication)

303. DEPARTMENT OF HEALTH AND ROYAL COLLEGE OF PATHOLOGISTS WORKING GROUP, *Draft Guidelines for Pathologists. NHS Breast Screening Programme.* Oxford: Breast Screening Publications, 1988.

304. DEPARTMENT OF HEALTH AND ROYAL COLLEGE OF PATHOLOGISTS WORKING GROUP, *Pathology Reporting in Breast Cancer Screening: Draft Guideance. NHS Breast Screening Programme.* Oxford: Breast Screening Publications, 1988.

305. MURRAY-SYKES, K., *Organising Assessment. NHS Breast Screening Programme.* Oxford: Breast Screening Publications, 1988.

306. AUSTOKER, J., HUMPHREYS, J., *Visiting Primary Care Teams to Explain their Part of the Screening Programme. NHS Breast Screening Programme.* Oxford: Breast Screening Publications, 1989.

307. ROYAL COLLEGES OF SURGEONS REPORT ON BREAST SCREENING. 1989.

308. DEAN, C., ROBERTS, M. M., FRENCH, K., ROBINSON, S., 'Psychiatric morbidity after sceeening for breast cancer', *J. Epid. Comm. Hlth.*, 1986; 40:71–5.

309. GOLDBERG, D. P., *Manual of the General Health Questionnaire.* NFER: Nelson, Windsor, NFER: Horsham, 1978.

310. ELLMAN, R., ANGELI, N., CHRISTIANS, A., MOSS, S., CHAMBERLAIN, J., MAGUIRE, P., 'Psychiatric morbidity associated with screening for breast cancer', *Br. J. Cancer*, 1989; 60:781–4.

311. FINLAY-JONES, R. A., BURVILL, P. W., 'Contrasting demographic patterns of minor psychiatric morbidity in general practice and the community', *Psychol. Med.*, 1978; 8:455.

312. WILLIAMS, P., TARNOPOLSKY, A., HAND, D., SHEPHERD, M., 'Minor psychiatric morbidity and GP consultation: the West London survey', *Psychol. Med.*, 1986; Supp. 9.

313. FORREST, A. P. M., The Welbeck Memorial Lecture 1988. 'Radiology and Breast Cancer', *Radiol. Today*, 1988; 55:13–20.

314. AITKEN, R. J., FORREST, A. P. M., CHETTY, U. *et al.*, 'Assessment of non-palpable mammographic abnormalities: comparison of a screening clinic and a breast clinic', *Br. Med. J.*, 1990, in press.

315. CIATTO, S., 'Usefulness of needle aspiration in a screening programme'. In: *Practical Modalities of an Efficient Screening for Breast Cancer in the European Community,* ZIANT, G. (ed.). Amsterdam. *Exercpta Med.*, 1989; 83–94.

316. BAINES, C. J., 'Evaluation of mammography and physical examination as independent screening modalities in the Canadian national breast screening study'. In: *Practical Modalities of an Efficient Breast Screening in the European Community,* ZIANT, G. (ed.). Amsterdam. *Exerpta Med.*, 1989; 3–10.

317. HENDRIKS, J. H. L. C., 'Technical requirements for mammographic screening illustrated by the Nijmegen project (14 years of follow-up)'. In: *Practical modalities of an efficient screening for breast cancer in the European community,* ZIANT, G. (ed.). Amsterdam. *Exerpta Med.*, 1989; 41–44.

318. THE UPPSALA-OREBRO BREAST CANCER STUDY GROUP. 'Sector resection with or without postoperative radiotherapy for stage I breast cancer', *J. Nat. Canc. Inst.*, 1990; 82:277–82.

319. FENTIMAN, I. S., FAGG, N., MILLIS, R. R., HAYWARD, J. L., 'In situ ductal carcinoma of the breast. Implications of disease pattern and treatment', *Eur. J. Surg. Oncol.*, 1986; 12:261.

320. HOLLAND, R., HENDRIKS, J. H. C. L., VERBEEK, A. L. M., *et al.*, 'Extent, distribution and mammographic histological correlations of breast ductal carcinoma-in-situ', *Lancet*, 1990; i:519–22.

321. VAN DONGEN, J. A., FENTIMEN, I. S., HARRIS, J. R. *et al.* 'In situ breast cancer: the EORTC concensus meeting'. *Lancet*, 1989; 2: 25–27

322. ZAFRANI, B., FOURQUET, A., UILCOQ, J. R., LEGAL, M., CALLE, R., 'Conservative management of intraductal breast carcinoma with tumorectomy and radiation therapy', *Cancer*, 1987; 57:1299–301.

323. FENTIMAN, I. S., 'Surgery in the management of early breast cancer', *Eur. J. Clin. Oncol.*, 1988; 24:73–6.

324. RIBIERO, G., 'Is breast conservation safe', *Lancet*, 1985; 1:1275.

325. VORHERR, H., 'Is breast conservation safe', *Lancet*, 1985; 2:282.

326. PAPAIOANNOU, A., 'Is breast conservation safe', *Lancet*, 1985; 2:282–3.

327. BARTELINK, H., 'Radiotherapy in the management of early breast cancer: a review', *Eur. J. Clin. Oncol.*, 1988; 24:77–82.

328. FISHER, E. R., SAAS, R., FISHER, B. *et al.*, 'Pathologic findings from the National Surgical Adjuvant Breast Project (BO6). 1. Intraductal carcinoma (DCIS)', *Cancer*, 1986; 57:197–208.

329. VAN DER SCHUEREN, E., VAN DONGEN, J. A., 'Management of early stage breast cancer: current status of treatment', *Eur. J. Clin. Oncol.*, 1988; 24:89–93.

330. *Protocol of the UK Randomised Trial for Management of Screen Detected Ductal Carcinoma-in-situ (DCIS) of the Breast*. NHS Breast Screening Programme: National Research Initiative. UKCCCR. 1989.

331. HOLMBERG, L., TABAR, L., ADAMI, H. O., BERGSTROM, R. 'Survival in breast cancer diagnosed between mammographic screening examinations' *Lancet*, 1986; ii:27–30.

332. MACMAHON, B., COLE, P., BROWN, J., 'Etiology of human breast cancer', *J. Natl. Cancer Inst.*, 1973; 50:21–42.

333. KELSEY, J. L., BERKOWITZ, G. S., 'Breast cancer epidemiology', *Cancer Res.*, 1988; 48:5615–23.

334. MILLER, A. B., BULBROOK, R. D., 'The epidemiology and aetiology of breast cancer', *N. Engl. J. Med.*, 1980; 303:1246–8.

335. BOYLE, P., LEAKE, R., 'Progress in understanding breast cancer: epidemiological and biological interactions', *Breast Cancer Res. Treat.*, 1988; 11:91–112.

336. HELMRICH, S. P., SHAPIRO, S., ROSENBERG, L. *et al.*, 'Risk factors for breast cancer', *Am. J. Epid.*, 1983; 117:35–45.

337. FEINLEIB, M., 'Breast cancer and artificial menopause', *J. Natl. Cancer Inst.*, 1968; 41:315–29.

338. GREENBERG, E. R., BARNES, A. B., RESSEGNIL, L. *et al.*, 'Breast cancer in mothers given diethylstilboestrol during pregnancy', *N. Engl. J. Med.*, 1984; 311:1393–8.

339. HUNT, K., VESSEY, M., 'Long-term effects of postmenopausal hormone therapy', *Br. J. Hosp. Med.*, 1987; 38:450–8.

340. PIKE, M. C., HENDERSON, B. E., KRAILO, M. D. *et al.*, 'Breast cancer in young women and use of oral contraceptives possibly modifying effects of formulation and age of use', *Lancet*, 1983; 2:926–30.

341. U.K. NATIONAL CASE-CONTROL STUDY GROUP, 'Oral contraceptive use and breast cancer risk in young women', *Lancet*, 1989; 1:973–82.

342. McMAHON, B., COLE, P., LIN, M. *et al.*, 'Age at first-birth and breast cancer risk', *Bull. WHO*, 1970; 43:209–21.

343. BRINTON, L., WILLIAMS, R. R., HOOVER, R. N., 'Breast cancer risk factors among screening programme participants', *J. Natl. Cancer Inst.*, 1979; 62:37–44.

344. HARRIS, B. M. L., EKLUND, G., MEIRIK, O., RUTQVIST, L. E., WIKLUND, K., 'Risk of cancer of the breast after legal abortion during the first trimester: a Swedish Register study', *Br. Med. J.*, 1989; 299:1430–2.

345. DOLL, R., PAGET, P., WATERHOUSE, J., *Cancer Incidence on Five Continents*. Berlin, Springer-Verlag, 1966.

346. KOLONEL, L. N., HARKIN, J. H., NOMURA, A. M., CHAD, S. Y., 'Dietary fat intake and cancer incidence among five ethnic groups in Hawaii', *Cancer Res.*, 1981; 41:3727–8.

347. WILLETT, W. C., MacMAHON, B., 'Diet and cancer: an overview', *N. Engl. J. Med.*, 1984; 310:697–703.

348. DeWAARD, F., CORNELIUS, J. P., ASKI, K. *et al.*, 'Breast cancer incidence according to weight and height of two cities in the Netherlands and in Aichi prefecture', *Cancer*, 1977; 40:1269–75.

349. HOLM, L–E., CALLMER, E., HJALMAR, M–L., LIDBRINK, E., NILSSON, B., SKOOG, L., 'Dietary habits and prognostic factors in breast cancer', *J. Nat. Cancer Instit.*, 1989; 81:1218.

350. GRAHAM, S., 'Alcohol and breast cancer', *N. Engl. J. Med.*, 1987; 78:1211–3.

351. BOYD, N. F., McGUIRE, V., 'Evidence of association between plasma high-density lipoprotein cholesterol and risk factors for breast cancer: correlation between level and risk of breast cancer', *J. Nat. Canc. Inst.*, 1990.

352. DeWAARD, F., BAANDERS-VAN HALEWIJN, E. A., HUIZINGA, J., 'The bimodal age distribution of patients with mammary carcinoma', *Cancer*, 1964; 17:141–51.

353. MACKAY, J., STEELE, C. M., 'Genetic aspects of human breast cancer'. In: *High Risk Factor: Breast Cancer*, RAGAZ, J., ARIEL, I. M. (eds). Heidelberg, Springer-Verlag, 1989, pp. 45–68.

354. KEY, T. J. A., PIKE, M. C., 'The role of oestrogens and progestagens in the epidemiology and prevention of breast cancer', *Eur. J. Cancer*, 1988; 24:29–43.

355. DANUTRA, V., TURKES, A., READ, G. F., WILSON, D. W., GRIFFITHS, V., JONES, R., GRIFFITHS, K., 'Progesterone concentrations in samples of saliva from adolescent girls living in Britain and Thailand, two countries where women are at widely differing risk of breast cancer', *J. Endocrinol.*, 1989; 121:375–81.

356. WOLFE, J. M., 'Risk for breast cancer development detected by mammographic parenchymal pattern', *Cancer*, 1976; 37:2486–92.

357. BERGKVIST, L., TABAR, L., BERGSTROM, R., ADAMI, H. O., 'Epidemiological determinants of the mammographic parenchymal pattern', *Am. J. Epid* 1987; 126:1075–81.

358. DeWAARD, F., ROMBACH, J. J., COLLETTE, H. J. A., SLOTBOOM, B., 'Breast cancer risk associated with reproductive factors and breast parenchymal patterns', *J. Natl. Cancer Inst.*, 1984; 72:1277–82.

359. GRAVELLE, I. H., BULSTRODE, J. C., BULBROOK, R. D., HAYWARD, J. L., 'A prospective study of mammographic parenchymal patterns and risk of breast cancer', *Br. J. Radiol.*, 1959; 701:487–91.

360. KALACHE, A., 'Risk factor for breast cancer: a tabular summary of the epidemiological literature', *Br. J. Surg.*, 1981; 68:797–99.

361. BULBROOK, R. D., HAYWARD, J. L., 'Abnormal urinary steroid excretion and subsequent breast cancer. A prospective study in the Island of Guernsey', *Lancet*, 1967; 1:519–22.

362. SHAPIRO, S., STRAX, P., 'The search for risk factors in breast cancer', *Am. J. Publ. Hlth.*, 1968; 58:820–35.

363. SHAPIRO, S., GOLDBERG, J., VENET, L., STRAX, P., 'Risk factors in breast cancer—a prospective study'. In: *Host Environment Interactions*, DOLL, R. (ed). pp. 169–81.

364. FAREWELL, V. T., 'The combined effect of breast cancer risk factors', *Cancer*, 1977; 40:931–6.

365. TOTI, A., PIFFANELLI, A., PAVANELLI, T., BURIANI, C., NENCI, I., ARSLAN-PAGNINI, C., ZANARDI, P., PECORARI, S., ROSSI, R., BARRAI, I., 'Possible indications of breast cancer risk through discriminant functions', *Cancer*, 1980; 46:1280–5.

366. DEWAARD, F., COLLETTE, H. J., ROMBACH, J. J., COLLETTE, C., 'Breast cancer screening with particular reference to 'high-risk' groups', *Breast Cancer Res. Treat.*, 1988; 11:125–32.

367. SCHECHTER, M. T., MILLER, A. B., BAINES, C. J., HOWE, G. R., 'Selection of women at high risk from breast cancer at initial screening', *J. Chronic Dis.*, 1986; 39:253–60.

368. ALEXANDER, F. E., ROBERTS, M. M., HUGGINS, A., 'Risk factors for breast cancer with applications to selection for the prevalence screen', *J. Epid. Comm. Hlth.*, 1987; 41:101–6.

369. DUFFY, S. W., TABAR, L., 'Screening for breast cancer'. *J. Chronic. Dis.* 1987; 40:907–8.

370. ALEXANDER, F. E., ROBERTS, M. M., 'The menopause and breast cancer', *J. Epid. Comm. Hlth.*, 1987; 41:94–100.

371. WHITEHEAD, J., COOPER, J., 'Risk factors for breast cancer by mode of diagnosis: some results from a breast cancer screening study', *J. Epid. Comm. Hlth.*, 1989; 43:115–20.

372. SIMPSON, J. S., MORRIS, T., PETTINGALE, K. W., GREER, H. S., RYAN, K., 'The selection of patients for breast cancer screening: is there a role for psychological testing', *Clin. Oncol.*, 1976; 2:232–6.

373. HILL, G. B., 'Selective screening', *J. Chronic Dis.*, 1986; 39:252–3.

374. GAIL, M. H., BRINTON, L. A., BYAR, D. P., CORLE, D. K., GREEN, S. B., SCHAIRER, C., MULVIHILL, J. J., 'Projecting individualized probabilities of developing breast cancer for white females who are being examined annually', *J. Natl. Cancer Inst.*, 1989; 81:1879–86.

375. PICKLE, L. W., JOHNSON, K. A., 'Estimating the long-term probability of developing breast cancer', *J. Natl. Cancer Inst.*, 1989; 81:1854–5.

376. GRAVELLE, H. S. E., SIMPSON, P. R., CHAMBERLAIN, J., 'Breast cancer screening and health service costs', *J. Health Economics*, 1982; 1:185–207.

230   REFERENCES

377. VAN DER MASS, D. J., 'The costs and effects of mass screening for breast cancer', *Netherlands: Medical Technology Assessment*, 1988.

378. DE KONING, H. J., VAN INEVELD, B. M. 'Cost/benefit evaluation of different screening strategies for breast cancer'. In: *Practical Modalities of an Efficient Screening for Breast Cancer in the European Community'*. ZIANT, G. (ed.). International Congress Series 865. *Exercpta Medica*, Amsterdam. p. 121–32.

379. JONSSON, E., HAKANSSON, S., TABAR, L., 'Cost of mammography screening for breast cancer after low-dose irradiation', *Lancet*, 1989; 1:629–30.

380. HOLMBERG, L., ADAMI, H. O., PERSSON, I., LUNDSTROM, T., TABAR, L., 'Demands on surgical in-patient services after mass mammographic screening', *Br. Med. J.*, 1988; 293:779–82.

381. HOLMBERG, L., 'The impact of mammographic screening on surgical treatment policies'. In: *Screening for Breast Cancer*, DAY, N. E., MILLER, A. B. (eds). Toronto, Hans-Huber, 1988, pp. 67–72.

382. VILLARD, L., MURPHY, M., VESSEY, M. P., 'Cervical cancer deaths in young women', *Lancet*, 1989; 1:377.

383. RAGAZ, J., GOLDIE, J. H., BAIRD, R., REBBECK, P., BASCO, A., 'Experimental basis and clinical reality of preoperative (neoadjuvant) chemotherapy in breast cancer'. Recent Results in *Cancer Res.* 1989; 115:28–35.

384. CANTRELL, M. A., ANDERSON, D., CERETTI, D. P., 'Cloning sequence and expression of a human granulocyte macrophage colony stimulating factor', *Proc. Nat. Acad. Sc.*, 1985; 82:6250–4.

385. WONG, G. C., WITECK, J. S., TEMPLE, P. A., 'Human GM-CSF: molecular cloning to the complementary DNA and purification of the natural and recombinant proteins', *Science*, 1985; 228:810–15.

386. DEARNALEY, D. P., SLOANS, J. P., IMRIE, S., *et al.*, 'Detection of isolated mammary carcinoma cells in marrow of patients with primary breast cancer', *J. Roy. Soc. Med.*, 1983; 76:359–64.

387. SCHLIMOCK, G., FUNKE, I., HOLZMAN, B., *et al.*, 'Micrometastatic cancer cells in bone marrow: in vitro detection with anti-cytokeratin and in vivo labelling with anti-17-1A monoclonal antibodies', *Proc. Nat. Acad. Sc.*, 1987; 84:8672–6.

388. RESKE, S. N., KARSTENS, J. N., GLOECKNER, W., and 4 other authors, 'Radioimmunoimaging for diagnosis of bone marrow involvement in breast cancer and malignant lymphoma', Lancet, 1989; i:299–309.

389. BRENNER, D. E., 'Liposomal encapsulation: making old and new drugs do new tricks,' *J. Nat. Canc. Inst.*, 1989; 81:1436–7.

390. JAIN, R. K., 'Delivery of novel therapeutic agents in tumours: physiological barriers and strategies', *J. Nat. Canc. Inst.*, 1989; 81:570–6.

391. TRAUTH, B. C., KLAE, C., PETERS, A. M. J., *et al.*, 'Monoclonal antibody-induced tumour regression by the activation of an endogenous suicide programme', *Science*, 1989; 245:301–5.

392. DEBATIN, K–M., GOLDMAN, C. K., BAMFORD, R., WALDMANN, T. A., KRAMNER, P. H., 'Monoclonal antibody-mediated apoptosis in adult T-cell leukaemia', *Lancet*, 1990; i:497–9.

393. SCHLOM, J., 'Monoclonal antibodies in cancer therapy: the present and the future', *Pharm. Ther.*, 1988; 12:56–60.

394. OSBORNE, C. K., 'Combined chemo-hormonal therapy in breast cancer', *Breast Cancer Res. Treat.*, 1981; 1:121.

395. LIPPMAN, M. E., CASSIDY, J., WESLEY, M., YOUNG, R. C., 'A randomized attempt to increase the efficacy of cytotoxic chemotherapy in metastatic breast cancer by hormonal synchronization', *J. Clin. Oncol.*, 1984; 2:28.

396. BONTENBAL, M., SIUWERTS, A. M., KLIJN, J. G. M. *et al.*, 'Cell-cycle kinetics of breast cancer cells', *Br. J. Cancer*, 1989; 60:688–93.

397. STEWART, H. J., 'Clinical experience in the use of antioestrogen tamoxifen in the treatment of breast cancer', *Proc. Roy. Soc. Ed.*, 1989; 95B:231–8.

398. FISHER, B., CONSTANTINO, J., REDMOND, D. C. *et al.*, 'A randomised clinical trial evaluating tamoxifen in the treatment of patients with node-negative breast cancer who have oestrogen-receptor positive tumours', *N. Engl. J. Med.*, 1989; 320:479–84.

399. BONADONNA, G., VALAGUSSA, P., TANCINI, G., DiFRONZO, G. D., 'Estrogen-receptor status and response to chemotherapy in early and advanced breast cancer', *Cancer Chemother. Pharmacol.*, 1980; 4:37–41.

400. FORREST, A. P. M., LEVACK, P. A., CHETTY, U., 'A human tumour model', *Lancet*, 1986; 2:840–2.

401. ANDERSON, E. D. C., FORREST, A. P. M., LEVACK, P. A., CHETTY, U., HAWKINS, R. A., 'Response to endocrine manipulation and oestrogen receptor concentration in large operable primary breast cancer', *Br. J. Cancer*, 1989; 60:223–6.

402. EPPENBERGER, U., GOLDHIRSCH, A. (Eds), *Endocrine Therapy and Growth Regulation of Breast Cancer*. Berlin, Springer-Verlag, 1989, vol. 113.

403. CALLAHAN, R., CAMPBELL, G., 'Mutations in human breast cancer: an overview', *J. Natl. Cancer Inst.*, 1989; 81:1780–6.

404. BENZ, C. C., SCOTT, G. K., SANTOS, G. F., SMITH, H. S., 'Expression of c-myc, c-Ha-ras 1 and c-erb B2 protooncogenes in normal and malignant human breast epithelial cells', *J. Nat. Can. Inst.*, 1989; 81:1704–8.

405. MORROW, C. S., COWAN, K. H., 'Mechanisms and clinical significance of multidrug resistance', *Oncology*, 1988; 2:55–68.

406. MOSCOW, J. A., COWAN, K. H., 'Multidrug resistance', *J. Nat. Canc. Inst.*, 1988; 80: 14–20.

407. CHABNER, B. A., SHOEMAKER, D., 'Drug development for cancer: implications for chemical modifiers', *Int. J. Radiat. Oncol. Biol. Physics*, 1989; 16:907–9.

408. MYERS, C. E., STEIN, Cy., LaRocca, R., COOPER, M., CASSIDY, J., McATEE, N., 'Suramin: an antagonist of heparin-binding tumour growth factors with activity against a broad spectrum of human tumours', *Proc. Amer. Soc. Clin. Oncol.*, 1989.

409. ROSENBERG, S. A., LOTZE, M. T., MULE, J. J., 'New approaches to the immunotherapy of cancer', *Ann. Int. Med.*, 1989; 108:853–64.

410. PETRAKIS, N. L., 'Oestrogens and other biochemical and cytological components in nipple aspirates of breast fluid: relationship to risk factors for breast disease', *Proc. Roy. Soc. Ed.*, 1989; 95B:169–84.

411. McGUIRE, W. L., NAYLOR, S. L., 'Loss of heterozygosity in breast cancer: cause or effect', *J. Natl. Cancer Inst.*, 1989; 81:1764–5.

412. MACKAY, J., ELDER, P. A., PORTEOUS, D. J. *et al.*, 'Partial deletion of chromosome 11p in breast cancer correlates with size of primary tumour and oestrogen receptor levels', *Br. J. Cancer*, 1988; 58:710–14.

413. MACKAY, J., STEELE, C. M., ELDER, P. A., FORREST, A. P. M., EVANS, H. J., 'Allele loss on short arm of chromosome 17 in breast cancers', *Lancet*, 1988; 2:1384–6.

414. THOMPSON, A. M., STEEL, C. M., CHETTY, U., HAWKINS, R. A., MILLER, W. R., CARTER, D. C., FORREST, A. P. M., EVANS, H. J., 'p53 Gene mRNA expression and chromosome 17p allele loss in breast cancer', *Br. J. Cancer*, 1990; 61:74–78.

415. MAREEL, M., VAN ROY, F., BRUYNEEL, E., BOLSCHER, J., SCHALLIER, D., DeMETS, M., 'Molecular biology of mineral invasion. Recent Results Cancer Res'. 1988; 106:14–20.

416. LIPPMAN, M. E., 'Steroid hormone receptors and mechanisms of growth regulation of human breast cancer'. In: *Diagnosis and Management of Breast Cancer*, LIPPMAN, M. E., LICHTER, A., DANFORTH, D. N. (eds). Philadelphia, W. B. Saunders Co., 1988, pp. 326–47.

417. LIPPMAN, M. E., DICKINSON, R. B., 'Growth control of normal and malignant breast epithelium', *Proc. Roy. Soc. Edin.*, 1989; 95B:89–106.

418. SALOMON, D. S., KIDWELL, W. R., KIM, N. *et al.*, 'Modulation by estrogen and growth factors of transforming growth factor-alpha and epidermal growth factor receptor expression in normal and malignant human mammary epithelial cells, Recent results', *Cancer Res.* 1989; 113:57–69.

419. DICKSON, R. B., KASID, A., HUFF, K. K. *et al.*, 'Activation of growth factor secretion in tumorigenic states of breast cancer induced by 17b-oestradiol or v-rasH oncogene', *Proc. Natl. Acad. Sci. USA*, 1987; 84:837–41.

420. CUZICK, J., WANG, D. Y., BULBROOK, R. D., 'The prevention of breast cancer', *Lancet*, 1986; 1:83–6.

421. JORDAN, V. C., 'Effect of tamoxifen (ICI46 474) on initiation and growth of DMBA-induced rat mammary carcinoma', *Eur. J. Cancer*, 1976; 12:419–24.

422. DE WARD, F., WANG, D. Y., 'Epidemiology and prevention: workshop report, *Europ. J. Clin. Oncol.*, 1988; 24:45–48.

423. FENTIMAN, I. S., 'The endocrine prevention of breast cancer', *Br. J. Cancer*, 1989; 60:12–4.

424. FORNANDER, T., RUTQVIST, L. E., CEDERMARK, B. *et al.*, 'Adjuvant tamoxifen in early breast cancer: occurrence of new primary cancers', *Lancet*, 1989; 1:117–9.

425. STEWART, H. J., KNIGHT, G. M., 'Tamoxifen and the uterus and endometrium', *Lancet*, 1989; 1:375–6.

426. JORDAN, V. C., 'Tamoxifen and endometrial cancer', *Lancet*, 1988; 2:1019.

427. LOVE, R. R., 'Prospects for antioestrogen chemoprevention of breast cancer', *J. Natl. Cancer Inst.*, 1990; 82:18–21.

428. POWLES, T. J., HARDY, J. R., ASHLEY, S. E. *et al.*, 'Chemoprevention of breast cancer', *Breast Cancer Res. Treat.*, 1989; 14:23–31.

429. POWLES, T. J., HARDY, J. R., ASHLEY, S. E. *et al.*, 'A pilot trial to evaluate the acute toxicity and feasibility of tamoxifen for prevention of breast cancer', *Br. J. Cancer*, 1989; 60:126–31.

430. NOLVADEX ADJUVANT TRIAL ORGANISATION, Controlled trial of tamoxifen as a single adjuvant agent in the management of early breast cancer', *Br. J. Cancer*, 1988; 57:608–11.

431. CHAUDARY, A., MILLIS, R., HOSKINS, O. L., HALDER, M., BULBROOK, R. D., CUZICK, J., HAYWARD, J. L., 'Bilateral breast cancer: a prospective study of disease incidence', *Br. J. Surg.*, 1984; 71:711–14.

432. CUZICK, J., BAUM, M. L., 'Tamoxifen and contralateral breast cancer', *Lancet*, 1985; 2:282.

433. RIBEIRO, G., SWINDELL, R., 'The Christie Hospital adjuvant tamoxifen trial status at 10 years', *Br. J. Cancer*, 1988; 57:601–3.

434. WAKELING, A. E., BOWLER, J., 'Novel antioestrogens', *Proc. Roy. Soc. Edinb.*, 1989; 95B:247–52.

435. PIKE, M. C., ROSS, R. K., LOBO, R. A., KEY, T. J. A., POTTS, M., HENDERSON, B. E., 'LHRH agonists and the prevention of breast and ovarian cancer', *Br. J. Cancer*, 1989; 60:142–8.

436. ANDERSON, T. J., BATTERSBY, S., 'The involvement of oestrogen in the development and function of the normal breast: histological evidence', *Proc. Roy. Soc. Edin.*, 1989; 95B:23–32.

437. PRENTICE, R., THOMPSON, D., CLIFFORD, C., GORBACH, S., GOLDIN, B., BYAR, D., 'Dietary fat reduction and plasma estradiol concentration in health postmenopausal women', *J. Natl. Cancer Inst.*, 1990; 82:129–34.

438. MACFAYDEN, I. J., PRESCOTT, R., GROOM, G. V., FORREST, A. P. M., 'Plasma steroid levels in women with breast cancer', *Lancet*, 1976; 1:1100–2.

439. WHITBY, L. G., 'Well population screening', *Proc. Roy. Soc. Med.*, 1968; 61:761–6.

440. MOORES, B. M., BOOLER, R., DOVAS, T., ASHBURY, D. L., 'Production and processing of digital ionographic images', *Brit. J. Radiol.*, 1985; 57:1157–60.

441. Report, *Br. Med. J.*, 1989; 299:877–8.

442. ACHESON, E. D., 'Haddow Memorial Lecture', *Proc. Roy. Soc. Med.*, 1989; 82:455–7.

443. *1989 Survey of Physicians Attitudes and Practices in Early Cancer Detection.* CA 1990; 40:77–101.

444. 'Breast cancer getting attention in Congress'. Report, *J. Natl. Cancer Inst.*, 1990; 82:11–12.

445. MILLER, A. B., HOWE, G. R., SHERMAN, G. *et al.*, 'Mortality from breast cancer after irradiation during fluoroscopic examination in patients being treated for tubercolosis', *New Engl. J. Med.*, 1989; 321:1285–9.